Authority, Autonomy, and Representation in American Literature, 1776–1865

Authority, Autonomy, and Representation in American Literature, 1776–1865

MARK R. PATTERSON

PRINCETON UNIVERSITY PRESS
PRINCETON, NEW JERSEY

Published by Princeton University Press, 41 William Street,
Princeton, New Jersey 08540
In the United Kingdom: Princeton University Press,
Guildford, Surrey

Library of Congress Cataloging-in-Publication Data

Patterson, Mark R., 1952–
Authority, autonomy, and representation in American literature, 1776–1865 / Mark R. Patterson.
p. cm.
Includes bibliographical references and index.
ISBN 0–691–06743–0 (alk. paper)
1. American literature—1783–1850—History and criticism. 2. Politics and literature—United States. 3. Authority in literature. 4. Autonomy in literature. 5. Representative government and representation in literature. 6. American literature—19th century—History and criticism. 7. American literature—Revolutionary period, 1775–1783—History and criticism. 8. United States—History—Revolution, 1775–1783—Literature and the revolution. I. Title.
PS217.P64P38 1988
810'.9'002—dc19 88–13999
CIP

This book has been composed in Linotron Baskerville

Clothbound editions of Princeton University Press books are printed on acid-free paper, and binding materials are chosen for strength and durability.
Paperbacks, although satisfactory for personal collections, are not usually suitable for library rebinding

Printed in the United States of America by
Princeton University Press,
Princeton, New Jersey

FOR LESLIE

CONTENTS

PREFACE

This is a study of the relationship between the origin of the United States' political identity as a representative democracy and the simultaneous rise of its self-conscious literary tradition. As such, this work's historical origin is 17 September 1787, the day the Constitutional Convention concluded its work and sent its completed document to the states to be ratified. From that moment to this, the fate of America's political and cultural life has been driven by the forces generated by the presuppositions and ideas embodied in this document. The Constitution itself presented a compromise between central authority and local autonomy in the form of proportional representation and separation of powers, but it was less a triumph of a rational, stable system than an often uneasy alliance of volatile claims. The Bill of Rights, Civil War, and continuing attempts to amend the Constitution testify to its imperfect, unfinished quality.

What this book investigates is the way in which the political solution of 1787 provides a means to understand the particular strains and stresses in American literature between the Revolutionary War and Civil War. American literature obviously did not begin in 1787, but a self-consciously national literary tradition did begin at this moment, and writers were quick to turn their talents to serving the new republic, a favor they hoped would be returned. And just as the central political issues between 1776 and 1861 turned out to be the location and character of authority in the nation and how that authority was to be represented, American writers attempted to define their own authority by creating new forms of literary representation.

What made this process difficult was the rise of popular democratic sentiment, constituting at once a volatile new political constituency and a difficult audience. Having questioned the traditional forms of authority and representation held by the British, Americans now raised the same issues during the internal debate over the nation's new political identity. The cry "No taxation without representation" worked fine to unify support against the British, but it worked equally well to divide support for the new American government during the unsettled period between 1787 and 1861. Of central concern to both writers and politicians was the need to reconcile traditional paradigms of literary and political authority with the new democratic conceptions of politics and society. However, the writers' politics are to be found not so much in the overt subject matter of their works as in the political conditions, the strategies of rhetorical engagement, we reenact when we read these writings.

In its discussion of how political issues were translated into literary terms, this work concerns three interrelated areas. First, it delineates the particular attitudes of American writers toward political and cultural authority. The peculiar history of American literature between the Revolutionary and Civil wars, the fact that this literary tradition was not born of any founder but was adopted as the stepchild of the Revolution, forced particular American writers into uneasy, often contorted attitudes toward American society. Second, it is concerned with how particular literary works enact these political attitudes by means of their rhetorical strategies. From Franklin's memoirs to Melville's subversions, writers adapted their narratives to correspond to particular political relationships ranging from authoritarian to revolutionary. Finally, by engaging those ideas central to the Constitution—the social bonding of authority, the problematics of identity in autonomy, and the epistemology of representation—I seek to understand how those issues continue to influence our own times. Although this book presupposes these matters to be in large part historically determined, the Constitution raised problems unforeseen by its creators.

Because of the historical scope and theoretical nature of this work, I have found it necessary to focus on several representative figures. The book itself is divided into two parts, the first consisting of three chapters on specific writers from the post-Revolutionary period, and the second part focusing on three writers in antebellum America. The first part discusses the writings of Benjamin Franklin, Hugh Henry Brackenridge, and Charles Brockden Brown within the context of the writing and ratification of the United States Constitution. In particular, I am interested in how each writer responded to the controversy between Federalists and Antifederalists over the Constitution and the growing democratization of American society. Franklin in his *Autobiography* and Brackenridge in *Modern Chivalry* chose very different literary responses to the historical disruptions created by the Revolution and Constitution. Brown's novels, on the other hand, reveal the internalization of America's political debate as authority seems to lie either in the "state" of his characters' unconscious motivations or in charismatic, demagogic villains. What unites these three writers is their constant fear of demagogues and their desire to educate their audience to the dangers facing American society.

The second part, including chapters on James Fenimore Cooper, Ralph Waldo Emerson, and Herman Melville, describes the ways in which three male writers of the American Renaissance responded to these same issues. The diversity of these chapters' issues testifies to the range of responses and the particular concerns each writer had when facing the democracy growing up in antebellum America. Cooper, for example, reacted to the changing democratic society by attempting to reestablish paternal authority as the key to political and social stability. Thus his reinterpretation of the Revolution and Constitution follows the increasing importance of paternal authority in his novels. Influenced by his own powerful father, Cooper establishes two contradictory forms of paternal authority: (1) his "white" fathers, associated with controversial historical origins and untransmitted patrimony; (2) his Indian or mythic fathers whose origins are natural and therefore prior to white (European) history, but whose powers are threatened by the incursion of historical forces. Choosing representative works from Cooper's early and middle career (particularly the early Leatherstocking novels and the Effingham novels), I discuss how Cooper attempts in vain to preserve a traditional, paternal authority in his novels and at the same time seeks to unite white father and native fathers, history and myth.

Rather than seeking to restore a lost patriarchal order, Emerson radically redefines the terms of the political argument. By reconstituting and internalizing the political concepts of authority, autonomy, and representation, he seeks to appropriate the ideals of democracy for his own spiritual ends. My concern in this chapter is to create a typology of his "heroes," including the Scholar and the Poet, and to trace the genealogy of the "representative man" by showing its relation to his theory of symbolism. When in "The Poet" Emerson claims, "the Poet is representative," he has in mind very specific political and literary issues. As a user of symbols, which are the active media of literature and politics, the representative acts for Emerson as a figure of a true representative democracy, for he is both representative and constituency. In essence, Emerson translates political questions into matters of his spiritual epistemology. By focusing on the volume *Representative Men* (1850), I argue that through the concept of the representative Emerson attempts to unite the literary and social impulses of his own psyche. For this reason, I view *Representative Men*, like Franklin's *Autobiography* and other American works concerned with reconciling authority and autonomy, as exhibiting an almost necessary impulse toward autobiography, that is, self-representation.

In my final chapter, I correlate Herman Melville's constant themes of subjection, mastery, and rebellion to his own experiments with narrative strategies in *Moby-Dick* and *The Confidence-Man*. As narrator of *Moby-Dick*, Ishmael insinuates himself between Ahab's desire for absolute autonomy and mastery of his crew and his own earlier attraction to self-abnegation within the ship's conventional forms of power and the metaphysical lure of the sea. For Ishmael, as for Emerson (although certainly in different ways), autobiographical self-representation provides a way to preserve forms of conditional identity that do not partake of Ahab's authoritarian claims. His narrative authority subverts Ahab's power while sustaining alternative visions of self-identity and social interaction. Here and in *The Confidence-Man* we recognize that democracy's drives to the extremes of absolute external authority or isolating autonomy not only impinge on social or political relationships but affect the very concept of self that exists within these bonds. Confidence therefore becomes the necessary condition for representation's ability to mediate between those absolutes. For this reason I read *The Confidence-Man* as a tough-minded but essentially affirmative vision of the necessity to have a conditional confidence, one still skeptical of social and political structures.

My decision to focus on representative figures has naturally limited my discussion of other writers who might have served me equally well. The Connecticut Wits in Part One, Hawthorne, Stowe, and Thoreau in Part Two are writers who were omitted for the sake of focus. For further discussion of the post-Revolutionary period, I would suggest Emory Elliott's work, *Revolutionary Writers*, and the recent study by Cathy Davidson, *Revolution and the Word*. Davidson's work unfortunately appeared too late for me to incorporate its insights. Hawthorne is certainly one writer who saw the interrelations of charismatic and paternal authority (*The House of Seven Gables*), the question of symbolic representation and social change (*The Scarlet Letter*), and the idea of the representative ("The Gray Champion"). And Harriet Beecher Stowe's *Uncle Tom's Cabin* provides a fascinating study of the conflict between political and narrative authorities. For my purposes, however, the six writers discussed here present six complex examples of how literature and politics converged after the Revolution.

* * *

As Emerson knew, each act of representation entails a form of self-representation. The seed of this book was unknowingly planted in the 1960s during sometimes heated discussions with my father and mother about the nature and necessity of authority. Over the years the arguments have become conversations, but I have learned much from my parents' examples. To their unconditional support and faith I owe a great debt. Emory Elliott advised a much earlier version of the book, but, more importantly, provided a lasting model of intellectual and personal generosity. Since then a number of people have, directly or indirectly, influenced the final shape of this work. Some of the following would no doubt be surprised at their influence, but it has its tangible fruit in the following pages: Martha Banta, Malcolm Griffith, Don Kartiganer, Robert Sattelmeyer, Willard Thorp, Beth Witherell. I would also like to thank Robert Brown at Princeton University Press for his support and my copyeditor Lise Rodgers for her work. This book was also aided by a Summer Stipend from the National Endowment for the Humanities. To Leslie Johnson I owe the biggest debt of gratitude for her unflagging faith and encouragement.

Earlier versions of some chapters appeared elsewhere. Portions of Chapter Two appeared in *Texas Studies in Literature and Languages* (28 [1986], 121–39); portions of Chapter Five appeared in ESQ: *A Journal of the American Renaissance* (31 [1985], 230–42); and portions of Chapter Six appeared in *Studies in the Novel* (16 [1984], 288–303).

INTRODUCTION

There is a representative scene in American literature recurring throughout the eighteenth and nineteenth centuries. In this scene, a speaker stands before a crowd of men and women, attempting to mitigate their natural suspicions in order to form a body of federated wills. Captain Farrago standing before the angry settlers in *Modern Chivalry*, Hugh Littlepage confronting the "Injins" in *The Redskins*, Ahab mesmerizing his crew aboard the *Pequod*, even Twain's Colonel Sherburn facing down the mob in Bricksville replay this quintessentially American drama of democracy and persuasion. Staged as a political drama, as would-be leaders seek to gain authority while the people guard their independence and autonomy, this scene is acted out essentially in literary terms, for each speaker reenacts the writer's need to gain the people's confidence, to become, for a moment, their representative. To this list I would therefore add the historical counterparts: Hugh Henry Brackenridge desperately speaking to the mobs during the Whiskey Rebellion; James Fenimore Cooper responding angrily to the people of Cooperstown over Three Mile Point; Emerson, Thoreau, and Twain seeking to cultivate and instruct their American audiences on the lecture circuit. Uniting these disparate scenes is a common dilemma of American democracy: How does one move or influence a crowd, mob, or nation of people who are suspicious of traditional forms of authority? That the solution to this problem conflates political and literary issues is the theme of my book.

The problem occurs in the continual redefining of authority throughout American history, a necessary process for a nation constantly reordering its identity. And it is the idea of democracy that stands behind the political and social definitions of identity that we see from the post-Revolutionary period to the Civil War. What the relationship is between a people and their governing structures and leaders, where true authority lies, has emerged with the founding of America as the principal problem of the colony and nation. Contemporaneous with the political transformation from colony to nation were the first works of American fiction, which themselves provide important models for the definition of authority in the young nation. Through fictional confrontations of speaker and audience, through Farrago, Littlepage, and Ahab, American writers rehearsed their own sense of authority even as they critiqued the state of American politics. Playing out their literary fantasies in the confrontation of speaker and audience, these writers necessarily reenact the political terms of the relationship. One essential intersection between writers and politicians is at the point where each seeks to create rhetorical strategies and narrative forms—that is, forms of representation and authority—in order to possess a sympathetic audience.

A succinct discussion of the problems of authority, autonomy, and representation is found in Benjamin Franklin's "The Way to Wealth," written in 1757. Composing the story for the twenty-fifth anniversary of his popular *Almanac*, which had been issued under the fictitious editorship of "Poor" Richard Saunders, Franklin explores the variety of ways authority may be achieved in American society. Speaking in Saunders's deftly humorous and engaging voice, Franklin sets this tale at a crowded sale of merchant goods. The sale is a fitting scene, for Poor Richard, musing on the reasons for his success, begins his narrative by equating the value of a book with its sales and the "authority" of the author with the number of his readers. Because his peers, the critics and other authors, have been miserly in their praise, Saunders decides "the People" who purchase and consume his books are the "best Judges of [his]

Merit."[1] He has discovered, as he says, "some Respect for my Authority" by hearing his name associated with the various proverbs and sayings he has compiled and printed under the name of Poor Richard.

Saunders's claim for authority is based on epistemic grounds: He is an acknowledged expert authority *in something* (in this case popular wisdom). Moreover, his claim includes its own legitimating terms: His authority is directly proportional to his book sales. Yet we already encounter problems here in the attribution of authority. The people, perhaps mistakenly, attribute to him the wisdom and authority of the proverbs. He, on the other hand, admits to being merely the *representative* (literally the one who *re*-presents the proverbs of others) of this authority. Although the people judge his merit by buying his books, and thus show respect for his authority, it is not clear whether this authority originates with them, since they are his judges, or whether the authority can be located in the wisdom and language of the proverbs themselves. Despite Saunders's own empirical standards for measuring authority, the nature of the relationship between himself and the people, that is, the direction and terms of authority, remain unresolved. To put the matter more simply for the moment: What is it that moves the people? Is it the figure of Poor Richard Saunders (the persona of Benjamin Franklin), the proverbs (seen in the power of language to express and represent traditional wisdom), or do the people move themselves as they listen to their wisdom, recognizing the alienated majesty of their own ideas reflected by Richard Saunders? Or, and this is a cynical possibility, are they moved by the same acquisitiveness drawing them to this sale?

These questions are quickly put to the test when the people at the sale, grumbling about the stiff taxes they have to pay, ask Father Abraham, the community patriarch, to speak to the "Badness of the Times." Copiously quoting Poor Richard as the authority on the subject, Father Abraham admonishes the people not to blame the taxes imposed by the government, but their own weaknesses and vices. Acting as Puritan patriarch and Jeremiah, he counsels them to be industrious, frugal, and prudent. The end of such vir-

[1] Benjamin Franklin, "The Way to Wealth," in *The Autobiography and Other Writings*, ed. Kenneth Silverman (New York: Penguin, 1986), p. 216. (Hereafter cited in text.)

tue, he tells them, is independence from debt: "Think what you do when you run in Debt; *You give another Power over your Liberty*" (223). As he later says, "Your Creditor has Authority." In his rousing climax, Father Abraham warns, "*The Borrower is a Slave to the Lender, and the Debtor to the Creditor,* disdain the Chain, preserve your Freedom; and maintain your Independency: Be *industrious* and *free*; be *frugal* and *free*" (224). It seems that Father Abraham complicates the problem of authority presented by Poor Richard Saunders. In the old man's terms, authority results in the subordination of one person (the borrower) by another (the creditor), a belief directly contradicting Poor Richard's view. If Father Abraham had his way, Poor Richard would lose his consumers *and* his authority. Freedom, which Father Abraham equates with independence, stands opposed to authority.

In his jeremiad, Father Abraham has presented the classic opposition of authority and autonomy.[2] One cannot be autonomous (in the absolute sense of producing one's own laws and in the more general sense of being independent) and still be under another's authority. Not only is the subordinate tied financially but his very terms of self-definition are controlled by the creditor. As Richard Sennett says, "the superior controls reality" by controlling the terms by which we associate ourselves with the world.[3] What is the relationship, however, between Father Abraham's fear of another's authority and Poor Richard's pride in his own? Both men use an economic metaphor to define the relations between authority and autonomy, and, it would seem, Father Abraham privileges autonomy or independence over authority. We can retain our independence only by resisting the external demands of others *and* the internal drives of our ambition or vanity, that is, by being self-possessed. Our autonomy is preserved at the expense of conventional authority. Absolute autonomy requires the rejection of external authority. Absolute authority over us, on the other hand,

[2] This opposition is clearly expressed by Robert Paul Wolff in his book *In Defense of Anarchy* (New York: Free Press, 1971), pp. 4–19, esp. p. 18: "The defining mark of the state is authority, the right to rule. The primary obligation of man is autonomy, the refusal to be ruled. . . . Insofar as a man fulfills his obligations to make himself the author of his decisions, he will resist the state's claim to have authority over him."

[3] Richard Sennett, *Authority* (New York: Alfred Knopf, 1980), p. 100.

demands the abnegation of autonomy, the loss of self-regulation. Our autonomy, therefore, guarantees our self-authority.

Poor Richard, in contrast, acknowledges his conditional dependence on the people who buy his books for both his economic success and literary value, but still insists on his authority. He thus places the importance of his authority, his social influence, over any concern for his lack of autonomy. He shows little interest in defining the exact conditions of his authority, and circumvents questions concerning the ultimate place of authority by presenting the issue as subject to quantifiable terms. Instead, he wants to determine how to *judge* authority and merit, and by obscuring other questions he presents his own authority as a *fait accompli.* As he moves people to buy his books, they judge his merit and also warrant his authority.

However, Father Abraham also wishes to influence and move the people, but toward greater virtue and better times and away from further economic consumption. In fact, he is called upon by the people much like the Roman *auctores*, those elders possessing a divine *auctoritas*, to provide guidance from his age and experience.[4] Unlike the Romans, however, this American audience listens to his lecture and then proceeds to ignore his sage advice. Tradition, age, and experience seem to have little authority in this country.[5] Having warned against bowing to others' authority and having proclaimed the absolute value of personal autonomy, Father Abraham assumes the burden of his own dependence on the people who have called upon him for advice. Desiring both authority and autonomy, he winds up with neither. Instead, he, like Poor Richard, becomes a kind of representative of the people.

Father Abraham presents an image of failed authority. But why does he fail to move the people, especially in light of Poor Richard's admitted success? In part, Father Abraham's "doctrine" cannot compete with the economic necessity and excitement of the

[4] On the etymology of the term *authority*, and its relation to Roman society, see R. Heinze, "Auctoritas," *Hermes* 9 (1925): 348–66.

[5] Max Weber's famous typology of legitimate authority (traditional, rational-legal, charismatic) remains a key study of authority in all of its complexities. See *A Theory of Social and Economic Organization*, trans. A. M. Henderson and Talcott Parsons (New York: Free Press, 1947). A good review of Weber's thesis is Dankwart A. Rustow, "The Study of Leadership," in *Philosophers and Kings: Studies in Leadership*, ed. Dankwart A. Rustow (New York: George Braziller, 1970), pp. 14–23.

sale. Poor Richard, on the other hand, has not only achieved some authority but he has done so within the economic terms respected by the people. By adjusting himself to these economic conditions by which the people themselves act, and by ignoring the detached aesthetic judgments of the critics, he allies himself with his audience. Thus, although both Father Abraham and Poor Richard share the same language and wisdom, their rhetorical strategies and poses distinguish them. The failure of Father Abraham's "harangue," as Poor Richard calls it, lies in its inability to articulate a common basis of sympathetic attachment between speaker and audience. As a Jeremiah he lectures the people directly, opposing their economically derived values of consumption with the alternate traditional value of self-discipline. Previously the jeremiad had been able to call on and even enunciate communally shared values, but its authority depended on a hierarchically descending (from God, to governors and ministers, to the people) definition of social relations. Because of dynamic changes in America's class structure, the decrease in religious fervor, and increasing influence of European custom, Father Abraham stands as an outsider and his form of address an anachronism.[6] By placing his values as well as his authority outside of the people, Father Abraham stands alienated; his very speech about authority and credit makes it clear that his own authority is conditional and representative, not absolute. He is the debtor to the people, but they no longer give credit to his opinions.

Despite Father Abraham's failure, Poor Richard has learned a valuable lesson from his representative. Having watched his own practical doctrines and language fail, he can better understand where and how success may be found. First of all, he learns that his success, and what freedom he might have, derives from his absence from the people, not his presence. More accurately, it is his detachment from a performing self that allows him to be spectator rather than actor. Printing is the ironic medium; its value and suc-

[6] Franklin, in fact, reveals the point at which the jeremiad loses its authority in this secular society. Sacvan Bercovitch has best described the "ideological consensus" sought by Father Abraham and other Jeremiahs in *The American Jeremiad* (Madison: Univ. of Wisconsin Press, 1981). On the intersection of Father Abraham's rhetoric and the issue of economic independence see Emory Elliott, "The Puritan Roots of American Whig Rhetoric," in *Puritan Influences in American Literature*, ed. Emory Elliott (Urbana, Ill.: Univ. of Illinois Press, 1979), pp. 109–11.

cess lie in its *difference*, its ability to disengage the writer from his language *and* the reader from the writer. Thus his most important discovery comes in his recognizing the need for representation, that is, for finding an indirect means or medium to present and re-present his doctrine. Father Abraham speaks for him, acts as his representative. Representation becomes the critical middle term between the absolutes of authority and autonomy. His books allow him some conditional authority, warranted by those who buy them, just as Father Abraham, or the creation of any persona or figural self, preserves a conditional autonomy. Recognizing the futility of Father Abraham's desire for authority *and* autonomy, Poor Richard frees himself to a certain extent through the irony inherent in his medium and through his ironic use of Father Abraham.

Between Poor Richard's claim for authority and Father Abraham's desire for autonomy, I would therefore interpose the crucial mediating term of representation. Unlike Father Abraham, Saunders understands that his authority can only be *represented*, in other words, can only be granted by his readers on certain reciprocal conditions. Although both men make claims to a kind of authority, only Poor Richard can take advantage of its conditional nature, conditioned, that is, by the people who buy his books and select Father Abraham to be their spokesman. If Father Abraham illustrates the paradox of authority (he preaches independence only at the cost of his subordination to the people), then Poor Richard reveals the power of representation to create a metaphoric territory in which both authority and autonomy are retained but in conditional and contingent forms. Representation itself can best be defined as the process by which something (an object, person, group, idea) is made figuratively present that is literally absent.[7] It is the "fiction" of representation, as Edmund Morgan calls it, that permits Father Abraham to speak for the people, just as Poor Richard speaks for Benjamin Franklin.[8]

Perhaps Poor Richard's shrewdest observation is his acknowledgment of the people's central role in this drama of command and influence. They not only judge his literary merit by buying his

[7] On the concept of representation, see Hannah Fenichel Pitkin, *The Concept of Representation* (Berkeley: Univ. of California Press, 1967).

[8] Edmund Morgan, "Government by Fiction: The Idea of Representation," *Yale Review* 72 (1983): 321–39.

books, they also pass sentence on his proverbs by ignoring Father Abraham's harangue. Their judgment includes both a critical assessment of literary representation and the selection (and rejection) of Father Abraham as their spokesman. If representation becomes the means by which we necessarily mediate between authority and autonomy, governor and people, writer and audience, then defining criteria for judging representatives or representations is an essential task. What became critical after the Revolutionary War was the difficulty in settling such criteria, for the power to define these matters fell increasingly, as Poor Richard anticipates, into the hands of the people themselves.

In its most basic form, judgment of any form of representation involves the epistemological problem of perceiving the relationship, the identity, between the represented object (the constituency, the world, the imagination) and its representation. We come to see how the representation shares an identity with its model, yet how they also remain essentially different. A representation actually creates a fictional territory, a metaphoric space, in which the inherent contradictions of the process are suspended. In this sense, senators and novels cohabit the territory of fiction, constructed, as it is, out of perceptions of identity and difference. But as Poor Richard understands all too well, political or literary judgment involves a more active participation than simple perceptual acknowledgment. We give assent or denial to our "representatives," sometimes simultaneously, and in so doing we place ourselves within the drama of political and literary representation.

Judgment, then, is a key element in the concept of representation; as readers or constituency we are involved at every step of the process. Such judging, however, is neither completely subjective, for we, like the crowd at the vendue, presume ourselves public beings as we judge, nor is it objective, for judgment mediates between our public expression and our personal desires. As Ronald Beiner has stated, "Judgment allows us to comport ourselves to the world without dependence upon rules and methods, and allows us to defeat subjectivity by asserting claims that seek general assent."[9] This is not to say that we judge without benefit of rules or methods, only that our judgments are a complex weave of public and private. Poor Richard's economic definition states this fact

[9] Ronald Beiner, *Political Judgment* (Chicago: Univ. of Chicago Press, 1983), p. 2.

best: To judge a writer's literary merit by buying his or her books conflates the act of fulfilling personal desires with the author's consequent public merit. Such public evaluation of literary worth has often been an untrustworthy guide for judging the merits of American writers.

Within the ironic counterpointing of Poor Richard's framing story and Father Abraham's sermon, there is the final irony that the only person moved by Father Abraham's speech is Poor Richard himself. The narrative detaches Saunders from his failure to move the people (in the guise of Father Abraham) and, having heard his own advice, he decides to forego any purchases at the sale. From this we might infer the moral of this parable: Even if one cannot persuade others to live virtuously, one should be reasonable enough to listen to one's own advice. Whether Poor Richard is moved by vanity, which he freely admits to, or by a true belief in the principles of hard work and restraint is not clear. What is clear is that the "echo," the representation, he perceives in Father Abraham resolves him to arrange his life more carefully according to such principles. Here Saunders's actions and beliefs are simply brought into closer alignment, the consequence of detaching himself from his own claims.

We must not confuse the simplicity of this story's moral with the complex texturing of its issues. To extrapolate: Throughout American literature, the instability and paradoxical qualities of many works of American literature arise from the struggle for mastery between competing conceptions and voices of authority and their consequent forms of representation. In "The Way to Wealth" we have the "ur-story" of Father Abraham and the people, which presents the struggle between locating authority in traditional forms like the jeremiad, or in the people themselves. Beyond this lies the less easily defined authority of Richard Saunders: Obscuring his attachment both to the wisdom of his proverbs and to the people, Saunders, unlike Abraham, at least understands the economic necessities of his position. By replacing the authority of aesthetic principles with the judgment of his readers, Saunders makes his own authority conditional and practical. Finally, there is the problematic issue of Franklin's authority as the true author of this story. We might call it "narrative authority" as he creates with us a particular social bond of illocutionary force, of narrative command and reader response. God-like, he remains aloof from censure through his ability to create fictional selves and the bond of humor through which we submit to his wisdom. Sensing a difference between Poor Richard's vision of the ironies and Franklin's wider vision encompassing even Saunders, we not only warrant this authority, but judge its aesthetic merit as well.

Thirty years after "The Way to Wealth," Franklin, among many others, was engaged in writing a more important text—the United States Constitution. Although much had changed in that time, one central problem facing the Constitutional Convention was familiar: Seeking to constitute a system of government and thus create a national identity, the participants had to balance the need for traditional, hierarchical authority against the growing claims for democratic independence and local autonomy. Like the earlier story, the final document negotiated a position between authority and autonomy by invoking the concept of representation. The Constitution certainly involves a more complex set of issues than Franklin's story, but fundamentally both rely on (1) language's ability to perform expressive, performative, and rhetorical tasks; (2) the power of representation to create mediating fictions; (3) the necessity of basing authority on the people's judgment. What neither Franklin nor the others could foresee were the startling challenges to American politics and literature created by these issues.

Between the Revolutionary and Civil wars, the destruction of traditional social and epistemic codes, combined with the rise of popular democratic ideals and industrial capitalism, required new tactics from both politicians and writers. No longer secure in their elected offices from the caprices of voters, political representatives sought new persuasive means to win votes, including populist symbols, slogans, and a rhetoric conflating corporate success and individual freedom. This same unstable audience, suspicious of both political and literary plots, led some writers to find safety in conventional forms, while others chose extravagance and experimentation. It was Alexis de Tocqueville who first reflected that the new democratic audience would lead to this "strong and bold" literary style: "Authors will strive to astonish more than to please, and to stir passions rather than to charm taste."[10]

[10] Alexis de Tocqueville, *Democracy in America*, ed. J. P. Mayer, trans. George Lawrence (Garden City, N.Y.: Anchor, 1969), p. 488.

More telling in this search for a constituency and an audience is the way in which the writers' rhetorical strategies reflect their particular attitudes toward political authority. Beginning with the unsuccessful attempts to ally themselves with the political heroes of the Revolution, writers most often came to regard themselves as the perennial opposition party. Brackenridge's failure to be elected to the Constitutional Convention, a political rejection that inspired his satiric *Modern Chivalry*, serves as a paradigm for other writers who used their talents to condemn the course of American society. The success of popular leaders, like the demagogues in Cooper's New York or Andrew Jackson and his followers, compelled these dissatisfied writers to divine the reasons for society's elevation of such men. Some, like Melville, would attack the psychological roots of the demagogue's power; others, like Emerson, found the problem to be epistemological; still others, like Whitman, emulated the populist rhetoric in order to gain a share of the people's attention.

In short, the purpose of this book is to follow out Tocqueville's claim that there are "always numerous connections between the social and political conditions of a people and the inspiration of its writers. He who knows the one is never ignorant of the other."[11] Implicit in each literary work (and often explicit) is a claim for authority that defines itself in relation to social and political forms of authority. America's unique history has prompted writers consciously to diverge from their political counterparts as they responded to the rise and idealization of popular democracy. In essence, as these writers attempted to influence political values and use their writings to establish the authority of letters in this young republic, they encountered the same Mephistophelian proposition facing the political leaders: either accommodate themselves to the pressures of public opinion or find new ways to instruct and move Americans. Unlike the politicians, they often chose to attack or subvert popular sentiments. From Hugh Henry Brackenridge to Herman Melville, certain writers assumed innovative, subversive, and combative styles as reaction against the combined success of political demagogues and popular literature. For each writer, an audience was not simply a group of passive respondents but an

[11] Ibid., p. 474.

assembly of potential judges (and voters) whose judgment was to be tested or trained. Each work, in other words, reenacts the struggle of American writers to define their place in American society, while engaging the writers in a narrative relationship with the reader.

In addition to its historical prescience, Franklin's story serves as a parable for how matters of authority, autonomy, and representation are enacted in communicative situations. To engage another in a communicative act presumes contractual claims about the relative positions of speaker and audience. First, we linguistically establish the relations and terms by which we recognize the social codes of the relationship; second, we share the states of affairs and knowledge according to those terms. Authority is not an attribute of personality or locatable in a person, object, or institution. Stated most simply, it is a "quality of communication" and as such its boundaries and terms are fluid and relational.[12] In its most basic form, authority exists as a command, a type of speech act that makes obedience to the conditions of the relationship the content of the utterance itself. The command is performative in that it constructs the roles of speaker and listener, roles created from the social and cultural codes of identity available to both of us. According to Jürgen Habermas, such "communicative actions are related to a context of action norms and values. Without the normative background of routines, roles, forms of life—in short, conventions—the individual action would remain indeterminate. All communicative actions satisfy or violate normative expectations or conventions."[13] We "do *X*," whether it entails carrying out the garbage, writing a term paper, or going into battle, because we understand, believe in, and follow the conventions that make "doing *X*" a reasonable, legitimate aspect of personal identity.

As a quality of communication, and dependent in large part on language, authority is subject to the momentary confusions and failures inherent in language. The language of authority is itself purposive and pragmatic: It seeks completion within the conditions and terms of a particular communicative structure, including

[12] Carl Friedrich, Introduction to *Authority*, ed. Carl Friedrich (Cambridge, Mass.: Harvard Univ. Press, 1958), p. 5.

[13] Jürgen Habermas, *Communication and the Evolution of Society*, trans. Thomas McCarthy (New York: Beacon Press, 1979), p. 35.

the underlying social and cultural codes. Thus the problem for one seeking authority is to find the proper form of address and expression by which the subordinate will recognize the authority's position and sympathize with his or her intention. In Franklin's case, the people recognize Father Abraham's position but are not moved to respond sympathetically to his intended end. On the other hand, the problem for the subordinate lies in the ability to perceive the command's appropriateness (its "felicity" according to speech-act theorists), recognize the commander's intention, and judge its legitimacy. This epistemological gap is generally satisfied by the codes enabling our recognition: institutional, in the case of a military command, or cultural, in a parent's directive.

What happens, however, when either the codes are not clearly perceived, or when the codes themselves are in a state of change? Returning to the paradigmatic scene of a speaker standing before a suspicious or hostile crowd, we can see the embodiment and consequences of these questions. Father Abraham's failure arises not from the inability of the people to recognize his intentions and authority, but in his ill-chosen rhetorical stance and his reliance on outmoded cultural codes. He is unable to gain that momentary identification of his intentions and his audience's judgment and belief that is his authority because (1) the code of traditional authority by which the people might recognize his allegiance to other Jeremiahs is missing; (2) he refuses to accept the people's desire for economic consumption; (3) he cannot fashion the relational ties by which the people recognize themselves in him.

As "The Way to Wealth" suggests, the concept of authority cannot be taken up alone, for implicit within each claim for authority is a concomitant redefinition of autonomy. Claiming the basic importance of autonomy, Father Abraham finds to his chagrin that it is the people who seem to practice it when they ignore his sermon. Authority implies the loss of autonomy on the subordinate's part, but the rhetorical nature of authority renders it conditional to the subordinate's judgment and compliance. Only absolute authority can create its own laws, invoke absolute autonomy. Mediating between these two terms of authority and autonomy, then, is representation—the metaphoric space creating a conditional authority *and* conditional autonomy for both commander and subordinate.

As Poor Richard teaches us, representation permits a conditional accommodation to the claims of both authority and autonomy. Acknowledging his dependence on his readers, Saunders can still preserve his distance through the office of his representative, Father Abraham. And here politics and literature intersect. A legislator's relation to his or her constituency appears to be a quite different phenomenon than the way in which language creates the illusion of presence of real or fictional objects. Yet both exist in the space of figural perception, particularly in our power to perceive a figural identity between two things—a representative and his or her constituents, a text and the world—that are literally different. Both political representation and linguistic representation rely on figural perception—on tropes—which themselves correspond and function according to cultural and linguistic codes. When these codes are subjected to the pressures of historical change or disruption, as in the truly volatile period of post-Revolutionary America, then both types of representation are put to the test. Father Abraham, in effect, offers himself as the social representative of the people and the literary representative of Poor Richard, just as Poor Richard represents, at a further remove, Benjamin Franklin.

This scene of Poor Richard and Father Abraham, then, sets the stage for future literary and political dramas. A century later, one of Herman Melville's confidence-men aboard the *Fidele* would claim, "To do, is to act; so all doers are actors," thus making authority available to all who could perform before a skeptical audience.[14] Unforeseen by Franklin, during the coming century authority would become less an attribute of fixed social codes and more a matter of those momentary enactments of the confidence game that makes possible the fictions of both politics and literature.

[14] Herman Melville, *The Confidence-Man*, ed. Harrison Hayford et al. (Evanston, Ill.: Northwestern Univ. Press and Newberry Library, 1984), p. 31.

ABBREVIATIONS OF FREQUENTLY CITED WORKS

AD Cooper, James Fenimore. *The American Democrat.* New York: Alfred Knopf, 1931.

AM Brown, Charles Brockden. *Arthur Mervyn.* Edited by Sydney J. Krause and S. W. Reid. Kent, Ohio: Kent State Univ. Press, 1980.

BF Franklin, Benjamin. *Autobiography.* Edited by Leonard Labaree et al. New Haven: Yale Univ. Press, 1964.

CC Cooper, James Fenimore. *The Chronicles of Cooperstown.* Cooperstown, N.Y.: H. & E. Phinney, 1838.

CM Melville, Herman. *The Confidence-Man.* Edited by Harrison Hayford, Hershel Parker, and G. Thomas Tanselle. Evanston, Ill.: Northwestern Univ. Press and Newberry Library, 1984.

CW Emerson, Ralph Waldo. *The Collected Works of Ralph Waldo Emerson,* vols. 1–4. Edited by Alfred Ferguson, Robert Spiller et al. Cambridge, Mass.: Harvard Univ. Press, 1971–1987.

HB Cooper, James Fenimore. *Homeward Bound.* New York: G. P. Putnam's Sons, 1895.

HF Cooper, James Fenimore. *Home as Found.* New York: G. P. Putnam's Sons, 1895.

JMN Emerson, Ralph Waldo. *The Journals and Miscellaneous Notebooks of Ralph Waldo Emerson.* Edited by William H. Gilman et al. 16 vols. Cambridge, Mass.: Harvard Univ. Press, 1960–1982.

LM Cooper, James Fenimore. *The Last of the Mohicans*. Edited by James A. Sappenfield and E. N. Feltskog. Albany, N.Y.: State Univ. Press of New York, 1983.

MC Brackenridge, Hugh Henry. *Modern Chivalry*. Edited by Claude Milton Newlin. New York: American Book, 1937.

MD Melville, Herman. *Moby-Dick: or, The Whale*. Edited by Harrison Hayford and Hershel Parker. New York: W. W. Norton, 1967.

O Brown, Charles Brockden. *Ormond, or the Secret Witness*. Edited by Sydney J. Krause and S. W. Reid. Kent, Ohio: Kent State Univ. Press, 1982.

P Cooper, James Fenimore. *The Pioneers; or the Sources of the Susqehanna*. Edited by Renee Schachterle and Kenneth M. Andersen, Jr. Albany, N.Y.: State Univ. Press of New York, 1980.

RB Melville, Herman. *Redburn; His First Voyage*. Edited by Harrison Hayford, Hershel Parker, and G. Thomas Tanselle. Evanston, Ill.: Northwestern Univ. Press and Newberry Library, 1969.

W Emerson, Ralph Waldo. *The Complete Works of Ralph Waldo Emerson*, vols. 5–12. Edited by Edward W. Emerson. Boston: Houghton Mifflin, 1903–1904.

WI Brown, Charles Brockden. *Wieland, or The Transformation*. In *"Wieland, or The Transformation" and "The Memoirs of Carwin the Biloquist,"* edited by Sydney J. Krause and S. W. Reid. Kent, Ohio: Kent State Univ. Press, 1977.

PART ONE

The Post-Revolutionary Period

CHAPTER ONE

Benjamin Franklin and the Authority of Imitation

Declaring Independence

When Benjamin Franklin began Part Three of his *Autobiography* in August of 1788, he was, for the first time, writing from his own home. Whereas the earlier sections had been composed in England (in 1771) and France (in 1784), he now wrote in his own library on Market Street. But home meant not only the city of Philadelphia or America, which, after all, has always been more a conceptual space than an actual geographical location; home in late summer of 1788 also included the recently constituted and ratified United States of America. In fact, as Franklin looked back over his accomplishments (no doubt with characteristic vanity), his role in helping to write and to ratify the federal Constitution must have seemed significant, for his efforts in Philadelphia the previous year had insured that his nation would have a permanent political and legal identity. It was therefore appropriate that, now assured of the Constitution's ratification, Franklin would turn to his memoirs. For Franklin, personal and national identities and fortunes were inseparable.

If the place of composition was significant, the moment Franklin chose to renew the writing of his life was even more so: Having (re)founded itself in the Constitution, and preparing now to secure its destiny, America needed a new guide in the wilderness. Thus, although the identity of Franklin under construction was that of a generic American, this particular historical moment provided the rhetorical impetus for that autobiographical act. And it is precisely the rhetorical nature of the *Autobiography* that mediates between the historical necessities facing Franklin and his contemporaries, those political squabbles requiring his skill at conciliation, and the representative, universal quality of his life. Over the past year, ever since the Philadelphia Constitution Convention had adjourned on 17 September 1787, debate over that document had threatened to splinter the fragile political unity achieved during the Revolutionary War into autonomous and bickering states. It was Franklin himself who made the closing speech at the convention, urging each person there to "doubt a little of his infallibility" and approve the Constitution. Part Three of the *Autobiography*, therefore, concerns itself with illustrating the very nature of fallibility, using Franklin's dealings with historical figures and events as heuristic anecdotes.

Putting aside for the moment the particular political issues addressed in Part Three, we must first regard this work's peculiar ability to combine the occasional and the universal.[1] Expressly begun to give Americans a model for personal and national success, the *Autobiography* also responds to the historical pressures at each moment of composition. The three places where Franklin composed the work therefore correspond to three crucial historical moments: Twyford in England when Franklin was negotiating with Parliament (1771); Passy in France where he remained minister after the Treaty of Peace with Great Britain was signed (1784); and Philadelphia after the Constitution Convention (1788). Because Franklin's "personal being," as Mitchell Breitwieser has noted, "is in the largest sense *rhetorical*," each historical moment influenced Franklin's rhetorical strategy and thereby dictated the self we encounter in each section.[2] Taken together, the selves we

[1] See Mitchell R. Breitwieser, *Cotton Mather and Benjamin Franklin* (New York: Cambridge Univ. Press, 1984), p. 231, for a discussion of Franklin's "occasional" style. Breitwieser, however, reads the *Autobiography* as leaving behind historical matters. See also Robert F. Sayre, *The Examined Self: Benjamin Franklin, Henry Adams, Henry James* (Princeton: Princeton Univ. Press, 1964), pp. 16–33.

[2] Breitwieser, *Cotton Mather*, p. 171.

encounter in the four parts of the *Autobiography* make up Benjamin Franklin, Printer and Representative American, but each self is also discontinuous, rhetorically composed to respond to the exigencies of the historical moment. Each section (taking the last two together), therefore, corresponds to the key documents of the Revolutionary period: the Declaration of Independence, Articles of Confederation, and Constitution.

By looking at the *Autobiography* as a series of related, but discontinuous, narratives, each bound to a particular historical moment and each with a specific rhetorical design on the reader, we discover that it is rhetoric itself which unites personal and national histories. What Franklin narrates is a life full of encounters with various forms of authority; what he assumes as narrator of that life is his own authority. In doing so he takes on the central issues of this period: the nature and location of authority and how that authority was to be represented. As Jonathan Boucher, the Tory minister, had said of the changes taking place during the Revolution, "Americans were making a truly revolutionary transformation in the structure of authority."[3] In each section of the *Autobiography*, Franklin describes his experience with competing figures of authority and, having internalized the most practical and efficacious, makes himself the representative, the narrator, of that authority for the reader.

* * *

Franklin begins his *Autobiography* as a personal declaration of independence. Describing his steady rise in society and growing influence in a country of equally great potential, Part One defines the qualities and efforts necessary for a republic not yet in existence and outlines the conditions that make Franklin himself the model governor. The Franklin we see at the opening of the *Autobiography* seeks independence, but not revolution. His goal is to become the paradigmatic American, but true to his practical nature he employs the standards at hand, using them as the foundation for his own authority. Authority alone, however, is not enough; Franklin couples it with a claim for autonomy. He initially defines this authority in terms of its imitability, but he preserves his inde-

[3] Quoted in Gordon Wood, *The Creation of the American Republic* (New York: W. W. Norton, 1972), p. 66.

pendence through a narrative strategy of detached (and detachable) reasonable discussion and exposition. He seeks to achieve, in other words, the voice of rational inquiry, witty and slightly ironic perhaps, but also self-assured and self-possessed. It is the voice of Benjamin Franklin, Printer: cool as the type itself, detached from the experience of past events and his younger selves and related to his readers by representing their desires for success. As he begins to give shape to his self, Franklin changes from the guise of traditional paternal authority speaking to his son to a social and theatrical role. Like Hawthorne's Robin Molineux, he transforms his conception of identity and authority from the fixed standards of familial ties to the arbitrary ties of social interaction and association.

In the first section, Franklin immediately establishes the rhetorical strategy of paternal authority by employing the traditional epistolary genre of fatherly advice. Here he attaches the reader to the terms of his authority:

> Twyford, at the Bishop of St. Asaph's 1771.
>
> Dear Son,
>
> I have ever had a Pleasure in obtaining any little Anecdotes of my Ancestors. You may remember the Enquiries I made among the Remains of my Relations when you were with me in England; and the Journey I took for that purpose. Now imagining it may be equally agreeable to you to know the Circumstances of *my* Life, many of which you are yet unacquainted with; and expecting a Weeks uninterrupted Leisure in my present Country Retirement, I sit down to write them for you. . . . Having emerg'd from the Poverty and Obscurity in which I was born and bred, to a State of Affluence and some Degree of Reputation in the World, and having gone so far thro' Life with a considerable Share of Felicity, the conducing Means I made use of, which, with the Blessing of God, so well succeeded, my Posterity may like to know, as they may find some of them suitable to their own Situations, and therefore fit to be imitated.[4]

[4] Benjamin Franklin, *Autobiography*, ed. Leonard Labaree et al. (New Haven: Yale Univ. Press, 1964), p. 43. (Hereafter cited in text as BF.)

The Ciceronian structure with which Franklin ends this passage, the style of elevated rhetorical persuasion, masks the personal appeal to William Franklin, his son and governor of New Jersey. Although William may actually stand for all Americans, the particularity of address enacts those cultural filiopietistic codes that define and grant his father authority. The person addressed may not matter, but the *form* of address does. In the first lines, Franklin not only invokes his own memory for this task, but draws upon his son's participation as well: "You may remember." A slight gesture in itself, this call to William Franklin asks that the son assist in the family's genealogical epic and reattach himself to family matters from which he had been estranged.[5] Having a son warrants Franklin's enterprise, and within this brief preface, he reconstructs the bonds of filial obedience and patriarchal authority. Evoking family history without threatening his son, Franklin suggests the dangers that filial disobedience and willfulness may pose to the continuity of the family's identity.[6]

As he invokes the issue of paternal authority, however, Franklin adds to it the problematic consideration of imitation. It is perhaps intuitively clear the kinds of emotional or financial powers a father may possess, but how does an original, an authority "figure," legitimately warrant its own imitation? Part One soon establishes the means by which we identify legitimate models of imitation by providing negative examples: his brother's arbitrary tyranny, the improper conduct of Governors William Keith and William Burnett, and the clumsy managerial skills of William Bradford and Samuel Keimer, whom, Franklin says, "I found poorly qualified for their Business. Bradford had not been bred to it, and was very illiterate; and Keimer tho' something of a Scholar, was a mere Compositor" (BF, 78–79). Beginning his *Autobiography* with claims of his representative character, Franklin also presents this power in such a way as to judge other familial, political, and economic authorities.

It is Franklin's own father who escapes these particular failures

[5] Approximately forty years old when Part One was written, William Franklin had been royal governor of New Jersey since 1762. Father and son continued on opposite sides throughout the Revolutionary War and never reconciled.

[6] For a contrasting reading of Franklin's attitude toward paternal authority, see Jay Fliegelman, *Prodigals and Pilgrims* (New York: Cambridge Univ. Press, 1982), pp. 106–12. On paternal authority in general see Sennett, *Authority*, pp. 50–83.

of duty and authority. Acknowledging his son's "Bookish Inclination," Josiah Franklin bound Benjamin to his brother; recognizing the quality of Benjamin's poetry, he luckily discouraged his son from being a poet, "most probably a very bad one" (BF, 60). The elder Franklin acts early in the *Autobiography* as a brake to his son's excesses, preventing young Benjamin from a potentially disastrous business venture with Governor Keith and stopping him from escaping, Ishmael-like, out to sea. To honor the memory of *his* father and mother, and presumably to present a model of filial piety for his own son, Franklin tells William how he provided his parents with a gravestone complete with inscription. With this act he initiates the principal theme of the *Autobiography*: the permanence and power of writing and the freedom one achieves from constructing (literally in this case) texts. Here he not only expresses filial values, but his words themselves have an illocutionary force in their enactment, and he recreates the value of filial piety in his letter to his son by publishing the text of the epitaph, thereby attaching himself to his father and his son to himself.

At this moment Franklin makes a crucial break in his narrative that marks a stylistic and rhetorical turn. "By my rambling Digressions," he writes, "I perceive my self to be grown old. I us'd to write more methodically. But one does not dress for private Company as for a publick Ball. 'Tis perhaps only Negligence" (BF, 56–57). It is an enigmatic declaration that serves several purposes. First, it reminds himself and his son of his advancing age, once again providing the possibility of sympathetic attachment between the two. At the same time, Franklin calls attention to the narrative itself, particularly its digressive quality which is dragging him into a moment of intimate self-revelation and away from his expressed intention to model himself. By foregrounding the moment of composition, Franklin creates divergent narratives: the story of his youth, and the continuing creation of a self shared by the reader. As he moves back into a discussion of his father, Franklin has announced his separation from that earlier life, announced his independence from the past.

Although Franklin's father provides one of the few constraints on the ambitious son, and one of the few positive models, his influence begins at this point to be shared by others. The series of male figures in this first section enact the varieties of competing authorities in the world. Father, boss, tyrant, counselor, all provide potential models of behavior and figures to whom the young Franklin can attach himself. The concept of attachment underlines the picaresque quality of Franklin's early life. If this early stage can be seen as a search for models and standards, these men do not so much serve as surrogate fathers as they reshape paternal authority according to new patterns. One constant remains: Authorities are those who are fixed and move others. Franklin, for example, is sent by his father to Philadelphia and to England by Governor Keith. In both instances he turns to printing to survive.

Yet the attachments provided by authority, even that of imitation, are necessarily based on inequality. Authority, as we see in "The Way to Wealth," implies subordination, debt, and constraint; the myth that Franklin creates in the *Autobiography* is one of active independence. As a result, Franklin's travels, usually inaugurated by authority, prove insufficient to keep him down or to contain his natural abilities. Just the opposite: He thrives in his new environments, changing *them* to suit his needs. By defining his ties to family and society in terms of credit or his famous metaphorical "errata," Franklin is able to make various forms of authority conditional to his ability to repay or correct them. In a sense, he repays his father's guidance through his act of "filial Regard," a gesture which also signals his own power. Because his errata are simply moral debts, serving only to create bonds that can be erased or broken upon repayment, then all social ties are found to be external and contingent. As he narrates his steady progress through the imitation of role models and his successful correction of errata and repayment of debts, Franklin describes the internalization of authority. This gradual movement toward an internal authority enacts his personal autonomy, that is, his ability to authorize or write his own self.

Throughout this first section, Franklin masters and exceeds his models. His most significant forms of imitation, and those most critical to his later success, are stylistic. Running across an old *Spectator*, Franklin decides to imitate its style:

> I took some of the Papers, and making short Hints of the Sentiment in each Sentence, laid them by a few days, and then without looking at the Book, try'd to compleat the Papers

> again, by expressing each hinted Sentiment at length and as fully as it had been express'd before, in any suitable Words, that should come to hand.
>
> Then I compar'd my Spectator with the Original, discover'd some of my Faults, and corrected them. (BF, 62)

Notice that his performance creates "my Spectator," as he lays claim to possession by force of language. In the same sense, to write "my Recollections" implies self-possession. After comparing other versions, Franklin announces he "had been lucky enough to improve the Method or the Language and this encourag'd me to think I might possibly in time come to be a tolerable English Writer, of which I was extreamly ambitious" (BF, 62). Franklin's discussion of literary imitation suggests that improvement in style implies not only an exceeding of the model, but also its ownership.

Shortly thereafter, reading Xenophon's "Memorable Things of Socrates," Franklin decides to imitate ("put on") Socrates' persona of the "humble Enquirer and Doubter" (BF, 64). By retaining this mask of diffidence, Franklin tells us, "I have had occasion to inculcate my Opinions and persuade Men into Measures I have been from time to time engag'd in promoting" (BF, 65). Here Franklin changes the terms of imitation somewhat, defining it in the theatrical sense of taking on a role. Hence, language and social interaction are not only forms of self-presentation, but also, as he suggests, means of persuading others while improving oneself and the world. Style *is* the self, but both are "put on" as in Franklin's famous instructions "not only to be in *Reality* Industrious and frugal, but to avoid all *Appearances* of the Contrary" (BF, 125). Models present us with imitable authorities whose roles we can then assume and re-present to others in order to achieve our own authority. As in the case of the *Spectator*, the most effective roles are received not from life, but from books. Once again Franklin turns away from real-life models, whose actions may undercut their imitable authority, in favor of sharply outlined, shadowless literary models. In this, Franklin clarifies an important point about the imitation of appearances: The authority of a model can be possessed and improved by imitation but the reality of the model remains separate and distinct from its representation. His own autobiography, therefore, is a "literary" representation, worthy of imitation because of its idealized nature, but always detached from its creator's experienced reality.

The drive of this first section is away from the authority of Franklin's models and toward the authority of himself as a model. As he is educated by experience he teaches us to judge between worthy and unworthy models. What he has accomplished in this section, however, is not merely to show his superiority to these various models, but to use these failed authorities to define his own. In other words, through the inclusion of his father, brother, Governor Keith, Keimer, and others, he creates the structure by which we *recognize* his authority. Authority depends on our ability to recognize it, and we do so through association with certain social and cultural codes. By accepting his father's paternal authority, Keimer's economic power, and Governor Keith's political conventions as legitimate, albeit improperly represented, Franklin can then show us how he fulfills their offices through his own actions. Franklin is hardly revolutionary; he accepts the conventions, the roles of society, for they provide him with the costumes and dialogue by which he represents himself as the model American.

The key term in Franklin's rise in society and subsequent popularity is *imitation.* For him, personal success and social order rely upon our ability to recogize worthy models of imitation and to properly play out these received roles in the *theatrum mundi.* In his utopian optimism, Franklin envisions the improvement of these roles and therefore of the persons playing them, so he defines the process by which he makes himself a role model. Although he begins this section of his autobiography expressing his paternal authority, he gradually transforms it into what I will call *mimetic* authority, the ability to make oneself into an autonomous original which others can then use as a model for their own behavior. Mimetic authority assumes a portion of paternal authority's inheritable power to link generations, but it revises feudal patriarchy's static succession by making the inheritance available to all on the open market. Recognizing that he has nothing to pass on to future generations but himself, Franklin abandons the specific role of father for the more persuasive position as American original, or, more accurately, original American.

By choosing imitation as the basis for American society, Franklin, however, runs into the same problem Plato describes in *The*

Republic: Imitation itself might actually be a dangerous form of social behavior in a society that lacks true standards for judgment. Doesn't imitation threaten to become mere impersonation, lacking the sincerity, the presence, of the original while disrupting social interaction through its ontological play? In *The Republic*, Plato places at the top of society his rulers, the Guardians, who have acquired the proper education and understanding to guide the utopian society. Their education, however, hinges upon the powers of *mimesis* as they learn by imitating the proper actions of heroes. Yet Socrates is aware that in the theatrical enterprise of *mimesis* the representation is not necessarily attached to the original, thereby introducing ontological and epistemological instability into the act of imitation. When he asks, "Do we want our Guardians to be capable of playing many parts?" he betrays the fear, much like Franklin's, that acting or imitation may lead to reality. Speaking of the Guardians, Socrates says, "if they act, they should, from childhood upward, impersonate only the appropriate types of character, men who are brave, religious, self-controlled, generous. They are not to do anything mean or dishonourable; no more should they be practised in representing such behaviour, for fear of becoming infected with the reality."[7] In part it is this very fear of impersonation that leads Plato to ban poets from his republic.

The idealist Plato and pragmatic Franklin may at first seem to have little in common, yet both exhibit a utopian impulse. Unlike Plato's utopian, authoritarian society, Franklin's vision individualizes political governance, incorporating the state within each person. And for both, the problem of a utopian government lies in the very nature of mimesis, that is, in the slippage between an original authority and its representations. Obviously, the chief difference lies in the fact that for Plato models of behavior are ultimately ideal forms, and thus have absolute authority. The Guardian's authority arises from *truly* representing these ideal forms, just as Philosophers, whose business it is to perceive these ideals, *must* necessarily be kings. For both Franklin and Plato, these leaders achieve their status through correct education; if one controls the environment and forms of learning, then one can create superior humans.

[7] Plato, *The Republic*, trans. F. M. Cornford (New York: Oxford Univ. Press, 1945), 395b–d (p. 83). On the subject of Plato and theatricality, see Jonas Barish, *The Antitheatrical Prejudice* (Berkeley: Univ. of California, Press, 1981), pp. 5–37.

Yet the problem of imitation remains: How can we *control* the fluid relationship between model and its representation, and how do we perceive the relation between the two? Plato excludes poets from his utopia because of their creation of "untrue" representations and in part because the act of representing acquires its own freedom. Wanting to restrict all change, Plato recognizes that mimesis in its theatricality threatens our ability to control it.

Charles Altieri has suggested that for Plato "Socrates becomes a figure of the performative sublime, dramatizing in actions principles of values which Wittgenstein properly insisted could not be stated in propositional terms."[8] Socrates is able to enact those virtues which he cannot in language represent. Similarly, for Franklin, authority arises in the acting itself, that is, in the production of *correct* rather than true representations of social codes. As long as Franklin consistently "puts on" the social codes, then those codes do not have to correspond to absolute values. Abandoning belief in a causal relation between a moral ideal and its representation, Franklin makes authority free to those who can act. Social control thus occurs within the terms of proper conduct, terms which are based on appearance, rather than on the ideals themselves. Franklin's famous program of achieving perfection with the help of his chart of thirteen virtues presents another exercise in mimesis. It is also a critique, tongue-in-cheek as it may be, of a Platonic republic.

Franklin's theatrical conception of the self in the first section allies him closely with traditional eighteenth-century notions of the public man.[9] He stands at the late boundary of the age which considered personal identity a function of social conventions. Within this theatrical world view, people conducted themselves according to standards of etiquette; the separation of public from private lives required them to dress, speak, and work according to carefully observed rules and codes. The magnificent powdered wigs and fine clothes of Franklin were presentations of self, and presenting such a fine image was a part of his social obligation as well as a communication of a legitimized identity. In essence, authority

[8] Charles Altieri, "Plato's Performative Sublime and the Ends of Reading," *New Literary History* 16 (1985): 251–74.

[9] This discussion follows Richard Sennett's study of capitalism, theatricality, and personality, *The Fall of Public Man* (New York: Alfred Knopf, 1977), esp. pp. 47–122.

was encoded in those expressions of self, tying one to a particular class, position, employment, and public office. Thus many of Franklin's anecdotes create the impression of *tableau*; walking into town with loaves of bread under his arm, or pushing the wheelbarrow through the streets, Franklin shows much of his success to be based on proper activities, rather than on virtuous action.

Behind this vision of the public man lay a conception of a homogeneous and hierarchical society, and behind *that* vision lay European, particularly English, conceptions of a static world. Such a world view did not neatly fit into the facts of America, even in 1771. The curious aspect of Franklin's conception of society in this first section is that it maintains the traditional hierarchical structure, and the theatricality involved in class association, but he gives it dynamic possibilities never considered in London. He explores the possibility that, outside the confines of British society, position and power might be held by performance arising not from proper breeding but simply through imitation. An industrious and talented man like Ben Franklin could rise socially because he knew the appropriate parts to play, but he required hierarchy in order to imbue the strata of society with representative moral values marking one's moral decline or progress.

Part One clearly shows the conception of society and culture held by Franklin and most of the signers of the Declaration of Independence. Like the Revolution itself, this vision was conservative in intent, seeking to maintain certain values which Americans believed the British themselves had abdicated.[10] The founders needed the traditional structures of society which they could imitate and improve upon, just as Franklin superseded his models. For these conservative revolutionaries, however, independence initiated unexpectedly profound social and political consequences. Attending independence was the increasing power of the individual voter, necessitated by the new state constitutions which privileged the power of representatives over the governors, and the rise of a republican ethos. The term *republican* now stood for the end of the monarchy, a new form of government, and the new moral

[10] On the conservative quality of the Revolution, see Samuel Eliot Morrison, *The Conservative Revolution* (Washington, D.C.: Society of the Cincinnati, 1976). See also Bernard Bailyn, *The Ideological Origins of the American Revolution* (Cambridge, Mass.: Harvard Univ. Press, 1967), pp. 94–143, and Wood, *Creation*, p. 10: "They revolted not against the English constitution but on behalf of it."

standards necessary for a nation newly raised on standards of the "common good."[11] Although the society ran on traditional models, the people could generally agree with Thomas Paine's claim that, because of the Revolution, Americans were now "really another people."[12] Charged with the energy of Puritan rhetoric, republican ideology claimed the transcendent power of this virtuous people united by voluntary obedience to its ideals.

Emphasizing the ascending consensual power of the people, republican ideology created troublesome consequences for the leaders. First of all, this consent could not be coerced by the leaders, nor could the people's wishes be constrained by force. Persuasion, not coercion, is the tool of a republican government. The people must be convinced to vote, to act, and to obey, that is, to subsume private interests to public virtue. Consequently, as Gordon Wood has commented, "[a] republic was such a delicate polity precisely because it demanded an extraordinary character in the people."[13] This need to instill the qualities of public virtue, to create "public men" again, suggests the degree to which the categories of public and private, basic to traditional conceptions of society, were changing. Without a performative self realized in public, politics threatened to degenerate into questions of personal preference and individual judgment. Perhaps recognizing the inherent dangers of republicanism to the conventions of society, the leaders sought to articulate the virtues needed by the individual republican.

In Part One, Franklin anticipates the republican emphasis on individual virtue and judgment made necessary by the events of 1776. He acquires independence by appearing virtuous, hoping perhaps, unlike Socrates, that the reality would be infected by appearance. Such independence is to be judged by the degree to which he internalizes his external constraints, makes himself, in other words, a republic governed by the self, *one that can represent that self*.[14] As in "The Way to Wealth," to *be* an authority by providing a model for proper action and yet to remain autonomous and

[11] For a discussion of republican values, see Wood, *Creation*, chapter 2, and Linda Kerber, "The Republican Ideology of the Revolutionary Generation," *American Quarterly* 37 (1985): 474–95.

[12] Thomas Paine, "Letter to Abbe Raynal," in *The Complete Writings of Thomas Paine*, ed. Philip S. Foner (New York: Citadel Press, 1945), 2: 244.

[13] Wood, *Creation*, p. 68.

[14] Breitwieser, *Cotton Mather*, p. 179, explains that "for Franklin, government is also an interior voice, but it is the self or *I*, rather than a counterweight to the self."

self-possessed, one must persuasively represent that authority. The sense of an almost pure exteriority we have when reading the *Autobiography* comes from the fact that we are seeing the representation, meeting the representative, of that authority. For Franklin, all authority is represented authority, which also means that autonomy is, paradoxically, a theatrical gesture projected against the background of social constraints, an achievement, that is, of a negative self. We judge Franklin's mimetic authority by those men—father, brother, boss, and governor—who fail to govern others or themselves, and we recognize his independence as a freedom from those bonds created by the failure of self-governance.

The first section presents an extraordinary collaboration of Puritan self-analysis and Enlightenment theatricality. And together these two influences supported the cause of republican government by emphasizing disciplined virtue acted out toward the end of individual independence. Beginning Part One as Father Benjamin, Franklin revises that role to become the imitable model of republican success, the authority "figure" of American independence, as well as the successful imitation, the representation of that authority.

The Failure of Confederation's Virtues

Proclaiming his personal independence five years before the nation's declaration, Franklin had accomplished a literary act that both made claim to his authority and enacted his autonomy. As he ended the first section, Franklin was beginning to describe the fruits of his industriousness: his personal success as printer; his club, the Junto; and the subscription library. To this he added the memorandum, "My Manner of acting to engage People in this and future Undertakings," marshaling, once again, his mimetic authority for public ends. For the next thirteen years, between this terminal point and the section written in 1784, political events of the Revolutionary period caused him to turn his attention to other forms of public service. However, when he returned to his *Autobiography* the presuppositions of his earlier work no longer easily applied to this new world. Like Rip Van Winkle, he wakes to a different historical moment; his principal concern is once again to make himself useful.

This crucial second section presents a revaluation of both paternal and mimetic authorities. In 1771 he had sought authority first as a father and then as a model of success. Beginning Part Two, he reemphasizes his position as an imitable model by including the letters of Abel James and Benjamin Vaughan. No longer must he write his own praises; now, like Poor Richard, he empowers others to represent him. But just as the Revolution transformed the terms of authority from monarchical and illocutionary to republican and persuasive, the model authorizing imitation proves to be quite different: His guides are not father, boss, or governor, but rather, the abstract precepts of his "Project of arriving at moral Perfection" (BF, 148). But how should a reader understand Franklin's account of his virtues, for they present an entirely different conception of imitation? Franklin's apparent ironic failure to imitate these virtues, unlike his earlier success at "possessing" the original *Spectator* essay by improving on it or "putting on" Socrates in a gesture of theatrical representation, suggests a new intention to persuade rather than to model.

The detached tone of this section constantly verges on the humorous, but it also masks Franklin's intentions, reminding us of Poor Richard's ironic contemplation of the restless countrymen at the auction. The America that Franklin contemplated in 1784 was not that run by homogeneous republican virtues. It had settled into chaotic bickering of regional and political factions, each seeking a voice and order in the new nation. In its vagueness, disorder, and lack of imitable power, Franklin's system of virtues most resembles the Articles of Confederation, the original constitution of the Revolution that worked principally through the necessity of war. But by 1784 the Articles were actually impeding unity because they did not provide a clear structure of order upon which to found a new nation.[15]

In much the same way, Franklin's plan for moral perfection fails to move us to imitate him because it collapses into abstraction. Reading each of these virtues, we can uncover any number of po-

[15] Wood, *Creation*, p. 359, notes: "Congressional power, which had been substantial during the war years, now began precipitously to disintegrate, and delegates increasingly complained of the difficulty of gathering even a quorum. By the middle eighties Congress had virtually ceased trying to govern." Like Franklin's plan, the Articles of Confederation contained thirteen articles.

tential imitative actions because they are written without practical parameters. "SINCERITY," for example, tells us to "Use no hurtful Deceit" (BF, 150), a useful suggestion until we realize that it fails to distinguish between rational action and rationalization. Although these remain positive instructions, they are not true models of behavior, and they provide few clues as to their applicability to particular situations. Only in his final virtue, "Humility," does Franklin look to human models. Yet even Franklin's explanation of this virtue—"Imitate Jesus and Socrates"—provides an impossibly ambiguous model for human behavior. Like Franklin, Socrates assumes humility as one of the best forms of argumentation, rather than as an ideal virtue.

The difference between Parts One and Two reveals how much America's situation had altered, and consequently how Franklin addresses the problem of virtue. Part One is cautionary: In it we see Franklin carefully plot his course toward success, using negative examples as warnings of possible failure. But within each failure lies his own potential for success. To see Governor Keith's inability to govern openly does not negate the necessity of his public office, just as Keimer's failure as a printer instructs the young Franklin how to succeed in his chosen vocation. In just the same way, Americans rebelled from England because it had corrupted its ideals, not because the principles themselves were bad. The Revolution insured independence even as its victory gave proof to the Americans' claim on the republican virtues England herself had abrogated. But once victory had been attained, the abstract principles of government did not serve as practical guides for establishing a new system of government. Part Two plays out the same problem in personal terms as Franklin recounts the difficulty of aligning personal weakness with an impossibly demanding system of ideal virtues.

Just as the Articles of Confederation proved useless at creating unity, Franklin too decides that his "Scheme of ORDER" gives him "the most Trouble" (BF, 156). In fact, he abandons the plan altogether, although retaining its ideal form on marble, just as he chronicles his failure to complete other projects. What remains, however, is his understanding of the contradictions inherent in his own search. Attempting to destroy pride, he only identifies it more clearly; seeking humility, he inevitably loses it in his search. In suggesting his own limitations, Franklin makes a crucial turn from the first section where he became his own model for success. Here *he* is the failed model, the one who in his failure negatively presents us with the structure of virtue to be imitated.

Franklin's conceptions of individual and social identity in Part Two circumscribe certain limits to his earlier utopian vision. The self remains fluidly progressive and improvable, but not perfectible on its own powers. Perfection becomes a useful fiction but its individual virtues are less qualities to acquire than the conventions of society to be put on. One does not simply perform before others in order to possess these virtues; rather, one presumes their ideal nature and works for an adequate representation. A model American, Franklin represents the need for objective authorities. As the optimism of 1776 began to wear off, and the nation's identity began to unravel for want of order, Franklin seeks to posit those virtues that, if properly practiced, might restore order.

In 1771, Franklin had unwittingly made what now seemed dangerously opposed claims. His concept of a theatrical, hierarchical society now seemed threatened by the very social mobility he embodied in his earlier memoirs. Mobility based on talent was one of the foundations of republican ideology, but by 1784 it seemed that every American, no matter his or her qualifications, talent, or background, claimed the right to rise in society. Franklin's true conception of success is best explained by Gordon Wood:

> Movement must necessarily exist in a republic, if talent alone were to dominate, if the natural aristocracy were to rule. But such inevitable movement must be into and out of clearly discernible ranks. Those who rose in a republic, it was assumed, must first acquire the attributes of social superiority—wealth, education, experience, and connections—before they could be considered eligible for political leadership.[16]

In characterizing republican ideology, Wood here also defines the concept of society that Franklin maintains from 1771 to 1788. What changes for Franklin is not his image of a republican society, but the forms of authority meant to achieve its order and stability. In 1784 he can ironically criticize the dangers of the loosely de-

[16] Wood, *Creation*, pp. 479–80.

fined Articles while simultaneously holding them up as ideals. By 1788 he seeks to posit an institutionalized authority and a corresponding vision of the self.

Reconstituting the Self

When Franklin begins the third section (in August of 1788), he refers to his plan for Moral Perfection almost as Father Abraham might. Based on his model of virtue, this "Society of the *Free and Easy*," he claims, aims for the autonomy of its members: "Free, as being by the general Practice and Habit of the Virtues, free from the Dominion of Vice, and particularly by the Practice of Industry and Frugality, free from Debt, which exposes a Man to Confinement and a Species of Slavery to his Creditors" (BF, 163). Franklin himself has been forced by "multifarious Occupations public and private" to abandon the project. Instead, two young men adopt the plan "with some Enthusiasm" on their way to wealth and autonomy. This remark seems at first another example of Franklin's ability to infect others with his paradigmatic self. However, as we encounter other "Enthusiasts," particularly George Whitefield's religious enthusiasm and General Braddock's military hubris, we must stop to reconsider the dangers of imitation for those seeking to realize such an ideal plan.

Like the first part, Part Three is littered with failures, although these work on a grander scale than James Ralph's fall into obscurity. Now personal frailty or excess leads to public disasters and the ignominy only history can document. If Part One narrates the success of one man according to the rules already laid down by society, then Part Three privileges society's advancement over the individual's. Franklin has reversed the code of success: In 1788, success and failure must be measured by the improvement or harm to society, and the standards for such evaluation now belong to Franklin himself. With this difference in mind, we can see that Franklin ends his discussion of the "Society of the Free and Easy" with an exhortation he himself has not heeded:

> And I was not discourag'd by the seeming magnitude of the Undertaking, as I have always thought that one Man of tolerable Abilities may work great Changes, and accomplish great

> Affairs among Mankind, if he first forms a good Plan, and, cutting off all Amusements or other Employments that would divert his Attention, makes the Execution of that same Plan his sole Study and Business. (BF, 163)

The self that Franklin presents in the final two sections is the maker of good plans. He is not so much a particular individual but the institutional representation of a self. In other words, we see Benjamin Franklin as he exists in the projects he has instituted or supported, and his authority no longer lies in a theatrically presented self, a role model for his children, but in the *constitutions* of his societies and institutions. Max Weber has called this type of authority "rational-legal."[17] In Franklin's conception, this institutional authority grows less out of a plan of abstract virtues than from the codified rules and laws constituting his fire companies, libraries, and the nation itself. If Franklin begins his *Autobiography* wanting to create a continuous identity, he realizes it cannot be done as a "Father" of the country, nor as a moralist, but as its inventor. He speaks to us *through* his institutions as their identities begin to merge.

Franklin's personal enterprise in Part Three is warranted by his participation in the public act of constructing and ratifying the Constitution. Although most readers have been aware of Franklin's emphasis on the power of print and of writing, it is in this section that writing first becomes "documentary," that is, becomes a truly public enactment and connection of personal and collective identities. And it is here that personal identity becomes entangled in history, allowing autobiography to assume documentary value. The moment of composition for this section corresponds to the sensitive point when ratification of the Constitution, once an uncertainty, appeared to be assured.[18] In the seventeen years since

[17] See Max Weber, *The Theory of Social and Economic Organization*, trans. A. M. Henderson and Talcott Parsons (New York: Free Press, 1947), pp. 57–58, 329–41, for a discussion of rational-legal authority.

[18] By 17 February 1788, Franklin was able to write to his friend, M. Le Veillard:

> Six States have already adopted the Constitution, and there is now little doubt of its being accepted by a sufficient number to carry it into execution, if not immediately by the whole. It has, however, met with great opposition in some States, for we are at the present a nation of politicians. And, though there is a

first beginning his autobiography, Franklin has gone from a model of individual success to one of collective identity. It is still a *written* identity, but it now critiques the power of individuals to impose themselves on society and the world. In Weber's terms, it preserves the rational-legal over the charismatic.

True to the course of Franklin's career, Part Three concerns itself with his public activities as organizer, diplomat, and scientist. Recounting his experiences *in* history, Franklin undoubtedly filtered these events through his knowledge that, as a member of the Constitutional Convention, he had helped *make* history. Once his duties had been fulfilled, and knowing he must have only a short time left to write, Franklin took up his memoirs with new urgency.[19] Yet it is also very likely that the political events of the last year added to his haste. Franklin never doubted ratification, but the Antifederalist opposition surprised him. Fought with exchanges of letters, pamphlets, and sermons, the battle for ratification had divided the Federalists (Franklin's party), who sought a strong executive and central government, from the Antifederalists (later to become the Republicans), who wanted the greatest share of authority to remain within semi-autonomous states. This debate of 1787–1788 expressed the issues of the Revolutionary War in national rather than international terms. The relatively rapid transformation of authority from hierarchical to republican, from the governors to the representatives (and eventually to the people), made problematic the very process of creating a new political identity. By decentralizing authority, the Antifederalists wanted to extend the revolutionary doctrines of independence; in effect, they

---

> general dread of giving too much power to our *governors*, I think we are more in danger from too little obedience in the *governed*.

From *The Works of Benjamin Franklin*, ed. Jared Sparks, 10 vols. (Boston: Hilliard Gray, 1840), 10: 337.

[19] On 22 April 1788, Franklin wrote to M. Le Veillard:

> My three years of service will expire in October, when a new president must be chosen; and I had the project of retiring then to my grandson's estate in New Jersey, where I might be free from the interruption of visits, in order to complete the work [the Memoirs] to your satisfaction. . . . But considering now the little remnant of life I have left, the accidents that may happen between this and October, and your earnest desire, I have come to the resolution to proceed in that work to-morrow, and continue it daily till finished, which, if my health permits, may be in the course of the ensuing summer. (*Works*, 10: 345)

wanted to remake America in their own image. Their efforts must have seemed a personal affront to Franklin, for he had spent years in public service, and had written the first two parts of his *Autobiography*, attempting to redesign America in *his* image.

To understand completely the historical moment of Part Three, and therefore its rhetorical and political strategy, it is useful to outline briefly what was at stake in the controversy between Federalists and Antifederalists. In this struggle, Franklin naturally gravitated toward those intent on preserving the document. His inclination, however, derived from social ideology as much as from political allegiance. The conflict itself arose from a tangle of issues, but the terms of the disagreement centered on authority: the image of central authority, the relationship between representatives and constituents, and the relative authority of individual states. Nevertheless, what was being argued was less the constitutional codes themselves than the concepts of social identity that informed the creation of these codes. In articulating their points of view, the two sides in effect created divergent definitions of American society: the Federalists, a hierarchical society of distinct, theatrically defined classes led by a social elite; the Antifederalists, an antiaristocratic society mirroring the desires of the quasi-democratic constituency.

The image of authority envisioned by the Federalists was basically that sketched by Franklin in the first section of his *Autobiography*: a theatrically presented and codified authority of the public man. The Revolutionary War had granted Americans independence from England while promising a new conception of national (and consequently, personal) identity in republicanism, but it did not easily replace the ideological conceptions of society that constituted British authority.[20] They shared a view, as Gordon Wood has suggested, found in the *Federalist*, "that all parts of the society were of a piece, that all ranks and degrees were organically connected through a great chain in such a way that those on the top were necessarily involved in the welfare of those below them."[21] At stake for the Federalists was more than the degree of political power; rather, it was the way in which political authority corresponded to

[20] See Bailyn, *Ideological Origins*, pp. 302–9.

[21] Wood, *Creation*, p. 499.

social power, enabling the leaders to define the underlying cultural and social rules, the very basis of personal and national identity by which this authority is transmitted.

As the Antifederalists responded to this image of authority they did so with a vehemence left over from the Revolution. Despite the Federalists' disclaimer of any personal interest or gain, their opponents wondered if they had defeated British aristocracy only to be governed by American aristocrats. Writing under the name Cato, George Clinton (then governor of New York) evoked the latent fears of courtiers and monarchy held by Antifederalists as he described the proposed president's cabinet: "The language and the manners of this court will be what distinguishes them from the rest of the community, not what assimilates them to it; and in being remarked for a behavior that shows they are not meanly born, and in adulation to people of fortune and power."[22] As another writer suggested, the cultural heritage of the Federalists invited closer ties to despotic foreign nations, making the representative unfit for "that generous system of policy which is founded on the affections of freemen."[23] Mercy Warren summed it up best when she called the proposed Constitution "dangerously adapted to the purposes of an immediate aristocratic tyranny."[24] The Antifederalists, in short, fought to dismantle the organic, hierarchical notion of social identity and authority presupposed by the Federalists, replacing it, they hoped, with an identity arising from the people themselves.

Federalist and Antifederalist alike agreed with Alexander Hamilton's republican vision that consent of the people should be the "pure original foundation of all legitimate authority."[25] Their agreement, however, was based on contrary assumptions. The Federalists considered that the authority inherent in the amor-

[22] George Clinton, "Letters of Cato," No. 7, in *Essays on the Constitution*, ed. Paul Leicester Ford (Brooklyn, N.Y.: Historical Printing Club, 1892), p. 262. Cecilia Kenyon has called the Antifederalists "men of little faith." See "Men of Little Faith: The Antifederalists on the Nature of Representative Government," in *National Unity on Trial, 1781–1816*, ed. E. James Ferguson (New York: Random House, 1970), pp. 11–47.

[23] James Winthrop, "Letters of Agrippa," No. 11, in *Essays on the Constitution*, ed. Paul Leicester Ford (Brooklyn, N.Y.: Historical Printing Club, 1892) p. 89.

[24] Quoted in Wood, *Creation*, p. 513.

[25] Alexander Hamilton, James Madison, and John Jay, *The Federalist*, ed. Benjamin Fletcher Wright (Cambridge, Mass.: Harvard Univ. Press, 1961), p. 199.

phous body politic would be invested and given form in the body of officers responsible to the nation. Going far beyond this, the Antifederalists wanted, at least to some degree, the people themselves "to act as sovereign, exercising authority as one body with undivided power."[26] Of course, this demand for popular sovereignty led to several problems: (1) how to find leaders who could reflect the general will of the people; (2) how to limit the representatives' office by minutely detailed laws; (3) how to keep the "body" small and in geographical proximity to its leaders. Despite the republican rhetoric, both sides shared a Hobbesian view of humankind as selfish and hungry for domination. As George Clinton declared, "rulers in all governments will erect an interest separate from the ruled, which will have a tendency to enslave them."[27]

At root, however, the Antifederalists feared the image of the theatrical public man described by Franklin and his Federalist allies. To put the problem another way: The fears of the Antifederalists were as much epistemological as they were ideological. They simply did not share the same faith in the cultural and social codes enacted by the Federalists, nor did they presume one's ability to judge those performances properly. Not easily able to assume the public personae of the Federalists, they also could not communicate with the same variety of social vocabularies. Antifederalists like Philip Freneau chose to see vanity and arrogance in the Federalists' deportment: "When I walk the streets of this city," he wrote, "I can instantly tell who are people in authority, simply by the assumed significant superiority of countenance, displayed on these occasions by the great men."[28] Unwilling to trust both the performers *and* performance of authority, the Antifederalists tried to separate social identity from authority by restricting the terms of authority to the fixed rule of law constituting each office.

The Antifederalists' mistrust of political authorities gave political life to the Puritan fear of actors. They reveal in their arguments an almost pathological fear of deception and impersonation. And in their fear of Franklinesque imitation (to "put on" another's au-

[26] Charles W. Hendel, "An Exploration of the Nature of Authority," in *Authority*, ed. Carl J. Friedrich (Cambridge, Mass.: Harvard Univ. Press, 1958), p. 23.

[27] Clinton, "Letters of Cato," No. 7, p. 278.

[28] Philip Freneau, *The Prose of Philip Freneau*, ed. Philip K. Marsh (New Brunswick, N.J.: Scarecrow Press, 1955), pp. 188–89.

thority), they threatened to undo the terms of mimetic authority described in Part One of the *Autobiography*. Like Plato, they feared that the representative's role as an elected authority might infect him with the reality. The geographical and legal separation of the representatives from the people, they believed, would necessarily lead to their independence, just as an actor achieves a frightening degree of ontological freedom when assuming a role. Displacing this fear onto the Federalists themselves, the Antifederalists called their opponents a "masqued aristocracy." One Antifederalist described the opposition as both actors and, anticipating Melville, confidence-men: "It is knavery that seeks disguise. Actors do not care that any one should look into the tiring room, nor jugglers or sharpers into their hats or boxes."[29] Mistaking public performance for illusion, the Antifederalists misunderstood the conventional foundation of the Federalists' world.

Given this mistrust of performance, it is perhaps not surprising that Antifederalists found even the language of the Constitution deceptive. Although the Federalists could claim that the Constitution "is expressed with brevity, and in the plain, common language of mankind," their opponents, desiring even greater exactness, found it dangerously ambiguous.[30] Unlike the Federalists, to whom language was a fixed and conventional social medium, the Antifederalists sought to define the Constitution's powers in precise, almost absolute terms. To fix its language would be to prevent arbitrary interpretation. The Antifederalist "Centinel" (George Bryan) wrote, "the science of government is so abstruse, that few are able to judge for themselves." Being unable to understand the language of legal complexities, and without the education to decide exegetical questions, the common people would easily become the "instruments of despotism in the hands of the artful and designing."[31]

Fear, it seems, was the binding motivation for most critics of the Constitution. Yet fear of authority, as Richard Sennett has suggested, actually involves three different objects: "In part it is fear

[29] George Bryan, "The Letters of Centinel," in *The Antifederalists*, ed. Cecilia Kenyon (Indianapolis: Bobbs-Merrill, 1966), pp. 17, 20–21.

[30] Oliver Ellsworth, "The Landholder," No. 5, on *Essays on the Constitution*, ed. Paul Leicester Ford (Brooklyn, N.Y.: Historical Printing Club, 1892), p. 156.

[31] George Bryan, "Letters of Centinel," p. 4.

of the authorities as seducer. In part it is fear of the act of seduction, of liberty yielding to security. In part it is a fear of the seduced, of the masses who might be weak-willed."[32] In a country where political action was often accomplished by the mob or assembly, the Federalists feared a government by mobs led by unscrupulous demagogues. Daniel Shays's rebellion in 1786 seemed to them the fruit of a truly democratic rule. The Antifederalists feared their representatives and governors as the potential seducers of the people. Moreover, they feared the performance of authority and the rhetoric of the Federalists as acts of seduction. Improper "confidence"—a term that should remind us of the political nature of the confidence game—is "frequently the parent of deception," one Antifederalist wrote.[33] Between them the Federalists and Antifederalists defined the political Scylla and Charybdis of the Federalist era: the charismatic and populist demagogue who charms the mobs of citizens, and the aristocratic tyrant, who, like Edmund or Iago, seduces the people in the tragedy of state.

For his own part, Franklin feared the rise of this opposition because it seemed to threaten the social foundation on which the Constitution stood. More specifically, the threat came from demagogues, those misrepresentatives whose power overcomes the individual's self-government. Writing in "A Comparison of the Conduct of the Ancient Jews and of the Anti-Federalists of the United States of America," he points directly at those who feign public service in order to achieve private ends. The Israelites, Franklin claims, suffered their "newly-acquired liberty . . . to be worked upon by artful men, pretending public good, with nothing really in view but private interest." As a result, "they were led to oppose the establishment of the new constitution, whereby they brought upon themselves much inconvenience and misfortune."[34] The millennial subtext serves to make clear the consequences of following such demagogues. For my purpose, Franklin's fear underscores the new emphasis on public duty and his antagonism toward charismatic leaders in Part Three.

Franklin was aware of the opposition's natural suspicion of the Federalists' intentions and their fears that the traditional leaders

[32] Sennett, *Authority*, p. 15.

[33] Clinton, "Letters of Cato," No. 7, p. 277.

[34] Franklin, *Works*, 5: 162.

would sacrifice the country's well-being for personal ambition. As he begins Part Three of his *Autobiography*, Franklin raises the issues of private versus public interest and the relation of both to political parties when he quotes from his reading notes from 1731, which he ingenuously claims had been "accidentally preserved": "That few in Public Affairs act from a meer View of the Good of their Country, whatever they pretend; and tho' their Actings bring real Good to their Country, yet Men primarily consider'd their own and their Country's Interest was united, and did not act from a Principle of Benevolence" (BF, 161). His conception that one's vanity may aid the nation, rather than hinder political confidence, does not contradict his earlier belief that society runs on the weaknesses and resulting interdependence of its citizens. But his description of bickering parties, and belief in a utopian "regular Body, to be govern'd by suitable good and wise Rules" (162) suggests a characteristic desire to assuage the controversy with practical consensus.

Much of Part Three, therefore, delineates one's responsibility to the collective public good and the means by which the fragments of a disordered body may be collected and given a new identity. To accomplish this act of persuasion, Franklin once again uses himself as a model of action, but here subordinates personal gain to public service. He sets himself the task of determining the proper and improper ways in which the public may be organized and moved, and once again employs alternative visions of authority in order to suggest indirectly the proper means to achieve order. Unlike Part One, in which Franklin gradually internalizes the codes for success while rejecting the flawed individuals who represent them, Part Three finds Franklin already admirably self-governed. With his internal constitution in place, he locates those alter egos who threaten to disrupt society. As with many Federalists of his age, Franklin finds in the charismatic demagogue the principal danger to national unity and personal autonomy.

Of course, Franklin himself remains central in this section. In fact, if the first part of the *Autobiography* consists of Franklin's peripatetic search for proper models, Part Three presents Franklin as being fixed in society and in his identity. Now governors, ministers, and generals seek *his* advice. When this advice is heeded, as, for example, when Gilbert Tennent follows Franklin's directions for fund raising, the result is successful. When General Edward Braddock arrogantly refuses to listen to Franklin's counsel, he is killed and his army routed. Whereas the figures in the earlier section are potential models, now men like George Whitefield are alter egos and rivals. In a nation struggling to identify itself through rational-legal authority, these men present the dangers of charismatic authority based on personality.

The complex treatment of Whitefield reveals the way Franklin fuses autobiography and history, narrative self and narrated self. Here he offers a slightly different self-portrait exemplifying the problem of reconciling order and independence in the United States of 1788. He first sets up Whitefield as the model of charismatic authority. In contrast to Franklin's strategy of presenting a humble demeanor, Whitefield's rhetorical posture aggressively seeks identificaton through "common Abuse" (BF, 175) of his admiring audience. Franklin unmistakably admires Whitefield's "Power over the Hearts and Purses of his Hearers" (BF, 177), for as projector and potential utopian governor he too seeks the proper leverage to move the people and to construct the institutions of society. From his vantage point in 1788, however, Franklin is acutely aware of the mesmerizing persuasive power that a Whitefield or Daniel Shays wields. For Franklin, like Plato, autonomy is allied with rationality, and the loss of the latter presumes the abdication of the former. Recounting Whitefield's sermon, Franklin reveals the power of the charismatic leader by himself bending to the minister's powerful rhetoric. But he once again finds a representative for his own skepticism, and points out the dangerous loss of reason and autonomy:

> At this Sermon there was also one of our Club, who being of my Sentiments respecting the Building in Georgia, and suspecting a Collection might be intended, had by Precaution emptied his Pockets before he came from home; towards the Conclusion of the Discourse however, he felt a strong Desire to give, and apply'd to a Neighbour who stood near him to borrow some Money for the Purpose. The Application was unfortunately to perhaps the only Man in the Company who had the firmness not to be affected by the Preacher. His Answer was, *At any other time, Friend Hopkinson, I would lend to thee*

> *freely; but not now; for thee seems to be out of thy right Senses.* (BF, 177–78)

The practical man and worldly philosopher has here dangerously placed himself in the hands of charismatic authority, only to be saved by a skeptic. More importantly, Whitefield's ability to sway listeners through his powerful presence suggests a kinship to the Antifederalist demagogues who likewise gathered crowds of Americans by the force of rhetoric.

At this point, Franklin commences his retaliatory critique of Whitefield. He tells us their relation was "a mere civil friendship," as if to emphasize the conventions of social intercourse that should bind them. Responding to the charismatic minister, the scientific Franklin circumscribes Whitefield's power by restating it in rational and social terms. He begins by measuring the distance from which Whitefield could be heard by the masses:

> Imagining then a Semi-Circle, of which my Distance would be the Radius, and that it were fill'd with Auditors, to each of whom I allow'd two square feet, I computed that he might well be heard by more than Thirty-Thousand. This reconcil'd me to the Newspaper Accounts of his having preach'd to 25000 People in the Fields, and to the antient Histories of Generals haranguing whole Armies, of which I had sometimes doubted. (BF, 179)

Distance is the answer to combating Whitefield's charismatic power, particularly the objective distance of rational inquiry enabled by inscribed language. His answer to Whitefield, in other words, involves not just the power of the written word, but its efficacy as the ironic medium by which we remove ourselves from immediate experience. But Whitefield is more than a failed minister, for Franklin's apparently offhand comment associates Whitefield with the other failed military leaders we encounter in Part Three. Whitefield finally becomes a prototype of the demagogues then fomenting dissension in the fields of Pennsylvania and Connecticut.

Whitefield's greatest mistake is to neglect the future consequences of his rhetoric. As Franklin tells us, perhaps with an admonishment to his own composing self, "[Whitefield's] Writing and Printing from time to time gave great Advantage to his Enemies. Unguarded Expressions and even erroneous Opinions del[ivere]d in Preaching might have been afterwards explain'd, or qualify'd by supposing others that might have accompany'd them; or they might have been deny'd; but *litera scripta manet*" (BF, 180). Whitefield does not anticipate the future by "recollecting" his life, nor can he therefore correct that life. His authority lacks the power to continue itself in his audience's imitation. Although his life, like Franklin's, becomes the words left in his absence, Franklin wins this contest, for the *Autobiography* is the correction of his life, *is* the life for future generations. The letter does outlive the voice; the *appearance* of presence supersedes the *reality* of absence. Finally, in Part Four, Franklin explains that he often sends a speech to the Assembly, rather than read it, "the Intention of which was only to reduce to a Certainty by writing, what in Conversation I had delivered *viva voce*" (BF, 264). Once again, writing provides the certainty of intention and deliberation. Those who neglect to write, Governor Keith earlier or General Lord Loudon in this section, fail to accomplish their purpose.

By writing his life, Franklin authorizes it. As he supersedes his rivals, he no longer submits to others. He has, in effect, narrated his life on his terms, thereby escaping the ignominy of subordination and his imitation. Franklin presents his life as exemplary in all of that term's meanings. It is, first of all, a life worthy of imitation by those who seek public success. Moreover, it provides the model, the exemplum, by contrasting itself with the failures who litter history. Yet it tells us not so much *what* to become as *how* to achieve success, that is, the rules and conditions by which abstractions like success can be judged. By explaining his life in terms of the conditions for proper judgment, he presents us not only with the image but also with the structure for recognizing its authority.

Franklin aims at creating an autonomous self, as independent and self-governing as the nation he seeks to serve. In this he mirrors the nation; self-government, autonomy, and authority *were* the political issues of the day—as they continue to be in our own. He presents his thirteen-step plan to moral perfection with deadpan irony, but despite its unworkability the plan points out the need to establish standards of behavior for the nation, to will the flux of identity into shape. The need to fix and settle and determine the standards and roles of authority characterizes much of the *Autobiography*. As it moves from the first section to the last, this work concerns itself less and less with Franklin as a model of accomplishment and more with him as a model of practical judgment. In his critique of Whitefield, Franklin illustrates the proper way to address would-be authorities: Armed with skepticism, scientific formulas (that is, conventions capable of the pragmatic truth test), and rationality, we can preserve our independence. If the first and earliest section of his work is the Declaration of Independence, the final sections, written in the crucial days of national self-analysis, are his Articles of Confederation, helpless in their unrealizable abstractions, and Constitution, provisional yet always capable of change and amendment. The dual character of his narrative—the plot of his life and the process of composing that life—exposes the differences.

His narrative authority, to borrow Max Weber's terms, shifts from the traditional to the rational-legal. Beginning with his own family history, Franklin presents his encounters with men who embody varieties of paternal and traditional control: tyrannic, advisory, admonitory, influential. The personal character of these attachments, however, leads inevitably to conflict and rebellion. The final sections define Franklin's role in creating institutions that bind people to an impersonal order. This order, as Weber says, is "for the administration of everyday profane affairs."[35] We remember Franklin today for the organizations he started—the fire company, post office, newspapers, libraries, the United States itself. In the end, Franklin *becomes* those institutions he invents; he melds his identity and authority with theirs. No longer is he the parent speaking to his children; now he speaks in a manner as detached as the bureaucracy he inspired. Readers often find the final sections a less vivid account of his life, but his bond with us, his readers, becomes, as it did with Whitefield, "merely civil." We are no longer his children but account for our relation to him by virtue of existing within the rational machinery of America.

Charisma, of course, becomes the one form of authority that Franklin must counter. Sympathetic attachment to men like Whitefield drives us out of our "right senses," destroying the rational

[35] Weber, *Theory*, p. 333.

organization of society. Because authority is a quality of communication, Franklin represses the irrational, personal forms of traditional authority; he is no longer Father Abraham, nor even the ironic Poor-Richard-like figure we encounter in the first section of the *Autobiography*. His authority is no longer economic, measured by those who buy his books, but rather mimetic, measured by the imitable power of the American dream, and rational-legal, conceived in constituted powers of government. The power he makes and the life he writes remain models to be superseded. But he himself remains independent and self-sufficient by this autobiographical act.

CHAPTER TWO

Hugh Henry Brackenridge and Representation

THE REVOLUTIONS OF REPRESENTATION

In the spring of 1781, Benjamin Franklin was minister to France and soon to act as commissioner to negotiate a peace settlement with England. On 12 March of this year, Franklin asked Congress to relieve him as minister, citing poor health: "I have been engag'd in publick Affairs, and enjoy'd public Confidence in some Shape or other, during the long term of fifty Years, an honour sufficient to satisfy any reasonable Ambition" (BF, 318). That same spring another Philadelphian, Hugh Henry Brackenridge, migrated from the most sophisticated city in America to the small frontier town of Pittsburgh. After having attempted a series of careers as literary editor, writer, chaplain, and lawyer, Brackenridge moved to the border of civilized America precisely to enjoy the same public confidence and to fulfill his ambitions as Franklin had in Philadelphia and Europe: "I pushed my way to these woods where I thought I might emerge one day, and get forward myself in a congress or some other public body."[1] Although Brackenridge eventually became a representative, and later a judge, he is best known as the author of the long picaresque novel, *Modern Chivalry* (published in

[1] Quoted in Claude Milton Newlin, *The Life and Writings of Hugh Henry Brackenridge* (Princeton: Princeton Univ. Press, 1932), p. 57.

seven volumes between 1792 and 1815). What Brackenridge eventually received in this territory, however, was not the public's confidence in him as a writer, or even representative, but its suspicion and hostility. If Franklin could now boast of his authority among the Americans, Brackenridge's fate reveals the problems for any public person, especially an aspiring writer, in the new nation.

Brackenridge's choice to reject the fixed and certain life of Philadelphia for the unsettled potential of the frontier town provides a new version of Franklin's travels to find a place where he could shape his identity through hard work. Ambitious and dissatisfied, Brackenridge, too, hoped to establish a new identity, and the unformed town of Pittsburgh must have seemed the ideal stage. But his restlessness also reflects the unsettled conditions of the United States, which was struggling at that moment to redefine itself, indeed to call itself into existence. In his study of recently independent Third-World countries, Clifford Geertz has described each new nation's need to challenge the "cultural, social, local, and linguistic categories of self-identification and social loyalty" that comprise its nationhood.[2] Settlement comes (if it comes at all) only after the uncertainty involved in the process of redefining these categories of knowledge, perception, and expression. Revolution and independence, in other words, call into question not only the identity of a nation and its citizens, but the very ways we come to know and establish an identity. Starting in the Constitutional period and lasting throughout the century, this process of recategorization and redefinition became the true American revolution, but one that threatened ambitious men like Brackenridge who sought to ally personal and public identities in a time when neither was assured.

The turning point in Brackenridge's career came when he attempted to "get forward" by running for the Pennsylvania state convention meeting to ratify the Federal Constitution. Having lost the election to William Findley, a weaver whom he considered unfit to represent the people, Brackenridge proceeded to write the first version of *Modern Chivalry* as a satiric antidote to demagogues and other false representatives. Near the end of the novel he makes its purpose explicit: "The great moral of this book is the evil

[2] Clifford Geertz, "After the Revolution," in *The Interpretation of Cultures* (New York: Basic Books, 1973), p. 239.

of men seeking office for which they are not qualified."[3] Consequently, a paradigmatic scene in the novel is the frontier election, the ceremony in which the principal issue involves judging the best representative and determining his proper relation to the people. In the United States, this act of election also defines and renews the nation's particular form of republican government, its political identity. But this novel quickly reveals that this identity was an unsettled and unsettling issue, for each election seemed to present new and sometimes violent problems for the people who had not yet developed the ties of national loyalty.

To limit attention to political representation, however, overlooks the more fundamental philosophical and social problems raised by the novel. Investigating the categories of self and social identity, the paradigms that constitute our knowledge of the world and which themselves are brought into question by these political elections, leads Brackenridge beyond politics to a more essential question: What *is* representation in this new country? In other words, this novel explores the problematic nature of representation, and particularly the ontological sleight of hand of presenting something as itself in another form or medium as well as the epistemological problem of perceiving the representation and its represented object as sharing an identity. These problems, inherent in any cultural or political act, had real consequences for Brackenridge, who as a writer (a user of language for truthful or fictive purposes), political representative (one who stands for others), and judge (one who ascertains the validity of truth claims) had to address them in a region and nation that had just called them into question.

Associated with representation are a number of concepts—imitation, agency, mediation—that link the novel's encylopedic discussion of politics, language, money, and law. Throughout the picaresque episodes the same issues appear: The relationship between the representative object or person and the things represented—between the world as represented by the novel's fictive language, as well as between the political representative and his constituents as constituted by the republican form of government. Bracken-

[3] Hugh Henry Brackenridge, *Modern Chivalry*, ed. Claude M. Newlin (New York: American Book Company, 1937), p. 611. (Hereafter cited in text as MC.)

ridge poses a series of questions in *Modern Chivalry*: How does currency represent value? How is language attached to the world? Perhaps the most important question is epistemological: How are we to distinguish true representations and representatives from false ones? In political terms he rephrased the question: "How do you distinguish the demagogue from the patriot?" (MC, 415). In short, Brackenridge diagnoses the social and political confusions in post-Revolutionary America as matters of representation, and he uses his novel to teach the reader to judge such matters.

Franklin's *Autobiography* attempts to mediate between the self's internalized authority and society's need to constrain individual autonomy by creating a representative self. *Representation* becomes the key, triangulating term in the constant struggle between the self's aggressively egocentric internal "states" and society's external roles. But Franklin was born into a society whose mixture of Puritan and Enlightenment paradigms provided the necessary tools to create a representative identity. In contrast, Brackenridge's novel and his experiences on the frontier reveal the dramatic changes taking place not only in the public structures of government but in the very nature of identity. Something of this change is evident in the sequence of the *Autobiography*'s composition, but in *Modern Chivalry* even Franklinesque hard work and practicality fail. Franklin restated the problem of authority in terms of representation; Brackenridge discovered that representation creates new problems.

* * *

As a picaresque novel, *Modern Chivalry* uses its episodic quality to contrast being fixed or settled with movement and contingency. Like Brackenridge himself, the novel's Captain Farrago and Teague O'Regan wander rootlessly through the frontier, comically reflecting the dynamic changes in America's class attitudes. More to the point, *Modern Chivalry* resembles *Don Quixote* as it makes these class differences symptomatic of a profound revolution of world views in the frontier society. Living on a historical as well as geographical boundary, he depicts the confusions and ambiguities resulting from competing ideas about the nature of personal and social identities. Thus the eccentric wanderings of Farrago and Teague through the countryside—the "frontier" and "marginal position" to which Michel Foucault assigns the poet and madman—reiterate the other unsettled and indeterminate areas of the novel: social classes that have lost their distinctions, characters who manifest ontological slipperiness, words that have no clear referents.[4]

The episodes that produce the greatest confusion and volatile humor are the elections of representatives. In part, the scenes serve as revenge on Brackenridge's neighbors for electing the weaver William Findley ("Traddle" in the novel) to the Pennsylvania convention ratifying the Federal Constitution.[5] But the novel transcends personal spite as it makes the act of election elicit a number of conflicting claims about the process of selection and the judgment required to choose a suitable representative. We confront these issues early on in the novel as Teague O'Regan, Captain Farrago's Irish servant, is asked to serve as a representative of the people. Wishing first to dissuade the people from electing either the weaver Traddle or Teague, Farrago argues from the position of static social roles: "You are surely carrying the matter too far in thinking to make a senator of this hostler; to take him away from an employment to which he has been bred, and put him to another, to which he has served no apprenticeship" (16). Farrago's politics are anchored in the fixity of class and identity. The people, however, argue from different rules:

> It is a very strange thing said one of them, who was a speaker for the rest, that after having conquered Burgoyne and Cornwallis, and got a government of our own, we cannot put in it whom we please. This young man may be your servant, or another man's servant; but if we chuse to make him a delegate, what is that to you. He may not be yet skilled in the matter, but there is a good day a-coming. We will impower him; and it is better to trust a plain man like him, than one of your high flyers, that will make laws to suit their purposes. (MC, 16)

Rather than believing in inherited ("bred") qualities, these new democrats see identity and ability as learned and incomplete ("a-coming"). Whereas Farrago sees representation as existential, as *being* or having the character of a representative, the people see

[4] See Michel Foucault, *The Order of Things*, (New York: Random House, 1970), p. 50.

[5] See Newlin, *Life*, p. 96, for this episode in Brackenridge's life.

the representative as *acting* for them. Virtue acquired through the Revolution's success thus resides in the people as a whole, who can delegate ("impower") that virtue, in effect, imbue Teague with the glory of the common man. Because such virtue is transferable, it is better to delegate a "plain man" who is amenable through his lack of fixed characteristics. The character and social class of a representative become arbitrary just as he exists metonymically to those who elect him. His identity, fixed by his constituents, is assured only as long as he resembles them.

Brackenridge himself believed, as did most Federalists, that those with the best education and breeding should represent the people. Responding to the confusion of rumor and exaggeration attending the Constitution's ratification, he wrote in the *Pittsburgh Gazette*, "The simplicity of those whom we send to represent us in the public bodies is at the bottom of this misfortune."[6] In particular, William Findley lacked the learning necessary to judge such vital matters: "Let him occupy the present interval to improve himself in books; for most assuredly he is not without the need of this. I am now in the fiftieth year of my age, and having been forty-five a severe student; and yet because I know something, I should tremble, were I to think of a seat in the legislature of the union, at not knowing more."[7] In short, as he was to write in *Modern Chivalry* ten years later, "There are but two characters that can be respectable as representatives of the people. A plain man of good sense, whether farmer, mechanic, or merchant; or a man of education and literary talents" (MC, 296–97). Implied here is the distinction between Franklin's public man, the man of letters whose occupation provides him with the proper tools of persuasion and rational detachment, and the private man attached to irrational self-interest. The choice, at least for the politically ambitious Brackenridge, seemed easy.

Brackenridge's stance was essentially little different from that of other supporters of the Constitution. Writing under the name of Publius, James Madison, a classmate of Brackenridge at Princeton,

[6] "Sermon in Favor of the Federal Constitution," *Pittsburgh Gazette* 29 March 1788. Reprinted in *A Hugh Henry Brackenridge Reader*, ed. Daniel Marder (Pittsburgh: Univ. of Pittsburgh Press, 1970), p. 134.

[7] From "An Address in Opposition to the Election of [William Findley]," in Brackenridge, *Reader*, p. 138.

said in *The Federalist* No. 57: "The aim of every political constitution is or ought to be first to obtain for rulers, men who possess most wisdom to discern, and most virtue to pursue the common good of society; and in the next place, to take the most effectual precautions for keeping them virtuous, whilst they continue to hold their public trust."[8] As he declared in the famous tenth essay of *The Federalist*, success for the republican government of the United States lies in the ability of the representatives to "*refine and enlarge* the public views," that is, to present local issues within the context of national concerns.[9] The superiority of a republican over a democratic government lies in "the *substitution* of representatives, whose enlightened views and virtuous sentiments render them superior to local prejudices, and to schemes of injustice."[10]

Both *Modern Chivalry* and *The Federalist* reflect the current national debate over the criteria for proper representation.[11] This period witnessed a dramatic transformation in the concept of the ideal political structure from one based on a governor's hierarchical authority to the now-familiar concept of authority resting in the people at large who delegate their authority to representatives. As representation replaced authority as the key issue, however, the problem of this "government by fiction," as Edmund Morgan calls it, became one of deciding between virtual representation (each representative standing for the entire nation) or actual representation (each representative standing for the narrower geographical interests of constituents).[12] Assuming the homogeneity of society and the similarity of interests among the people, virtual representation "implied that the representative was a superior so com-

[8] Hamilton, Madison, Jay, *Federalist*, p. 383.

[9] Ibid. p. 134; my emphasis. On the metaphor of refinement, see Garry Wills, *Explaining America* (New York: Penguin, 1981), pp. 223–37.

[10] Hamilton, Madison, Jay, *Federalist*, p. 135; my emphasis. Madison later discussed the bonds linking the representative and constituents: "Duty, gratitude, interest, ambition itself, are the chords by which they will be bound to fidelity and sympathy with the great mass of the people" (No. 57, p. 385). Wills comments: "Representation is itself a sign of trust and surrender—the agent, the delegate, is put in charge of man's affairs. There is a commitment *of* the agent to seek his *client's* good; but in a scheme of republican virtue there is also a commission *to* the agent to seek the *public* good." *Explaining*, p. 217.

[11] On current debates over representation, see Wood, *Creation*, pp. 162–96, 596–600; see also Bailyn, *Ideological Origins*, pp. 161–75.

[12] Morgan, "Government by Fiction," pp. 321–39.

pletely possessed of the full authority of all the people that he must be solicited, never commanded, by his particular electors and must speak only for the general good." Actual representation, on the other hand, was motivated by social heterogeneity: The representative was "simply a mistrusted agent of his electors, bound to follow their directions."[13] In the elections themselves, these issues combined the epistemological and social problems of identifying the proper representative.

Reacting to Antifederalist fears that representatives, detached from their constituents, would become a new aristocratic tyranny, Madison balanced the need for a national perspective against local circumstances. His use of contradictory metaphors, however, suggests either an unconscious confusion of the meanings of representation or a deliberate elision of the problem. To be a "substitute" as he calls the representative in *Federalist* No. 10 is simply to stand in a metonymic relation of the part to the whole; that is, he is empowered by the whole body of the people to act for them. To "refine and enlarge" the people's views, however, verges on a metaphoric displacement of the people as the representative himself is figuratively transformed from a private to a public person.[14] The linguistic confusion reveals the epistemological slippage inherent in the relationship between representative and electors. Avoiding the central problem, Madison wisely transforms representation into a matter of degrees of attachment by discussing it in terms of frequency of election and numerical proportion of electors to representatives. He hopes that virtuous, learned men will be elected and, by "virtue" of their public office, will conduct their local affairs with a national conscience. In other words, Franklinesque *performance* of an office will infect the representative's role with the office's virtues.

To see political representation as a form of troping locates these particular points of contention in terms of how people identify relationships between parts and wholes. Like a rhetorical trope, a representative's identity is essentially relational, involving the dis-

[13] Wood, *Creation*, p. 189.

[14] My discussion of Madison's circumvention of the problem of representation supports Albert Furtwangler's view that writing *The Federalist* was as much an act of "self-persuasion" as a "coherent and fixed theory of government" (see *The Authority of Publius* [Ithaca: Cornell Univ. Press, 1984], pp. 80–97).

placement and transfer of meaning that occurs from perceiving distinctions of similarity and difference between terms. The *fiction* of representation occurs as we create figurative ties of identity to someone who acts for us. Such a fiction requires a general congruence between perceptual categories and social codes. As an example of metonymy (the part standing for the whole), the representative's success lies in being able to transport the meaning of the larger term of the constituency in a reduced state.[15] He is most representative who can, by his common association with the whole, embody the essence of the whole. To use Madison's term, he is a substitute, but he must in some way be able to resemble the electors, act as their delegate, and mediate between them and the institutions of the government. This metonymic model requires some sort of obvious logical reference between the two terms; *hands*, for example, standing for *workers* involves the recognition of functional similarity. Actual representation is thus defined by functional association and perceived contiguity: the representative is the agent or delegate of the people because he or she exhibits easily perceived ties to them. Most important, the delegate can substitute for the people, be made to signify by them, because they recognize an association and resemblance. Just as metonymy is the trope of realism in its ability to create the illusion of mimetic reference, the metonymic representative assuages the constituents' suspicions by creating a likeness of them. A metonymic representative is one tied to the whole; his significance is achieved at the expense of his autonomy.

[15] For the sake of convenience, I am subsuming synecdoche under the general heading of metonymy, following Roman Jakobson's example in "The Metaphoric and Metonymic Poles," in *Fundamentals of Language* (The Hague: Mouton, 1956), pp. 76–82. Although I agree with his association of metonymy with contiguity and metaphor with similarity, some later discussions need clarification. Subsequent developments have mistakenly linked metaphor with substitution, confusing the perception of similarity for an act of substitution of one term by another. *Substitution* is actually the term employed by classical rhetoricians to describe metonymy (see, e.g., Quintilian, *Institutio Oratorio*, 8.6.23). Metaphor does not substitute one term for another, but, rather, relies on the conjunction of identity *and difference* in the figurative relationship between the two terms which remain yoked but necessarily autonomous. Here I follow Paul Ricoeur, *The Rule of Metaphor*, trans. Robert Czerny (Toronto: Univ. of Toronto Press, 1977). For a useful discussion of the problems associated with tropes, see Jonathan Culler, "The Turns of Metaphor," in *The Pursuit of Signs* (Ithaca: Cornell Univ. Press, 1981), pp. 188–209.

Metaphor, though declaring a similarity between terms, asks that we see this similarity in terms of their difference. In saying, "My love, a rose," we make a more radical perceptual shift when we consider the figurative relation between "my love" and "rose," one that moves from the literal absurdity of the association to a cognitive satisfaction conceiving an identity. Turning a private individual into a public *figure* through election involves, I would argue, not only a delegation of voice but the transformation of personal identity into a figural self. A representative is different in kind. Brackenridge, like Madison, wanted a representative to resemble his constituents' interest *through* his difference and to transcend local prejudice by virtue of what Kenneth Burke calls "perspective."[16] In this form of representation, the representative *creates* an identity for his constituents through his performance, even as he retains his autonomy.

Watching the outcome of actual frontier elections, Brackenridge had doubts as to the wisdom of a republican government. The people willfully committed themselves to electing the plain, the uneducated, even the corrupt. In short, they elected men who resembled them in their faults rather than embodied their collective republican virtues. Hoping to assuage Antifederalist fears, Madison had elegantly described the degree of attachment of representative and people without detailing its exact nature. As a victim of the new democratic notions of election, Brackenridge sought to explain true representation in terms of detachment and independence, that is, to define a metaphorical attachment, which does not require literal resemblance. Although he wanted to create a place for his own public talents, his political concerns were less personal than philosophical. That people would elect the William Findleys and Teague O'Regans seemed to him symptomatic of a habit of mind, a literalness of perception, that undermined a republican government and threatened all social relations. Thus election becomes the paradigmatic scene of deception, misperception, and misrepresentation. And at the center of each election scene in the novel stands Teague O'Regan whose presence has a peculiarly unsettling effect on the people's judgment.

[16] Kenneth Burke, "Four Master Tropes," in *A Grammar of Motives* (Berkeley: Univ. of California Press, 1969), p. 504.

Teague's role in the novel has largely been overlooked because he is too obviously the butt of the humor. Yet he creates the confusions and entanglements precisely *because* his malleable character reveals and accentuates the contradictions of the young republic. If the ideas of his master Farrago are "drawn chiefly from what may be called the old school; the Greek and Roman notion of things" (MC, 53), then Teague (like many later characters in American fiction) is a new man. As a recent immigrant, he is uneducated, uncultured, and uncouth—"plain" as the people like to call him—in an equally undefined nation. "You have nothing," Farrago tells him, "but your character Teague, in a new country to depend upon" (MC, 17). Except for his ambition, he is defined by his absence of signification.

What, then, makes Teague attractive to so many people? In the course of the novel he is sought as a representative to Congress, Indian chief, scientist, tax man, actor, and military leader. Sheer Franklinesque ambition or talent does not account for these bewildering possibilities. He is most often drawn into these deceptive situations by the ingenuous efforts of others, and it is precisely this unfinished quality of Teague's character that makes him attractive to electors. Because he can be completed by the people, or, rather, be made to signify when empowered by them, he does not possess independence or autonomy but promises to identify his interest with theirs. In electing him, the people seek a kind of literal identification.[17] Representation thus demands a (con)fusion of intention and identity that exceeds mere delegation of authority by the sheer intensity of attachment.

Jay Fliegelman has shown that affectional ties—the bonds of "fidelity and sympathy" that Madison mentions in the *Federalist*—took on a threatening, sinister quality in America in the 1790s.[18] In particular, he points to the long Christian tradition of *simile simili gaudet*: "One loves those in whom one perceives one's own image." The transformation of this religious belief (God loves humankind in His image) into a republican government threatens to become a kind of electoral narcissism as we elect those in whom we see ourselves *or* who look (or can make themselves look) like us.

[17] Pitkin, *Concept*, pp. 60–91, terms this "descriptive representation."

[18] Fliegelman, *Prodigals and Pilgrims*, pp. 227–35.

Representation then becomes an impossible attempt to copy oneself and resemblance becomes the chief criterion for judgment and approval. Attachment, in other words, becomes a kind of self-love as the object of affection is substituted by self-interest.

In a seemingly extraneous section of *Modern Chivalry*, Brackenridge points out the political and social consequences of self-love and sympathetic attachment. Having been taken to Washington by Captain Farrago to learn to dress and act like a cultured representative, Teague finds himself irresistible to the Capitol's ladies who are taken by his rough frankness and protean abilities. In a crucial observation, the narrator explains the reasons behind his success.

> A Teague O'Regan has no sentiment of his own, and therefore he approves all the reason, and laughs at all the wit of the lady; so that putting her in love with herself, she becomes in love with him. . . . Again, a Teague O'Regan is repressed by no sense of honour, or regard to a permanent happiness, from passing himself for what he is not, and practising imposition, he imposes; talking of his great relations when he has none. (MC, 241)

This description differs only in degree from Franklin's habit of persuasion through humble deportment. As a representative or lover, Teague's lack of an independent self mirrors our desire for attachment based on self-love. If we are motivated by self-love in electing a representative, his success can be measured by the degree he "plays," "re-presents," or mirrors us. In the desire for attachment and identification with others we can be deceived by them and by our own desires. This Washington society borders on madness because there is no permanent attachment to the things of the world. Teague interposes himself between the lovers and reveals the illusory desire for floating signifiers, for the actors of the world. By extension, the electoral process repeats this desire, revealing in the process the frightening convulsions of a society reordering its categories of meaning and identity.

If Teague is a signifier without a referent, a character who can be made to appear as almost anything in this society, Farrago represents the opposite extreme: one who believes in stasis, fixity, and the necessary unity of signifier and signified. Within the contrast of these two, Brackenridge himself attempts to find some conditional stability.

Like Don Quixote, Captain Farrago has an attachment to a way of life that has passed suddenly without his awareness. The new world continually surprises him with its possibilities. Assured by a man that Teague can be transformed into an Indian "in about nine days," Farrago responds, "Is it possible that such deception can be practiced in a new country?" (MC, 56). The confidence-man's response is to the point:

> The government . . . is at a great distance. It knows no more of Indians than a cow does of Greek. . . . How is it possible for men who live remote from the scene of action, to have adequate ideas of the nature of Indians, or the transactions that are carried on in their behalf? Do you think the one half of those that come to treat, are real representatives of the nation? Many of them are no savages at all; but weavers and pedlars, as I have told you, picked up to make kings and chiefs. (MC, 56)

On the unsettled frontier, Franklin's advice to "appear" takes on frightening consequences as those appearances acquire ontological validity. And if representation involves the making present of something absent, then geographical distance here replicates the gap between represented object (Indian chief) and representation (Teague)—the awareness of absence existing in the act of representation.

Farrago, on the other hand, wishes to believe in a world of presence. Things for him are simply presented rather than represented. The exchange between Farrago and a member of the Order of Cincinnati over the organization's emblem underscores his efforts to fix meaning. For Farrago, the emblem is a misrepresentation because it is unnatural ("the eagle, a bird of Jove . . . grasping the lightning in its claws") and unrealistic. A more serious objection is that "the motto does not at all express that in which the merit of Cincinnatus did consist. It was not in leaving every thing to accept the commission of the Roman senate; but in resigning his commission, and, the work done, going to his plough again" (MC, 73). Again Farrago's obsession with place: Cincinnatus, unlike Teague, returns to his proper station. Most problematic, however, is the fact that the emblem arbitrarily excludes the soldiers who fulfilled the moral duty symbolized by the emblem but who simply do not belong to the organization. He complains that the consequences of this exclusion is the necessity "to keep alive attachment to what is arbitrary, and founded, not in utility, but caprice" (MC, 75). Only if the insignia referred to all Revolutionary soldiers would it truly signify. "Every thing," he claims, "ought to be preserved *sui generis*; as nature makes no honourary animals; a bear is a real bear, a sheep is a sheep; and there is no commixture of name, where there is a difference of nature" (MC, 75). The emblem *and* the institution mislead because their significance is unfixed and thus ultimately divisive. The epistemological uncertainty of the image (it is a "molten" image), the moral ambiguity of the motto's language, and the autocratic presumption of the institution to speak for the Revolutionary soldiers and the nation, all provide support for Farrago's perceptive criticism.

Yet the criticism cuts both ways. Is it true that "a bear is a real bear"? Wanting to fix the meanings of institutions and words, Farrago fails to recognize that, though "nature makes no honourary animals," human beings do. Confusion over the ability to create new identities becomes the principal source of humor in the novel, and the irony is heightened as Farrago himself adds to the problems. When confronted with two men claiming to be ministers, one with the clerical garb and the other with the proper papers, Farrago counsels the imitator to continue the ruse because there are "few bodies, ecclesiastical or civil, in which there [are] more than one or two men of sense; that the majority of this consistory, might be as easily humbugged, as the lay people" (MC, 100). The false minister proceeds to give a practical and successful thirty-second synopsis of the Bible that does convince the people. The humor, aimed at these fickle, ignorant people, returns to Farrago with a barbed point. What, then, is a minister? Farrago has successfully proven that a representative need only establish credibility through feigned presentation rather than exist *sui generis*, or through legitimate ties to an institution and congregation. Throughout the novel this question of identity is constantly posed until the narrator places it in a political context: "How do you distinguish the demagogue from the patriot?" (MC, 415). This epistemological and linguistic doubt lying at the heart of most eighteenth-century comedy requires that we judge Farrago by his own untenable desire for a static society and world.[19]

Teague and Farrago, then, present opposing perspectives on the problem of representation. Moving from consideration of political elections to their philosophical and social analogues, Brackenridge implies that it is not what the representative does or means that is important but rather how we come to judge and select representatives. The question becomes, What are the criteria for judging between true and false representatives? Teague presents frightening possibilities because the people select him for his absence of character and qualifications. He expresses the arbitrariness of meaning, or, perhaps, the fact that meaning in this new world is discovered only in the process of defining and interpreting. Farrago, on the other hand, attempts to impose a classical, static order on the frontier. For all his good intentions, he reveals the contradictions of the elitist opposition: Wishing to separate truth from error, he must add to the deceptions of the world; desiring to fix the fluid character of American society, he himself wanders picaresquely; claiming to have the independent public good in mind, he too is moved by self-interest.

Turning from thematic concerns, in which the theme of political representation and election becomes paradigmatic for problems of signification in general, I want to suggest that *Modern Chivalry* actually enacts a form of representation that ties together Brackenridge's literary and political ambitions. Through its peculiarly American unfinished roughness of style, the novel represents the proper relationship of author to reader.

The Representative Style of *Modern Chivalry*

In what ways does a literary work itself exist as a representation? How does language make present that which is not only absent but often nonexistent, that is, fictional? In short, how is language attached to the world and to the reader? Using the now familiar metaphor of fixity, Brackenridge presents one part of the problem in the novel's first sentence: "It has been a question for some time

[19] My discussion of Captain Farrago follows that of Emory Elliott, *Revolutionary Writers* (New York: Oxford Univ. Press, 1982), pp. 183–89. Like Elliott, I see Farrago as an object of satire rather than Brackenridge's spokesman.

past, what would be the best means to fix the English language" (MC, 3). Continuing on, the reader soon discovers that language is "fixed" neither in terms of its standards nor its referents. Proliferating throughout the novel are literary styles from elevated to Hudibrastic, dialects, literary genres including orations, sermons, poems, the discourse of science and philosophy. Rather than linguistic fixity, this novel describes fluidity and disjunction. The overabundant styles and genres force us to consider seriously the narrator's claim that his novel will "consider language only, not in the least regarding the matter of the work" (MC, 3). We might rephrase this to say that style, the troping of representation, *is* the matter.

Chapter 1 anticipates this self-reflexivity by testing its own initial claims. Although the narrator begins with a description of Captain Farrago, he says only of Teague O'Regan, the servant, "I shall say nothing of the character of this man, because the very name imports what he was" (MC, 6). Thus Teague is not merely a representative type—the ignorant, sensual bogtrotter of literary caricature—but he is "fixed" by his name, turned by that name itself into a static object. Yet immediately after this comment we are asked to consider the ability of language to fix meaning. On their very first adventure, Farrago and Teague meet several jockeys traveling to a race. When asked if he has a horse to enter, Farrago replies, "Not at all . . . this is but a common palfrey, and by no means remarkable for speed or bottom; he is a common plough horse which I have used on my farm for several years and can scarce go beyond a trot" (MC, 6). Hearing this claim, "the jockeys were of opinion, from the speech, that the horse was what they call a bite, and that under the appearances of leanness and stiffness, there was concealed some hidden quality of swiftness uncommon" (MC, 6–7). The confusion here arises from willed disbelief; the jockeys doubt Farrago *because* of his speech, not in spite of it. Language, even when supported by seemingly empirical evidence, creates uncertainty because of human mistrust in the intentions of others. In such communicative situations, one's ability to imagine the intentions of others momentarily aligns the linguistic and social codes of the relation, allowing consensus in such matters as reference—what they are pointing at—and authority—what their respective social positions might be. But such codes seem not to work in

Brackenridge's revolutionary world. What Farrago calls a "plough horse" (a type of horse) they call a "bite," but a "bite" does not refer to a real horse, nor even to a representation of a horse, merely to the idea of a misrepresented horse, one whose real status is questionable. When the Captain refers to his horse he sees a nag; when the jockeys point to the same horse, they see a "bite," an illusion. This is a world ripe for confidence-men.[20] What, then, of Teague O'Regan? How does, or rather, how can his name signify and fix his character?

Thus from the first chapter the novel portrays life in America as fluid and deceptive. Describing the revolutionary world of *Don Quixote*, Michel Foucault could be presenting the problems raised in *Modern Chivalry*: "Writing has ceased to be the prose of the world; resemblances and signs have dissolved their former alliance; similitudes have become deceptive and verge upon the visionary or madness, things still remain stubbornly within their ironic identity: they are no longer but what they are; words wander off on their own, without content, without resemblances to fill their emptiness."[21] The theme of settlement, so prevalent in American literature, extends its metaphorical possibilities to include the detachment of language from the world and identity from social class. Without means or standards to judge the qualifications of representatives or the truth of language as a representation of the world or a person's intentions, we wander as aimlessly as Farrago and Teague.

What unites political and literary representation is the ease with which, in America at any rate, they can become misrepresentations. The possibility for deception and misapprehension always exists in the figurative space created in the act of representing. Language is not fixed and can deceive; men can shift identities and loyalties. In the course of writing his novel, Brackenridge became more concerned with the process of judging true from false representations. This was a particularly difficult task in a century that defined itself in an oddly contradictory love of theatricality and paranoid fear of deceit and in a country fearful of the fictionaliz-

[20] For the theme of the confidence-man, see Wendy Martin, "The Rogue and the Rational Man: Hugh Henry Brackenridge's Study of the Con Man in *Modern Chivalry*," *Early American Literature* 8 (1973): 179–92.

[21] Foucault, *Order of Things*, pp. 47–48.

ing powers of the imagination.[22] The mistrust evident in the episode with the jockeys exemplifies the skeptical attitude of Americans toward all forms of authority and representation. Brackenridge's task in the novel is to assist in determining the categories of self-definition that constitute self and society. "It is my object," he announces, "only to assist the democracy with general observations; and by democracy, I mean not so much the tribunals that are to judge, *as the people that delegate the judgment*" (MC, 497). Brackenridge's problem was to create a style that would strengthen his distrusting democratic readers' judgment.

Brackenridge adapts a style to his American readers that represents them without becoming demagogic. Yet, it also involves the deception inherent in all literary forms of representation. The mark of a true writer, he claims, is that he is "able to deceive the world, and, never let it come into their heads that he has spent a thought on the subject." In defining what is *not* a good "stile," Brackenridge defends a degree of deception: "That stile, is not good, where it appears that you have not dared to use a word without thinking a long time whether you ought to use it; that, in the disposition of words, you have carefully studied which ought to go first and which last; and, that your sentence has a cadence which could not come by chance; but is the effect of design and art" (MC, 161). Brackenridge's advice to American writers to seem intentionally unintentional nicely characterizes his own ad hoc style, one that Lewis Leary has termed "elastically adaptable."[23]

By his own admission, Brackenridge follows the demands of his democratic office, for an author must accommodate his independent spirit in order to serve the public. Taking his comments on style one step further, we can see that the style itself is meant to represent contingency, that is, to adapt itself to the changeable whims of experience in this erratic society. Each sentence does not direct thought toward the closure of a generalizing sentiment, as in the classical Ciceronian mode. Rather, thought unfolds in time, always capable of responding to new perceptions, chance encounters, and a listener's response. Most importantly, the lack of a *telos*,

[22] Fears of conspiracy were epidemic at this time. For a discussion see Gordon Wood, "Conspiracy and the Paranoid Style: Causality and Deceit in the Eighteenth Century," *William and Mary Quarterly*, 3rd ser. 39 (1982): 401–41.

[23] Lewis Leary, *Soundings* (Athens, Ga.: Univ. of Georgia Press, 1975), p. 170.

of "design" or "plot," frees the reader from fears of deceitful hidden intentions. The sinister implications of a designing rhetoric employed by a writer to keep something hidden from the reader submit to the openness of this democratic style. Late in the novel, Brackenridge repeats this political aesthetics in formal terms: "Though I have all the matter of the book in my head, I have not arranged it in the series and junctures of the particulars, so that I can tell before hand what will come next. . . . And this unconcern arises from a consciousness that I have no harm in my mind, and therefore none can come out; I mean actual and intentional harm" (MC, 756).

The chief deception here lies in Brackenridge's acknowledged distinction between the desired democratic effects and the necessary intentional design. A precursor to the American colloquial style, Brackenridge seeks somehow faithfully to represent the experience of American life and yet remain palatable to common American readers. Recreating the effect of spontaneously emergent speech serves to attach the reader to a voice uttered with sincerity and candor. The style of *Modern Chivalry* "represents" as it reproduces the fluid character of the American self and society, all the while involving the reader in the act of self-definition. Thus the style and novel itself aim not at what the new nation and frontier mean, but at how we refine and train our judgment to arrive at meaning. This process of instruction is finally meant to settle the volatile American mind. For this reason, Brackenridge claims "it is Tom, Dick, and Harry, in the woods, that I want to read my book. I do not care though the delegated authorities never see it" (MC, 471).

Standing in opposition to Brackenridge are the demagogues, those who deceive through their feigned resemblance to the people. "The demagogue," Farrago says, "is the first great destroyer of the constitution by deceiving the people" (MC, 507). Ambitious men slip into office by mirroring the appearance and prejudices of the voters who out of self-love desire to see themselves in power. Brackenridge means to overcome the ambition and self-love associated with demagogues as part of his public duty as a writer. "It is not good policy in republicans," he admonishes, "to declare war against letters; or even to frown upon them, for in literary men is their best support" (MC, 401). The very act of writing makes Brackenridge a type of representative, but at a crucial moment in his life, and in the composition of his novel, Brackenridge was forced to test his aesthetic and political theories. How he aligned the two during the Whiskey Rebellion reveals a good deal about the problems of being a writer with political ambitions in this era.

Writing the Rebellion

I began my discussion of Brackenridge with the biographical fact of his crucial decision to move to the frontier in order to rise in society. Something remains to be said about the consequences of his actual encounter during the Whiskey Rebellion with the Toms, Dicks, and Harrys that constituted his new audience. Franklin invented a model for achieving social authority by creating a self that is both easily imitable and detached. Brackenridge, despite his Franklinesque ambitions, chose a very different path when he made the trip to Pittsburgh. The concept of "public" no longer implied a socially instituted place elevated above petty self-interest; rather, it consisted of a particular rhetorical relation to the people. In Part One of the *Autobiography*, Franklin presents strategic humility and industry as the proper means for achieving public approval. But Brackenridge encountered a more suspicious and volatile audience, requiring a new rhetorical strategy. From 1781 to his death in 1816, Brackenridge constantly tested his ties to this audience, who were his neighbors but also frequently his enemies. As a result, Brackenridge too transformed his life into art, but in a manner never envisioned by the worldly statesman Franklin.

In 1794, as he was working on the fourth volume of *Modern Chivalry*, Brackenridge became embroiled in the Whiskey Rebellion. It was to be, as his son later recounted, "the most important epoch" in Brackenridge's life, for during the crisis he confronted firsthand and with frightening clarity the social disruptions he had caricatured in earlier volumes of the novel. More than an instance of life imitating art, the events of the Whiskey Rebellion altered the method of Brackenridge's art in the subsequent volumes of his picaresque novel—true, as I have already suggested, to the flexible manner of its composition. During the rebellion, Brackenridge's efforts to control and persuade the mobs of angry settlers parallel in fascinating ways his attempts to establish the proper mode of attachment to the readers of his novel. More relevant here, however, are the ways Brackenridge dissociated life and art as he interrupted the writing of *Modern Chivalry* to publish his history of the Whiskey Rebellion (*Incidents of the Insurrection*, 1795) and then recast those same events in his novel. The difference between the two versions of the Whiskey Rebellion defines the social pressures affecting the post-Revolutionary writer. Given a chance finally to be the literary representative, Brackenridge discovered it a more dangerous office than expected.

The immediate cause of the Whiskey Rebellion was the imposition of a federal excise tax on the region's chief source of income—liquor. Underlying the unpopularity of this law, as Brackenridge's son pointed out, was the fact that "the people would not distinguish between a law of their own legislature, and the attempt to bind them in all cases whatsoever by a legislative body in which they were not represented."[24] In other words, the issue at stake was the familiar battle between virtual and actual representation, and the people naturally placed their local interests above national laws. Feeling geographically and politically isolated from the legislative process, the people refused to be bound by its laws. When John Neville, the excise officer, came to collect the taxes, he was chased off by an angry crowd of his own neighbors, who then burned down his house. At this point several men sought legal advice from Brackenridge who thought little of their chances to enforce the laws or to stand against the mob. Rather, it was his idea to "put by the tempest for the present, until the civil authority could interpose."[25] Over the next few days he tried to deflect the people's passions in a series of increasingly dangerous and hostile encounters with them, but he succeeded mainly in drawing their suspicions as well as those of the Federal government, which mistakenly considered him a ringleader of the rebellion. After being held by the Federal troops brought in to put down the rebellion, Brackenridge proceeded to write his *Incidents of the Insurrection* as

[24] Henry Marie Brackenridge, "Biographical Sketch of H. H. Brackenridge," *Southern Literary Messenger* 8 (1842): 5.

[25] Hugh Henry Brackenridge, *Incidents of the Insurrection in the Western Parts of Pennsylvania, in the Year 1794*, 4 vols. (Philadelphia: John McCulloch, 1795), 1: 7. (Hereafter cited in text.)

a way to vindicate his actions and "to explain my conduct, which has not been understood" (1: [5]).

The recurring, representative scene in *Incidents of the Insurrection* involves the confrontation between a suspicious crowd and an orator determined to persuade and lead them. It must have seemed almost providential to Brackenridge as he found himself placed in the mediator's role, for his rhetorical training under John Witherspoon at Princeton and his desire to assert a public position among the people coincided at this particular moment. *Modern Chivalry* thematizes the representative power of language; *Incidents* investigates language's persuasive powers. In its overt intentionality, and its power to create the illusion of presence and referentiality, oratory's promise was "the power of speech" as "the great means of keeping men together" (MC, 559).

During the real-life events of the Whiskey Rebellion, Brackenridge's most important opportunity to engage his persuasive powers came on 21 July 1794. It occurs at the key moment in *Incidents* when Brackenridge finds himself forced to make a speech that will label him either as opposed to popular sentiment or as too conciliatory to the rebels. Brackenridge's belief in the representative's independence (including the writer's role) and in the persuasive power of language were both at stake here. Speaking before him were David Bradford and James Marshall, who "under a subordination to popular influence" capitulate to the crowd. *Popular* is the operative term here, just as it operates the ironic machinations in *Modern Chivalry*. For Brackenridge, to be popular was to be read, or elected, but it also required "subordination" to the people. Yet throughout *Incidents*, Brackenridge fears the loss of his own popularity with the people. He had a "popularity obtained," he claims, "doubtless, by failing a little with the popular gale, at least not opposing it, but chiefly by a steady and upright demeanor in my profession" (2: 110). His Franklinesque professional dedication was to be tested now.

The problem facing Brackenridge at this moment becomes paradigmatic for the man of letters in America. Given the shifting codes of social loyalty, on what terms can he approach his audience? By what strategies can he move them? At bottom the problem becomes not only how can he represent the truth to them, but how can they agree on what constitutes the truth? His choice now seems to be either popularity or truth, a dilemma that presents the preconditions for his representative act as evasion, hidden intentions, and feigning. The problem turns upon the suspicions of the audience, the epistemological confusion of the speaker's self-presentation, and the ambiguities—the lack of "fixture"—in language. Whereas Franklin's popularity warrants his *Autobiography*, possible failure prompts Brackenridge. In this case, Brackenridge faces a hostile audience, having just heard two men capitulate to the rebels by imitating the inflammatory rhetoric of demagogues and presenting themselves as images of democratic virtue. "It was the people led them," Brackenridge writes, "It was the mass of people commanded; and it was fear of them, that operated on the minds of the more conspicuous individuals" (1: 105). How, then, can Brackenridge distinguish himself from them and their language, preserve his autonomy, and still maintain the bonds of popularity and confidence with the people?

In retelling the incident in question, Brackenridge breaks off the narrative to heighten the suspense: "After [Bradford] had spoken there was dead silence. The question would be taken; support or not support? My situation was delicate. There was but a moment between treason on the one hand and popular odium on the other, popular odium which might produce personal injury before I left the ground. To withdraw would be the same thing as to oppose" (1: 32). Notice that Brackenridge describes himself as a mediator between treason—the government and law—and popular odium—the people—and must construct a space for himself by his rhetoric alone. He calls upon language not to create an imaginative "world elsewhere," but, as many American writers would soon discover, to effect a rhetorical world here and now that would mediate between his independence and the people's power. "Having settled some outlines" in his mind, Brackenridge stands like Captain Farrago before the crowd, and at this moment we see the essential differences between the two. Unlike his fictional character, Brackenridge humors the crowd "as a substitute for saying anything directly to approve what had been done. Putting them in good humor, I ventured to touch upon the subject more seriously" (1: 33). Humor, jokes, the need to "laugh immoderately" (1: 54) with the people become the evasive strategies to accommodate himself to the people without capitulating to their demands. Here humor redefines the goals and expectations of both speaker and audience, and creates, in Kenneth Burke's words, "the purest rhetorical pattern: speaker and hearer in partisan jokes made at the expense of another."[26] Time and again Brackenridge employs humor to ease himself out of tight places.

Humor thus becomes a political and literary solution to the excesses of popular democracy. More to my point here, it becomes for Brackenridge an act of representation in that it establishes a relationship, a bond of *momentarily* shared values and codes. In his hands, humor becomes the frontier equivalent of the Puritan jeremiad, itself a form of address more cultural than literary. Whereas the jeremiad transforms the speaker into a prophetic figure speaking for America itself, speaking with the intent to align the people with the belief in their place in redemptive history, the humorist accommodates himself to the people through his colloquial style. Yet humor is always double-edged; it invites misapprehension by turning language back upon itself and transforming the speaker into an actor, a storyteller. Brackenridge recounts the particulars of his speech before the crowd "because it has been misconceived; and the pleasantry which I indulged in the subject of Indian treaties, construed with a contempt of the executive" (1: 34). Time and again he resorts to humor as the best means to control, deflect, and persuade.[27]

Unlike the older generation of Federalists, Brackenridge discovers that to remain in power he must adjust his elitist ideology to meet democratic demands. By "not opposing" the gale, as he confessed, he hoped to harness and direct its energies, or at least weather the storm. This act of personal and literary accommodation reflects the strategy of many Federalist men of letters of the time. Noah Webster, for example, attempted to fix the American language, in effect institutionalize it as Franklin might have, in his dictionary as a means of maintaining control. The present political transformations, Webster argued, forced him and others to ac-

[26] Kenneth Burke, *Rhetoric of Motives* (New York: Prentice-Hall, 1950), p. 38.

[27] Robert A. Ferguson, *Law and Letters in American Culture* (Cambridge, Mass.: Harvard Univ. Press, 1984), p. 99, has noted a similar fate for other lawyers: "Humor represented the cardinal achievement of the lawyer in post-Revolutionary literature. . . . Humor furnished an acceptable means of escape; it distinguished the new generation from the old, and it created alternative modes of expression."

quire new strategies: "Honest, independent men of talents should yield so far to popular opinion, as to retain the confidence of the people; for without that confidence, they are lost in the scale of political measures. But with it they may gradually wean the people from their foolish schemes and correct their opinions. . . . If they do not lead the people, fools and knaves will."[28] This seems precisely Brackenridge's motivation for humoring his audience during the Whiskey Rebellion.

Nevertheless, it is in their political lessons that *Incidents of the Insurrection* and *Modern Chivalry* diverge. Brackenridge's humor manages to restrain the people and deflect their passions during the rebellion, but it also obscures his intentions and raises the suspicions of the people and the government. Moreover, humor undercuts the independent qualities of public man and orator. When the government's forces finally moved in to restore order, it was Brackenridge whom they held and whose life they threatened.

Brackenridge was not finished with the Whiskey Rebellion. In the fourth volume of *Modern Chivalry* (published in 1797), he returns to these events, but in an oddly oblique manner. As he recast these events for his novel, Brackenridge employed them to a new purpose. Curiously, the fourth volume tells us little about the events themselves. Having found himself yet another job for which he is unqualified, Teague O'Regan plays the comic role of the excise officer hounded and eventually tarred and feathered by the mob. Like Brackenridge himself, Farrago acts as a reasonable diversion to the mob's excesses and is likewise subjected to their suspicions. In fact, we see here a closer identification between Farrago and his creator than ever before. The following might be a description of Brackenridge's own role during the Rebellion:

> The Captain . . . had been employed during the occasion, reasoning with the people, and endeavouring first to divert them

[28] Quoted in David Hackett Fischer, *The Revolution of American Conservatism* (New York: Harper and Row, 1965), p. 152. Fischer presents a well-documented account of the Federalists' accommodation to the changes in American society. But accommodation often resulted in frustration for American writers. For discussions of their continuing disillusionment, see Benjamin T. Spencer, *The Quest for Nationality* (Syracuse: Syracuse Univ. Press, 1957), pp. 25–72; Linda Kerber, *Federalists in Dissent* (Ithaca: Cornell Univ. Press, 1970), pp. 1–22; Joseph Ellis, *After the Revolution* (New York: W. W. Norton, 1980), pp. 24–38.

> from the outrage, and afterwards to convince them of the error of it, and the dangers of the consequences. Instead of allaying their fervour, and convincing their judgments, it had begun to provoke, and irritate exceedingly; and gave birth to surmises that he was an accomplice of the excise officer. (MC, 308)

Prepared to hear Farrago's speeches to the mobs (as in earlier volumes), the reader suddenly discovers the Captain's oratory is missing. We hear no didactic speeches, no persuasive rhetoric. In fact, Farrago suddenly escapes from the mob into the mountains, where like Rip Van Winkle he finds himself in a strange symbolic territory, complete with a French marquis, an exile from revolutionary France. Safe in the world of allegory, Farrago and the marquis contemplate the excesses of revolutionary fervor. What surprises us is not their conservative sentiments, but the violent transition from the events' realistic depiction to their symbolic interpretation.

This transformation from realism to symbolism, although consistent with Brackenridge's figurative representation, seems an oddly counterproductive evasion. The strange mixture of realism, caricature, and symbolism reveals how difficult he finds it to turn fact into fiction. These scenes address none of the issues raised by the Whiskey Rebellion, nor do they aim at the people who fomented it. Instead, the volume and Farrago's role in the events end abruptly as he is taken into government custody and then quickly released with the terse statement: "His account and explanation was understood, and he acquitted from the suspicion of having swerved from the duty of a good citizen" (MC, 326). By this point Brackenridge has replaced autobiography with wish fulfillment and in doing so has discovered the limitations of figurative representation. Using Madison's term, I would argue that Brackenridge here attempts to "refine and enlarge" the events of the Whiskey Rebellion by translating them first into allegory and then by rewriting a new conclusion. Brackenridge's fulfilled wish is not that the events would be different but that his own account would be transparently understood and acknowledged by the authorities. In contrast to the comic judge, the humorless Farrago is immediately exonerated and let free. Whereas Brackenridge argues against flight from danger, he permits Farrago to slip into the safety of allegory.

Perhaps the most interesting consequences of Brackenridge's experience in the Whiskey Rebellion are the changes that occur in the later volumes of *Modern Chivalry*. The second part of the novel (published in three installments: 1804, 1805, 1815) presents us with a new problem for Farrago. Almost as a counter to its picaresque form, the novel describes the difficulties of founding a new community—with Captain Farrago as the leader. Besieged by conflicting demands, confusion over legal rulings, and the problem of how to make paper money represent value, Farrago once again finds himself caught in the unending complexities of representation.

CHAPTER THREE

Charles Brockden Brown, Authority, and Intentionality

The late eighteenth century in America was a frightened age. The social aftershocks of the Revolution continued to shake the United States' political structure as the country neared what appeared to be the apocalyptic end of the eighteenth century. In the 1780s and 1790s, America found itself tested by the internal conflicts as the two parties, the weakening Federalist party and the ever-more-powerful Republicans (the opposition party arising from Antifederalist sentiment), fought for control. Aggravating these internecine battles were fears of an international conspiracy stemming from the French Revolution.[1] The projected fears eventually gave rise to the Alien and Sedition Acts of 1798; added to these fears of contamination by Europe's political troubles were the very real crises as the yellow-fever epidemics swept through New York and Philadephia. According to Marshall Smelser, "The United States

[1] For a discussion of this period, see Marshall Smelser, "The Federalist Period as an Age of Passion," *American Quarterly* 10 (1958): 391–419. For the specific battle between Federalists and Republicans see Richard Buel, Jr., *Securing the Revolution: Ideology in American Politics, 1789–1815* (Ithaca: Cornell Univ. Press, 1972), pp. 185–213. And for Brown's place in this society, see William Hedges, "Charles Brockden Brown and the Culture of Contradictions," *Early American Literature* 9 (1974): 107–42.

in 1798 was a scene of fear and hate, warmed by seven or eight years heating."[2] The year 1798 was also the year that Charles Brockden Brown published *Wieland.*

These political and social unpheavals effectively diverted ambitious writers from employing traditional genres. Instead of writing the *Lyrical Ballads,* they were often asked to turn their pens to writing transparent polemics and satires in support of a particular cause or party. In his essay, "Federalism and the Crisis of Literary Order," Lewis P. Simpson suggests that Federalist writers hoped to create a "Republic of Letters," thereby instituting a link to the political republic that would aid in stabilizing the nation. These Federalist men of letters perceived an analogy between literary order and political order and declared faction and democracy common enemies.[3] Believing the political consequences of democracy to be lawless chaos, the Federalists feared the literary effect would be unconventional mediocrity. For such men, writers and reviewers could wield power equivalent to the executives and judges of the republic; as the government enacted laws and dispensed justice, the writers too might encode and constitute the as yet incomplete powers of literary practice and interpretaton. We can detect the insecurity of these Federalist writers in their zeal to erect legitimizing structures of literary taste and performance. In other words, the Federalists' desire for stability included recognition of themselves as the true governors of taste.

In America, of course, work as a writer was scarcely considered gainful employment. Witness the various professions of Franklin, Brackenridge, and the Connecticut Wits. Being a writer was an almost inherently suspicious profession, for it was associated either with the dangers of the imagination or the partisanship of politics. As the tumult of America threatened the livelihood of potential writers, it also left a vacuum for someone like Charles Brockden Brown to fill. Entertaining hopes for a prominent place in American culture, Brown saw, as his earliest biographer noted, "the advantage of publication suited to a new state of manners and political economy."[4] As a novelist, however, Brown placed himself in a

[2] Smelser, "Federalist Period," p. 412.

[3] Lewis P. Simpson, "Federalism and the Crisis of Literary Order," *American Literature* 32 (1960): 258.

[4] William Dunlap, *Memoirs of Charles Brockden Brown* (London: Henry Colburn, 1822), pp. 2–3.

very different relation to the political conditions than did his immediate predecessors. Franklin, Brackenridge, and the Connecticut Wits had attempted to unite their public offices with the vocation of writer, hoping to retain the eighteenth-century ideal of writing as a public duty, comparable to that of statesman, general, or scientist.

Brown's conception of fiction reflects that moment in American literary history when writing diverges from social and political authorities and finds itself more often than not in opposition to their demands. Nevertheless, Brown claims for the poet or writer the intellectual power to transform society. In 1799, at the height of his astonishing creativity, he published a description of a poet's power in his *Monthly Magazine and American Review*:

> A man, whose activity is neither aided by political authority nor by the press, may yet exercise considerable influence on the condition of his neighbors, by the exercise of intellectual powers. His courage may be useful to the timid or the feeble, and his knowledge to the ignorant, as well as his property to those who want. His benevolence and justice may not only protect his kindred and wife, but rescue the victims of prejudice and passion from the yoke of those domestic tyrants, and shield the powerless from the oppression of power, the poor from the injustice of the rich, and the simple from the stratagems of the cunning.[5]

Behind this passage's assertive tone stands the troubling presupposition that the writer himself stands as an outsider and potential victim. Living in a ruthless, predatory society, the poet may interpose himself between the poor and social tyranny or injustice, but to him belong none of the institutional or social powers. In speaking for the disadvantaged, the poet becomes their representative, but he does so without any support apart from his own talents.

Ten years previous, Brown had seemed more assured of his art and social position. Writing in *The Rhapsodist*, he granted the romantic writer superiority over his subject, much as Emerson would the Poet forty years later: "[The rhapsodist] contrives a chariot and a train for his hero, worthy the greatness of his exploits, and gives

[5] Charles Brockden Brown, *The Rhapsodist*, ed. Harry Warfel (New York: Scholars' Facsimiles and Reprints, 1943), p. 153.

him the dignity and grace of an immortal.—He then pulls down the pageant from his exalted station, strips him of the purple and the crown, turns him loose among the rabble and places himself on the vacant seat."[6] Dreams of dignifying, almost deifying, the writer's status seem realizable, until we recognize him as the usurper of imperial power whose own legitimacy is based on revolution. Shortly thereafter, Brown himself deflates the poetic imposter: "He swells with unusual transport, at this new instance of his countrymen's applause, for such, in this momentary paroxism of his frenzy, he *imagines* it to be."[7] The writer's real power over his subjects—the heroes and leaders of society—reveals itself to be as imaginary as the applause of his readers. What prevents the writer from achieving authority, however, is not those leaders, but the lack of applause. How does he move these new readers in whom all authority now seems vested?

These two ambivalent discussions of the writer's social position contain a common theme: It is a role *imagined*, not given. Without a preestablished office, complete with the conventions of communicative address, the writer must, Brown implies, establish a rhetorical space out of his "intellectual powers." In short, he must establish a proper relation with his reader, but he can do so only in conventional terms. Franklin had acquired his success by imitating and surpassing the conventions of society; Brown finds no ready-made office to occupy. Furthermore, in an age and society torn by paranoid fears of designs, Brown, like Brackenridge, acknowledges the need for an unconventional, that is, an artless and unpremeditated, style. Writing in the first essay, *The Rhapsodist*, he announces what becomes the problematic notion of literary style: A rhapsodist, he claims, "will write as he speaks, and converse with his reader not as an author, but as a man."[8] Collapsing speech and writing presents the true relation between writer and reader in terms of social equality, transparent intentionality, and presence.

Brown's poetics of sincerity raises the problem of locating the origin of the speaker's identity. To speak directly to another by revealing an inner self previously hidden behind social conventions necessitates defining an authentic, individual personality.

[6] Ibid., p. 11.
[7] Ibid.; my emphasis.
[8] Ibid., p. 5.

American society was revolutionary precisely because it praised personal autonomy and required individual judgment as a necessary part of the political process, but it did so by internalizing the idea of identity. When social conventions hinder rather than facilitate personal expression, then the very concept of identity and the means to represent it must be redefined. With something of this awareness, but having different political axes to grind, Franklin attempted first to internalize the idea of government and then relied on benevolent, paternal social institutions to provide the bonds of proper engagement. Franklin's striking lack of an articulated interior self requires the full complement of public roles and conventions by which to construct identity. But Brown's definition of the writer's power presupposes the malevolence of social institutions and makes it the writer's duty to overcome conventions. No longer could one publicly enact the self by representing it before an audience, as Franklin did so well; now it was preserved behind a public mask.[9] If, as he says in *Arthur Mervyn*, books "talk to us behind a screen," then the author must theoretically demolish the screen in order to reveal his true identity and establish sincere ties with the reader.[10]

When we turn to Brown's novels with this theory in mind, however, we find a sharp contrast between this critical stance and his deceptive, confusing narratives and insincere characters. Recent criticism has emphasized the duplicity of his characters and narratives, concluding often that both are subversive or indeterminate. What thwarts our readings of Brown's novels is precisely the opaque intentions and seeming lack of sincerity of his characters. In other words, these novels explore the consequences of writing outside of the forms and institutions of society, and they describe the dangers of relying on a self lacking Franklinesque self-government. While Franklin's *Autobiography* narrates the transformation of paternal authority into the beneficent, paternal institutions of society, Brown most often explores the critical moments when both

[9] See Sennett, *Fall*, p. 261: "Personality in public destroyed the public by making the people fearful of betraying their emotions to others involuntarily. The result was more and more an attempt to withdraw from contact with others, to be shielded in silence, even to attempt to stop feeling in order for the feelings not to show."

[10] Charles Brockden Brown, *Arthur Mervyn*, ed. Sydney J. Krause and S. W. Reid (Kent, Ohio: Kent State Univ. Press, 1980), p. 427. (Hereafter cited in text as AM.)

paternal authority and social institutions fail, leaving the ill-governed youth to the mercy of charismatic characters such as Carwin, Welbeck, and Ormond.

Like Franklin, Brown often suggests the need to escape paternal control, but his fathers bear little resemblance to Josiah Franklin. Facing the father's palpable absence (*Wieland*), weakness (*Ormond*), or tyranny (*Arthur Mervyn* and "Memoirs of Carwin the Biloquist"), the youth of these novels have set before them the familiar task of making their way in the world without the help and guidance of their fathers. In limiting the direct role of paternal authority, Brown responds to contemporary attacks on the entire idea of a familial aristocracy, or, as he described it, a "prejudice by birth, by which a father transmits to son absolute authority over the property, liberty and lives of millions."[11] Here Brown refers not so much to paternal authority, the *symbolic* relations between father and son, but patrimonial authority, the tangible economic powers passed on primogenitively from father to son. This crucial distinction plays an important part in his characters' search for authorities to replace their absent parents, for the children are driven by the need to recover their lost economic and symbolic inheritances. The union of paternalism and patrimonialism serves to entangle the complex bonds of psychological demands, social duties, and economic expectations holding father and son.

Franklin would have been shocked at what Brown shows to be the consequences of rejecting paternal authority. Fathers prove poor models in Brown's novels, while social institutions fail to create stable associations. Brown's youths, like Franklin, strike out on their own, but the figures they encounter are schemers who provide dangerous models of social climbing. Having little desire for manual labor, Arthur Mervyn is driven from his father "who did not see why he should treat as a son one who refused what was due to him as a father" (AM, 23). The elder Mervyn perceives the bond traditionally: Filial obedience is rewarded by the child's economic success. As Arthur flees from the country to his encounter with Welbeck in the city, the economic terms of relations are transformed from the reciprocity of labor exchange to the psychological and economic dependence of creditor and debtor. To take another

[11] Brown, *Rhapsodist*, p. 147.

example, Carwin escapes his father's brutal restraint, only to fall into the manipulative grasp of Ludloe, of whom, Carwin explains, "I could plead none of the rights of the relationship; yet I enjoyed the privileges of a son."[12] By circumventing the *legal* bonds of duty and inheritance, ties binding father and son reciprocally, Ludloe links himself psychologically with Carwin. Whereas Franklin's Governor Keith and Keimer revealed themselves as inadequate representatives of social and personal government, Brown's mentors advance themselves by negotiating outside these conventions. Franklin's fear of charismatic figures seems justified as we see the ease with which these men move into the vacuum of authority in America.

If traditional patriarchal authority is absent, and the institutions of society are impotent, where does authority lie in Brown's novels? To put the question in familiar terms: What moves the characters and events in these novels? Apparently the figures who slip into the vacuum of power are those who can dissemble and modulate their tones to the listener's expectations. Carwin, Welbeck, and Ormond stand as embodiments of the age's paranoia. Although they resemble Gothic, romantic anti-heroes, or the seducers of feminine virtue like *Clarissa*'s Lovelace, these villains have even more striking political parallels. Masters of dissembling, they represent political demagogues feared by both parties. They are completely theatrical; their identities arise from the chameleon-like ability to insinuate themselves into the confidence of others. They rise and progress in society by masking their intentions, creating, as Franklin might have, only the *appearance* of sincerity. But their power in these novels occurs in the ease by which they move others. The following description of Ormond presents his psychological relations in political terms:

> Ormond aspired to nothing more ardently than to hold the reins of opinion. To exercise absolute power over the conduct of others, not by constraining their limbs, or by exacting obedience to his authority, but in a way of which his subjects should be scarcely conscious. He desired that his guidance

[12] Charles Brockden Brown, "The Memoirs of Carwin the Biloquist," in "*Wieland, or The Transformation*" and "*The Memoirs of Carwin the Biloquist*," ed. Sydney J. Krause and S. W. Reid (Kent, Ohio: Kent State Univ. Press, 1977), p. 271.

> should controul their steps, but that his agency, when most effectual, should be least suspected.[13]

Ormond seeks a power, an authority, without his victims' being aware that he is its author. His goal is to "plot" a design without a recoverable authorial intention, a goal reflecting his particular vision of the world: "The universe was to him, a series of events, connected by an undesigning and inscrutable necessity, and an assemblage of forms to which no beginning or end can be conceived" (O, 180). In other words, he sounds much like the mysterious author of his own novel.

Brown thus plays out the consequences of absent paternal and institutional authority in distinctly literary terms. For him, authority and authorship are closely allied, but they are both problematic powers. The term *author* is most commonly applied to his morally ambiguous characters. In *Wieland*, the narrator (Clara Wieland), believing Carwin responsible for the Wieland family's destruction, calls him the "author of this black conspiracy" and the "author of these horrors."[14] In *Arthur Mervyn* (even the name implies his role), Arthur is accused by Welbeck as being the "author of the scene that you describe, and of horrors without number and name" (AM, 337). In both cases the attribution of authorship/authority carries with it a number of ambiguous presuppositions about the authority of authorship. First of all, an author is one who creates or causes an action. Working from this definition, Clara assumes that each act may be traced back, via the logical steps of causality, to the calculations of authorial intention. Theodore himself shares some of his sister's understanding when he refers to God—"the author of my Being"—as the ultimate cause of his actions. For Theodore, his "author" is also an authority who can command him to any action, including the destruction of his own family. More important for Clara, the design, and perhaps the authority, may be recovered by history or memory. Hence the need for her cautionary

[13] Charles Brockden Brown, *Ormond, or the Secret Witness*, ed. Sydney J. Krause and S. W. Reid (Kent, Ohio: Kent State Univ. Press, 1982), p. 177. (Hereafter cited in text as O.)

[14] Charles Brockden Brown, *Wieland, or The Transformation*, in "*Wieland, or The Transformation*" *and* "*The Memoirs of Carwin the Biloquist*," ed. Sydney J. Krause and S. W. Reid (Kent, Ohio: Kent State Univ. Press, 1977), pp. 214, 25. (Hereafter cited in text as WI.)

autobiographical tale. Each narrative we encounter in Brown's writings seems either an attempt to locate its own originating authors, or a disclaimer of any intentional harm, of any real authority.

In Clara's linking of authority, authorship, and design, we find one of the key problems facing Brown's reader. She assumes, in other words, the authority of a beginning, of "origin-ality." It is precisely this form of authority that seems to be missing in both *Wieland* and *Arthur Mervyn*, for we can never safely trace events back to their authors. The absence of originality proliferates a number of provisional authorities to which Clara and we turn: traditional or paternal (Wieland's father); rational-legal (the court); and charismatic (Carwin). As we search for the origin of events, for the reason Theodore Wieland murders his wife and children, we naturally turn to the story of his father's religious obsession and inexplicable death, for we assume either an inherited weakness, or a psychological reiteration of generational themes. Yet these connections between father and son are founded on the mere resemblance of events, whereas the consequences suggest dissimilarity: The elder Wieland may have been mad, or driven by some supernatural spirit, but he did not kill his family. Seeking a cause, we discover only its image.

If generational pressure provides no adequate explanation, then social institutions also promise no protection. In the face of Theodore Wieland's crime, we turn to the legal documents of his trial to provide us with the truth. But rational-legal authority appears as ineffective at shedding light on the cause of the events as the prison at restraining Wieland's madness. The law can only judge the consequences. In fact, Theodore's defense of his actions in court presents a frighteningly rational and airtight argument. *His* narrative alone of all the testimony we hear in the novel describes the origins of the crime clearly: He was simply commanded by God. Given the patriarchal foundations of both his religion and society, his accession to his heavenly father's authority, to his "author's" command, seems oddly rational in this novel's irrational world. But for us to find the murders' origin here would be to accept too much. Rather, his obedience to divine authority explodes the ineffectual basis of society's rational paternalistic constitution. At no point in his defense does Theodore step outside of the beliefs professed by his judges. To rephrase Ahab's claim, only his actions appear mad; his reasons are quite sane.

As we turn to Carwin's responsibility as the author and authority of these events, we find ourselves in the same paradox as Clara. If we accept the sincerity of his claims, he escapes the requirements of intentionality and his powers seem at best only indirectly related. He also raises the possibility that human agents have no authority, that authority can be discussed only in terms of its consequences rather than in its origins. Perhaps more disturbing, however, is the possibility that authority exists in the power of language itself as a creative agency. In this novel, language performs the creative task of giving shape to disembodied fears or ideas. As Mark Seltzer points out, "On every level of the narrative, one finds a confusion, a transformation, of ways of saying into modes of being," which subverts the laws of causality and "grants language the power of conferring reality on its images."[15]

As characters and readers attempt to find causal links between events, language overturns causality by no longer representing these events but actually invoking and authorizing them. Shortly after Clara asks "all-seeing heaven to drag to light and to punish this betrayer [Carwin]" (WI, 217), he appears in her room, but only, he claims, as the "undesigning cause" of the events. Wieland himself had prayed that "an unambiguous token of [God's] presence will salute my senses," only to be faced with the terrifying consequences of God's possible presence. In this novel shadows are transformed into human figures; reality, into shadowy resemblances. Early on Clara claims, "There are means by which we are able to distinguish a substance from a shadow, a reality from the phantom of a dream" (WI, 98). But as she soon discovers, her foreshadowing dream of her brother comes to haunt her reality.

As she deliberately weighs the events, seeking either their human or supernatural author, Clara herself stumbles onto this frightening possibility that authority may exist in language itself. "Some relief," she tells us, "is afforded in the midst of suffering, when its author is discovered or imagined" (WI, 214). If by author she means one who, either sincerely or insincerely, has created a meaningful, intentional design—a plot—then no such author ex-

[15] Mark Seltzer, "Saying Makes it So," *Early American Literature* 13 (1978): 84–85. See also Michael D. Bell's discussion in *The Development of American Romance* (Chicago: Univ. of Chicago Press, 1980), pp. 46–48.

ists, for there is no design. Clara apparently comes to this same understanding, for immediately upon hearing Carwin's tale she exclaims, "ruffian or devil, black as hell or bright as angels, thenceforth [Carwin] was nothing to me" (WI, 260). She realizes, moreover, that the issue of his veracity no longer matters: "Such is his tale, concerning the truth of which I care not" (WI, 261). Authority exists in its ability to convince us of its veracity, not in its verifiability. Language outstrips intention, spoiling the design and creating havoc with unforeseen consequences. The reality of the voices, the truth they may or may not express, matters less than the belief in the reality they constitute. Authority, in other words, is made the responsibility of the hearer who warrants its legitimacy. If we act in response to the voices, then they *are real* and have authority.

What we look for in Brown's novels is the singleness of purpose, the unity of design, and the transparency of intention. In other words, we seek the *authority* of the author. But we find instead the multiplicity of purpose, discontinuity, and opacity. Even as they narrate the insincere words of others, Brown's novels generally open with announcements of intention, each acting with a kind of illocutionary force. *Wieland*, for example, begins with Clara's clearly announced intentions to fulfill her audience's queries: "I feel little reluctance in complying with your request. You know not fully the cause of my sorrows" (WI, 5). In fact it is the reader as much as Clara who seeks the origin and cause of the narrative. In *Ormond*, we have an oddly similar situation of a woman narrator speaking to an unknown, yet named, listener, I. E. Rosenberg: "You are anxious to obtain some knowledge of the history of Constantia Dudley. I am well acquainted with your motives, and allow that they justify your curiosity" (O, 3). Who is I. E. Rosenberg? What are his motives? It seems that we readers must somehow supply them in order to warrant Sophia's narrative. In short, if we read for "plot," that is, order to understand the link between original motivations and their consequences, then we discover that *our requests* are the true origins, the true authority of each narrative.

A comparison with the opening paragraph of *Arthur Mervyn* helps clarify these problematic openings:

> I was resident in this city during the year 1793. Many motives contributed to detain me, though departure was easy and commodious, and my friends were generally solicitous for me

> to go. It is *not my purpose to enumerate these motives*, or to dwell on my present concerns and transactions, but merely to compose a narrative of some incidents with which my situation made me acquainted. (AM, 5; my emphasis)

As in the other openings, Dr. Stevens sidesteps the question of personal motives and intentionality. Rather, he seems to separate motives—the originating factors of action—from purpose—the final end of that object. His purpose is merely "to compose a narrative," to engage in the act of writing itself. When Dr. Stevens comes to open the second volume (published a year later) he again ignores his own intentions, wishing now only to substantiate the purity of Mervyn's: "By the aid of pure intentions, [Arthur] had frustrated the wiles of an accomplished and veteran deceiver" (AM, 219). The trusting rescuer (and new father?) of Arthur Mervyn, Dr. Stevens believes him because "the face of Mervyn is the index of an honest mind" (AM, 229–30). Stevens has a Federalist's faith in appearances; a friend, however, wisely reproaches him that his "confidence in smooth features and fluent accents should have ended long ago" (AM, 249). As we read of Stevens's desire to remake Mervyn, to "render that life profitable to himself and mankind," do we also locate motives that belie his disclaimers of disinterest?

Each of Brown's novels (*Edgar Huntley* is no exception), then, opens either as a reaction to an outside request, or to circumvent possible questions of the speaker's motivation or intentions. In each instance, however, Brown has also added a "pre-text" in the form of a preface (for *Arthur Mervyn* and *Edgar Huntley*) or advertisement (for *Wieland*). The effect of these pretexts is to suggest the presence of a real author, and an originating authority with its transparent intentionality, behind the fictional narratives. In recounting his "purpose" in writing *Wieland*, Brown declares it "is neither selfish nor temporary, but aims at the illustration of some important branches of the moral constitution of man" (WI, 3). Following hard upon the heels of this rather lofty claim are a series of defensive maneuvers by Brown, who seeks to forestall the reader's doubts by asserting the verifiable truth of the events and by defining the reader's role in judging the novel's worth. When he admits that "the reader must be permitted to decide" the value or worthlessness of the novel, he essentially acknowledges the reader's authority over him. He extends this power in the final line by telling us that the novel's sequel (the "Memoirs of Carwin") "will be published or suppressed according to the reception which is given to the present attempt" (WI, 3). If Brown grants the reader the power to judge the value *and* verifiable truth of his novel, he also establishes the proper criteria for judgment: "If history furnishes one parallel fact, it is a sufficient vindication of the Writer; but most readers will probably recollect an authentic case, remarkably similar to that of Wieland" (WI, 3). Allen Axelrod has described the public knowledge of the famous murder in 1781 by James Yeats of his family.[16] Presumably the common knowledge of this event fulfills the second part of the reader's duties.

But who is Brown's implied reader and what is his or her actual place in the design of the novel? In *Wieland*, Brown specifically describes the reader's identity, or at least the fictional context into which he situates the reader: "This narrative is addressed . . . to a small number of friends, whose curiosity, with regard to it, has been greatly awakened" (WI, 3). In other words, we find ourselves in a social setting of intimate friendship exactly parallel to that created by the Wielands and Pleyel, and we, like those characters, are addressed by ambiguous messages. However, if we reenact the inquiries of Clara, Wieland, and Pleyel about the source of the voices, the object of our "curiosity" is not Carwin's voice, nor the voice that Wieland hears, but Clara's. Nevertheless, we assume the conditions of authority defined by the novel—that is, authority as an original action unfolding a coherent design—and thus may extend our own authority by completing the design of the novel in warranting the publication of Carwin's memoirs. In other words, we are asked to legitimize Brown's voice, grant him authority, even after being placed in a situation like that of Clara, Theodore Wieland, and Pleyel in which authority of just such a voice is shown to be dangerous.

My purpose in discussing Brown's advertisement is to show the way in which our search for authority in his novels always comes back to us as readers. In Clara's search for the author of the murders, authority continually recedes from her grasp, for no design-

[16] Alan Axelrod, *Charles Brockden Brown* (Austin: Univ. of Texas Press, 1983), pp. 53–58.

ing and intentional origin can be found. Following Clara's example, we look for the authority of this novel, encountering as we do the protestations first by Carwin and then by Clara that they are not the origins but the transmitters, the mere representatives, of these events. Carwin cannot be said to be the author, for his motives and intentions—if they are recoverable by Clara or the reader—do not cause the events. In addition, Clara claims the intention only of providing an instructive tale, but the motive must originate, in part, in the reader's curiosity. It is, of course, the same kind of curiosity that motivates Carwin. Finally, Brown himself minimizes his own authority by placing the events as prior to his creation and making the reader the final judge. Much like Poor Richard's privileging of the reader's economic power, Brown assumes his own powers are subordinate to those who buy his books. But to this he also adds the reader's judgment of his novels' moral value, and thus implicates the reader at every mazy turn. As consumers we complete the narrative's design, as moral judges we warrant the possible social application and effects of the novel, and as implied readers we grant authority to Brown's and Clara's voices as we act on these same moral lessons.

These concerns about the relative authorities of author and reader make an implicit political point. In *The Federalist* No. 10, Madison makes as one of the principal foundations of his argument for representation over direct democratic participation the belief that "no man is allowed to be a judge in his own cause, because his interest would certainly bias his judgment, and, not improbably corrupt his integrity."[17] "Interest" here means egocentric self-interest and derives from one's legal concern or share in something, especially one's title to property.[18] By pitting preface against narrative, Brown asks the reader to judge the narrative on a variety of levels while making the reader's motives and curiosity a necessary part of the narrative's origin. The reader's "interest" surely clouds his or her judgment, just as Clara mistakenly accuses Carwin because of her own unacknowledged interest in both him and her brother. Clara's case serves as a paradigm for all of Brown's ambiguous characters: Their attempts to judge their own

[17] Hamilton, Madison, and Jay *Federalist*, p. 131.

[18] See Wills, *Explaining*, pp. 201–10, on the definition of *interest*.

narratives not only reveal their *self*-interest but actually conjure up repressed selves. Clara's dreams, Edgar Huntley's sleepwalking, Arthur Mervyn's contradictory actions, all betray the lack of "integrity," of a coherent and consistent self.

Madison's essay was an attempt to salvage a kind of conditional unity in the face of factionalism spread by competing interests. *Wieland* narrates the disintegration of a community because avowed public and rational motives mask the subtle, irrational self-interests of the characters. Whereas Franklin conceived of a society in which desire and duty could be reconciled by providing a model of self-governance, Brown remains skeptical. Aware that the reader actively engages in both constructing and judging meaning, his novels endlessly play out variations on the theme of an unsuspecting reader seduced by his or her desire.

Brown's novels are critiques of what Gordon Wood has termed the "paranoid style" of the eighteenth century. This particular perception of social and political interaction "presumes a world of autonomous, freely acting individuals who are capable of directly and deliberately bringing about events through their decisions and actions, and who thereby can be held morally responsible for what happens."[19] This is Franklin's active world run by a concept of individual agency, but with a sinister twist. Discovering the real intentions of individuals now seemed impossible. To account for apparent discrepancies between cause and effect, men and women like Clara Wieland discovered deception all around them. But against such claims of conspiracy and deception, Brown argued in the *Monthly Magazine* that "actions and motives cannot be truly described."[20] Brown's skeptical view of the "uncertainty of history" prompts him to turn his novels into subversive histories, leading us by subtle hints into the blind alleys of our own desires for unity and logical progression.

The growing realization that the people held authority transformed literary as well as political performances. Brown is, in effect, considering the possible dangers and consequences to society of this relocation of political power. If sovereignty and ultimate authority lie finally with the people, that is, if they move their rep-

[19] Wood, "Conspiracy," p. 409.
[20] Brown, *Rhapsodist*, p. 147.

resentatives as they themselves are moved, then we must look at the motivations not of their leaders but of the people themselves. We discover in Brown an acute understanding of democracy's consequences: the internalization of authority and the creation of private, rather than public interests. As the Federalist ideology of hierarchy and public performance began to collapse, these issues of intentionality and motivation became increasingly troublesome. Republicans inherited the Antifederalist concern over individual interpretation of intentionality and the maintenance of individual autonomy in the face of political seduction.

* * *

The election of a Republican President, Thomas Jefferson, in 1800 signaled a change in American politics. More effectively than his Federalist predecessors, Jefferson constructed an image of authority that accommodated the new realities of democratic power lying in the hands of the people. Charles Brockden Brown's eventual failure in the same period prophesied many of the difficulties facing future writers. The Mephistophelian proposition of accommodation to the new ideology of both voters and literary audience presented an uncomfortable consequence to both politicians and writers: If they were representatives of the people, then representation no longer meant what it had a few years before. They were now being asked to mirror their audience's desires in actual representation, rather than uplift and teach "by virtue" of their social positions.

The democratization of authority, the literalization of representation, and the internalization, the privatization of judgment and interpretation were the consequences of vast social and philosophical changes in the Western world. As authority came to be located in the people, or in their power to elect their representatives, the coercive strength of traditional hierarchical authority was necessarily transformed into new modes of persuasion. As Jay Fliegelman has pointed out, this transformation coincides with, and perhaps indirectly leads to, new patterns of familial authority. Privileging filial liberty over paternal tyranny promised future prosperity, but it left an ominous vacuum to those who could lead the children astray. In proposing mimetic authority and then by trying to imbue institutions with a paternal symbolism, Franklin, for example, had hoped to provide constraints for the new democracy.

Perhaps the greatest consequence of this new image of authority was its foregrounding of representation as a possible factor mediating between hierarchical and democratic conceptions of authority. The rapid rise of the Republican party testifies to the relative ease with which politicians responded to social changes, but writers found it difficult to overcome their cultural biases against democratic culture. The problem facing many of the writers was not so much their reader's antipathy as the general lack of definition of their audience. In a very real sense they were faced with creating and instructing the ideal reader. But given the suspicious nature of Americans, to accomplish this task required the masking of designs on the reader's sympathy. Artlessness and humor provided some success for Brackenridge, but Brown's subversively moral tales found few readers willing to learn his cautionary lessons. Nevertheless, both Brown's and Brackenridge's concerns with their readers mark an important change in the history of the American writer.

What these writers witnessed in the late eighteenth century was important steps in the transformation of authority from public performance to private judgment. Besides locating authority in the people, democracy permitted the internalization of political issues. With their emphasis on the voter's judgment and the representative's relation to his constituency, modern politics parallel the increasing power of private experience. Brown's concerns with his reader's motivations and judgments suggest that the real political issues of his day became epistemological: How do I uncover false representatives? How do I distinguish true authority in someone's narrative? To an even greater extent than Franklin or Brackenridge, to whom language was a social medium, Brown uses language to represent private thoughts and hidden emotions. The many letters, notes, and especially Clara's secret journal become the repository for secret and guarded thoughts. Theodore Wieland's voices are ambiguous precisely because they might very well be representations of unconscious and repressed emotions. In this, Clara and Theodore represent initial stages in the gradual impingement of individual private authority into public matters. In contrast, Brackenridge's dialect casts his characters in categories, rather than depicting personal and intimate thoughts and emotions. In Brackenridge's case, rhetoric is always public, political decisions are carried out in the open air. But for Brown, political questions have been pared down to his characters' psychologies. Political decisions, this transformation implies, are now made in the privacy of one's home, rather than the ballot box or legislative rooms. Finding ways to reach the independent reader and to establish a relationship that recovers the proper political relationship was to become an increasingly difficult process for American writers, for the politics of narrative mirrored the chaotic state of American politics for the next sixty years.

PART TWO

The Antebellum Period

CHAPTER FOUR

Myth from the Perspective of History: James Fenimore Cooper and Paternal Authorities

HISTORY AND MYTH: THE DIS-COURSES OF EMPIRE

In 1787, six years after Brackenridge had moved west to establish a name for himself on the frontier, William Cooper laid out plans for the wilderness town that was to bear his name, Cooperstown, New York. A strong Hamiltonian Federalist, William Cooper quickly saw the economic advantages of order and unity; he settled the region, like his counterpart in Pittsburgh, by betting his personal fortunes on the Constitution's success. When he was appointed first judge of the Court of Common Pleas of Otsego County in 1791, William Cooper soon added legal authority to his social power. In such an energetic and progressive nation, it did not take long to assume the status of civic leader and patriarch. When he wrote a history of this area, *A Guide in the Wilderness*, he also became the first man of letters and historian of the region. In 1838, his son, James Fenimore, anonymously published another history, *The Chronicles of Cooperstown*, which he hoped would be of interest to "those whose fathers were active in converting the wilderness around about us, into its present picture of comfort and civilization."[1] It was very much as the son of a founding father,

[1] James Fenimore Cooper, *The Chronicles of Cooperstown* (Cooperstown, N.Y.: H. & E. Phinney, 1838), p. [3]. (Hereafter cited in text as CC.)

then, that James Fenimore Cooper began his own career, and as such he was burdened with the glory and expectations that history held for him.

Given his own intimate ties to the Federalist founder of Cooperstown, it is not surprising that James Cooper would make the logical association between personal and national histories. Forty years after the writing of the Constitution, he looked back at the document and its supporters as the moment of a community's founding. In *Notions of the Americans* (1828), he identifies the Constitution as the central term by which a national community may be defined: "The very word *constitution* implies the control of all those interests which distinguish an identified community."[2] If the Revolution initiated historical disruption and discontinuity, the "constitution of 1787 wrought a vital change in this system [of confederation]. The Americans now became one people in their institutions, as well as in their origin and in their feelings."[3] This document provided an institutional origin, a beginning that united history, law, and affectional ties in an alliance corresponding to Judge Cooper's office in Cooperstown. Patriotism for his son could be at once a public and a personal sentiment.

The Constitution, however, proved a problematic origin for future generations because it represented an inimitable moment in history.[4] Speaking of these Federalist fathers in the "now" of 1828, Cooper presents them as existing and working *in* history, but history itself seems a realm completely divorced from the present: "The older members of the [Federalist] party sometimes act together, now, from habit and intimacy, but the generation that is just appearing on the stage, already read of the party struggles in which their fathers struggled as matters of history."[5] Equating fathers with history grants a founder like William Cooper an exalted status, but it also demarcates the boundary beyond which a portion of the founder's power cannot be transmitted. James Cooper here describes history not as a link to his father but as a barrier. So

[2] James Fenimore Cooper, *Notions of the Americans*, 2 vols. (London: Henry Colburn, 1828), 2: 200.

[3] Ibid., 2: 201.

[4] Robert A. Ferguson has pointed out that the Constitution's preamble requires change to be a necessary part of the United States. See *Law and Letters in American Culture* (Cambridge, Mass.: Harvard Univ. Press, 1984), p. 62.

[5] Cooper, *Notions*, 2: 221.

quickly in America people and events become history, thus losing the power to perpetuate themselves in future generations. More specifically, the fathers who make history cannot be redeemed from its flux.

Despite the proximity of national and familial origins, it seemed odd to Cooper that these origins were rapidly being obscured by historical change. Lost was the authority contained in those origins, an authority at once patriarchal, legal, and social. Writing in the introduction to his *Chronicles of Cooperstown*, Cooper admits his purpose in pursuing the past is that "posterity may know the leading facts connected with the origin and settlement of the village of Cooperstown, and that even the present generation may be set right in some important particulars, concerning which erroneous notions now prevail" (CC, [3]). History here means two very different things: the experience of temporal flux that threatens to erase origins through the process of change, and the representation of that change in literary form that can restore these origins, create temporal continuity, and defend against change and flux. The writing of history, in other words, may "set right" the "erroneous notions" that have occurred in the fifty years since Cooperstown's founding, but the implicit impetus to write history is the fact that America has gone off course, has been diverted from its founders' original intentions. Constitutional founding quickly signals, and perhaps generates, dangerous social changes and proves a burden to the son whose duty it is to right—or write—them.

United States history could begin with the ratification of the Constitution only because the Revolution violently disengaged us from English history. Like many revolutionary moments, the events of 1776–1787 proleptically shaped the fates of those who came after by creating the patterns which the descendants might imitate in hopes of inheriting their authority. Thus these descendants of the founders could enjoy the freedom and prosperity arising from the Revolution and Constitution but their power (as Franklin would have wanted it) could come only through *imitation* of the original laws, characters, and personalities. For a nation like the United States to have a purely historical origin—as opposed to primitive or mythological origins—means that its originality and priority are relative terms only, earned by disrupting one linear movement and diverting it to another end. Because of its association with disruption and revolution, United States history, ratified in the Constitution, promised only divergence from its origin. In other words, as it arose through historical change, the Revolution could not guarantee its descendants perpetuity but only more change; because it marked an origin, it also carried the dual threat that any future attempt at originality would have to be equally revolutionary and subject to the power of historical change.

In his second novel, *The Spy* (1821), James Cooper used the Revolutionary War to celebrate and explore the United States' origins as well as to exhibit his own literary originality and filial piety. As he later noted, he "chose patriotism for his theme," a sentiment that prompted his use of native materials as well.[6] Included in this novel is a fictional portrait of George Washington as a stern, aloof general and revered leader. He acts literally as a *deus ex machina*: In his brief appearances he is the representative of Justice and final arbiter of the characters' fates. Washington softens this awful presence, however, when he describes himself as a benevolent father: "All who dwell in this broad land are my children, and my care" (*Spy*, 412). Yet Harvey Birch, the eponymous hero of the novel, discovers that obedience to this father ultimately entails the loss of his own identity. Unable to reveal that Birch is his spy, working under his command, Washington requires him to live out his life in ignominy on the margins between society and wilderness. If Washington is indeed a father to his people, Cooper acknowledges the harsh obligations and uncertain future that filial piety demands. As Cooper implies, in the young Republic the fathers might have provided models of leadership and justice but the sons have no means to imitate them.

Revolution, change, and divergence, therefore, underlie the peculiar nature of American history. Consequently, any ties to this "new origin," this historical, legal founding, are necessarily complicit in its *relative* position. Law itself does not connect the children to their revolutionary parents, but rather measures the gulf between them. Like the second- and third-generation Puritans, the sons of the founding fathers mixed their praises with veiled, per-

[6] James Fenimore Cooper, *The Spy* (New York: G. P. Putnam's Sons, 1895), p. vi. Further references to Cooper's works, except those in the new SUNY edition, will be to this edition and cited in the text.

haps unconscious, complaints about the difficulty of living up to their parents' models.

In the famous opening to *The Pioneers* (1823), the narrator reveals this generational tension as he presents us with both a prospect and retrospect of the Otsego geography. Describing the effects of civilization on the wilderness, the narrator explains "the whole district is hourly exhibiting how much can be done, in even a rugged country."[7] Like many of Cooper's visual set pieces, this description conflates the temporal and visual and ends with an unsettling association of absolute change and conditional permanence:

> The expedients of the pioneers who first broke ground in the settlement of this country, are succeeded by the permanent improvements of the yeoman, who intends to leave his remains to moulder under the sod which he tills, or, perhaps, of the son, who, born in the land, piously wishes to linger around the grave of his father.—Only forty years have passed since the territory was a wilderness. (P, 16)[8]

In a hesitating and nostalgic tone, the narrator not only places his novel in historical flux but also sets up an uneasy alliance between progress ("permanent improvement") and decline. Behind each description of landscape lies an awareness that land, always subject to historical change as a result of founding, offers only instability. History grants each locus a relative value, just as it relativizes its own authority. For Cooper land itself is the repository of values, but those values must themselves be subject to the disruptions of historical transmission. In this first paragraph we discover that the pioneering world described in the novel has already been superseded by the yeoman but the yeoman himself is absent, a vic-

[7] James Fenimore Cooper, *The Pioneers; or the Sources of the Susquehanna*, ed. Renee Schachterlee and Kenneth M. Andersen, Jr. (Albany, N.Y.: State Univ. Press of New York, 1980), p. 16. (Hereafter cited in text as P. Whenever possible, I am using the text and explanatory notes from the Cooper editions being published under the directorship of James Franklin Beard.)

[8] For discussions of Cooper's visual style and its association with his sense of temporality, see Blake Nevius, *Cooper's Landscapes* (Berkeley: Univ. of California Press, 1976), pp. 23–24; Donald A. Ringe, *The Pictorial Mode* (Lexington: Univ. Press of Kentucky, 1971); and William P. Kelly, *Plotting America's Past* (Carbondale, Ill.: Southern Illinois Univ. Press, 1983), p. 13.

tim of historical change. Only the son remains, but he does not cultivate the soil nor, presumably, continue the region's development. Rather, his age is retrospective; filial piety brings an end to productivity and progress.

Taken together, *The Spy* and *The Pioneers* provide the paradigm describing the difficulties of historical transmission from father to son. The disruptive forces of the father's revolutionary founding threaten the son's identity, an identity tied to his inheritance of land. Interposed between the father's patrimony and the child's inheritance, history threatens to negate this tie by making the transmission of land subject to the power of historical change and divergence. Time and again in his fiction, Cooper reenacted this establishment of a new community in the wilderness to serve as the nexus of his personal, social, and literary concerns. In his earliest novels, this founding is associated with some form of patriarchal authority: of Washington the political father in *The Spy*, of Judge Temple the autobiographical and legal father in *The Pioneers* (1823), of Mark Heathcote the Puritan father in *The Wept of Wish-ton-Wish* (1829). These founders might represent Cooper's Oedipal dueling with his own father, but we must remember that these are *historical* fathers, tied quite specifically to history in ways that should extend any psychological reading of their authority to include the question of history's authority as well. Cooper's obvious fascination with fathers is ultimately tied to his sense of historical change so that the issue of patriarchal authority must be seen not only as Freudian dissent but as part of a larger concern with the transmission of the father's virtues and authority and the ability of succeeding generations to possess or imitate those values. *Descent* may appear to be *dissent*, but the more powerful conflict in Cooper's work is between historical change—the movement away from an origin—and the possibility of permanence—the presence of that origin in succeeding generations.

We can trace part of Cooper's ambivalence to his own role as the son of Judge William Cooper, the founder and patriarch of Cooperstown.[9] Certainly the burden and honors of family descended

[9] See Stephen Railton, *Fenimore Cooper* (Princeton: Princeton Univ. Press, 1978), for a psychoanalytic view of their relationship. There is a wealth of material in Cooper's novels and his journals and letters to make a case for the importance of William Cooper to his son's writings.

more heavily on James Cooper than on most. As Federalist, landowner, judge, and even historian, Judge Cooper must have been an imposing figure to his young son who later in life proudly introduced himself as a "Cooper of Cooperstown."[10] Thus property and family identity were conjoined early for him, an association no doubt strengthened and publicized in the later controversy over his father's property at Three Mile Point. Throughout his life, Cooper was embroiled in land disputes that made him all too aware of the difficulties of patrimonial inheritance. In fact, much of Cooper's life preceding his first novel, *Persuasion*, was spent untangling the legal problems and debts of his father's estate. In the decade following Judge Cooper's death in 1810, his four oldest children died, leaving James to bear the weight of bad investments and heavy spending by his brothers.[11] After taking out loans and involving himself in expensive and complicated legal actions, James Cooper learned firsthand the difficulty of securing his patrimony.

Cooper's struggle to preserve, and later to reclaim, his patrimony entangled him in two types of authority, each involving a different form of transmission. Distinguishing patriarchy from both a patrimonial society and paternalism, Richard Sennett defines a patriarchy as "a society in which all people are *consciously* related by blood ties."[12] In both a patriarchy and a patrimonial society, all property is inherited through the male relatives. The difference between the two, as Sennett says, is that in a patrimonial society (like America's), "people do not conceive of the social relationships exclusively in terms of family." The distinction between paternalism and the other two forms of power is important for my reading of Cooper: "Paternalism differs from patrimonialism in the most basic way: the patrimony itself does not exist. Property

[10] *The Letters and Journals of James Fenimore Cooper*, ed. James Franklin Beard, 6 vols. (Cambridge, Mass.: Harvard Univ. Press, 1960–1968), 3: 42. (Hereafter cited in text as *Letters*.)

[11] See Wayne Franklin, *The New World of James Fenimore Cooper* (Chicago: Univ. of Chicago Press, 1982), pp. 16–29, for a discussion of Cooper's financial problems. Like Franklin, I am also indebted to Beard's notes to his edition of Cooper's letters and journals. See also Michael Paul Rogin, *Fathers and Children: Andrew Jackson and the Subjugation of the American Indian* (New York: Alfred Knopf, 1975), pp. 79–81, 90–104, for a discussion of Jacksonian anxieties over possession of land.

[12] Sennett, *Authority*, p. 52.

no longer passes legally from father to eldest son according to the principle of primogeniture. Nor does society legally guarantee that the position held by a person in one generation will be held by a relative in the next."[13] In other words, the father retains a strong emotional and *symbolic* bond with his offspring, but has relatively little *material* control over the offspring's future. Paternalism tends to link the generations in an ambiguous fashion: Fathers offer protection and nurturance but no real security. As Sennett comments: "Paternalism is male domination without a contract."[14]

In *Notions of the Americans*, Cooper addresses the virtue of inheritance versus the inheritance of virtue in America. His ambivalence about the propriety of inherited virtue suggests a similar uncertainty about paternal authority. It would be impossible, the narrator writes in the first volume, "to destroy the influence of education, talents, money, or even birth." But having established these powers, he continues:

> Now, if some portion of the consideration of the father were not transmissible to the descendant, the latter clearly could in no degree presume on his birth. It is fortunate here, as elsewhere, to be the child of a worthy, or even of an affluent parent. The goods of the latter descend, by process of law, to the offspring, and, by aid of public opinion, the son receives some portion of the renown that has been earned by the merit of the father. (1: 209)

The narrator here establishes two mechanisms meant to insure transmission of a father's merit: the law and public opinion. Although he later claims law is the "only supreme authority in this republic" (2: 291), Cooper had already witnessed the law's inability to insure his inheritance. And over the next few years he faced the reality that public opinion, rather than insuring the inheritance of a father's virtue, actually threatened dissolution of the bonds between father and son. In truth, "it is not enough," the narrator tells us, "simply to be the son of a great man" (1: 211).

From the moment the Puritans landed in America, questions of a child's birthrights and obligations sparked conflict between fa-

[13] Ibid., p. 53.
[14] Ibid., p. 54.

thers and sons. Control of the land was a basic issue and the first-generation Puritans maintained strict control over the inheritance of land and therefore over the children's future.[15] Strengthening the parents' grip was their complete domination over their children's religious lives. Unable to live up to the political achievement of the founders, the children could not even sustain the Puritan religious fervor. The Half-Way Covenant was a critical statement of the children's moral and legal inferiority. This pattern of manipulation and dependence fostered feelings of insecurity and doubt in the second and third generations. In Sennett's terms, the Puritans created a patimonial society but used the patrimony to regulate obedience in order to insure the community's religious survival.

The strongly patrimonial control over inheritance and religion diminished in time, but the fathers had created a powerful symbol of authority. Authority, leadership, and fathers came to be linked symbolically in the Election sermons, even as the patrimonial society gradually changed. Speaking to the magistrates in his Election sermon, *The Serviceable Man* (1690), Cotton Mather, for example, made this relationship explicit: "We do this Day commit ourselves unto your Care, and we will now look upon you as our Fathers."[16] The strength of this metaphor becomes clear when we find it intact nearly a century later, in the critical year 1787, as Joseph Lyman claimed that "to be the father of his people, is the magistrate's duty."[17] Thus, despite the weakening of parental controls in colonial and post-Revolutionary America, familial ties continued to provide political and social power. Without a true aristocracy, the recently moneyed merchants gained authority in large cities, but in many medium-sized towns, or even villages like Cooperstown, "political benefit to be derived from having a prominent father was considerable."[18] Even John Adams believed "the people, by their

[15] See Emory Elliott, *The Power and the Pulpit in Puritan New England* (Princeton: Princeton Univ. Press, 1975), pp. 26–34; see also Kenneth Lockridge, *A New England Town* (New York: W. W. Norton, 1970); Sumner Powell, *Puritan Village: The Formation of a New England Town* (Middletown, Conn.: Wesleyan Univ. Press, 1963).

[16] Cotton Mather, *The Serviceable Man* (Boston, 1690), p. 60.

[17] Joseph Lyman, *A Sermon Preached before His Excellency Jonas Bowdoin, Esq.* (Boston, 1787), p. 19.

[18] Edward Cook, *The Fathers of the Towns* (Baltimore: Johns Hopkins Univ. Press, 1975), p. 98.

elections, will continue the government generally in the same families from generation to generation."[19] In these cases the family provided normative power of tradition and continuity for both community and offspring. Equating the magistrate's legal powers with a father's stature imbued the bonds of obedience and protection with an emotional commitment that often exaggerated the strains of the legal relationship.

As Cooper spent great effort to recover his father's inheritance (something he was not to accomplish until 1834), he equated his material patrimony, transmitted historically by the nation's laws, with the symbolic image of paternalism. When his inheritance itself became "neutral ground," territory to be contested, this patrimony became largely symbolic property. In short, the very sources of patrimonial authority maintained by Puritan and Revolutionary fathers—property, tradition, and law—became symbolically associated with Judge William Cooper by the very difficulty of their transmission.[20] As the historical son of a maker of history, Cooper, like Harvey Birch, was faced with the possibility of anonymity. Unable to maintain the material ties of patrimony to his father, Cooper strengthened the symbolic power of paternalism. Associated with the historical founding of the United States, Judge Cooper was thereby implicated in historical change, the process that renders inheritance problematic. As representative of the new ideals of economic speculation, geographic and class mobility, and individualism, William Cooper stood as one of the new Federalists who balanced political ideology with personal expediency. But change proved the key link between Judge Cooper's economics and the ideology of American democracy, in which, as Alexis de Tocqueville says, "each generation is a new people," by destroying the traditional, transmissable bonds of social hierarchy.[21] It is Tocqueville who astutely assesses the influence of democracy on the family: "But as soon as the young American begins to ap-

[19] John Adams, *Works*, ed. Charles Francis Adams (Boston: Little, Brown, 1850–1856), 3: 124. Marius Bewley discusses Adams's theory of society in *The Eccentric Design* (New York: Columbia Univ. Press, 1959), pp. 24–37.

[20] Henry Nash Smith in *Virgin Land: The American West as Symbol and Myth* (Cambridge, Mass.: Harvard Univ. Press, 1950), p. 62, has noticed that in *The Pioneers* "all aspects of authority—institutional stability, organized religion, class stratification, property—are exhibited as radiating from the symbol of the father."

[21] Tocqueville, *Democracy*, p. 473.

proach man's estate, the reins of filial obedience are daily slackened. Master of his thoughts, he soon becomes responsible for his own behavior. In America there is in truth no adolescence. At the close of boyhood he is a man and begins to trace his own path."[22] Democracy not only threatens historical disruption but it forces the children into adulthood too rapidly.

The concept of historical authority for Cooper, then, resides in the complex figure of the white father. But as we have already seen, Cooper's fathers themselves exist as a configuration of forces and qualities; their authority consists of several parts history, law, land, and symbolism. The challenge this authority presents the children is not one of obedience, for most of Cooper's children are excessively reverent, but the need to recover it for themselves. Just as the American Revolution relativized history, thereby privileging change over continuity, and the Constitution substituted a historical, legal origin for a traditional foundation, Cooper found his own location in time and space continually under attack. It seemed that all ground became, in his own terms, "neutral ground" and the only antidote was to somehow recover some stable, originating father.

* * *

If Cooper's writings associate white fathers with history, then sons inevitably become historians, literally and literarily lingering around the graves of their fathers. Serving as representatives to the memories of the fathers, the sons commit themselves to writing history, the mode of writing which equates representation with filial imitation. But as Cooper acknowledges in the opening to his *Chronicles of Cooperstown*, there is another origin for America, one displaced from history and historical fathers altogether—its native origins. "The site of the present village of Cooperstown," he begins, "is said to have been a favorite place of resort with the adjacent savage tribes from a remote period" (CC, 5). As he continues, Cooper suggests a different attitude toward the past, one which places his subject—the geographical site of Cooperstown—in the landscape of myth:

> The tradition which has handed down this circumstance, is rendered probable by the known abundance of the fish and

[22] Ibid., p. 585.

> game in its vicinity. The word 'Otsego,' is thought to be a compound which conveys the idea of a spot at which meetings of the Indians were held. There is a small rock near the outlet of the Lake, called 'Otsego Rock,' at which precise point the savages, according to an early tradition of the country, were accustomed to give each other the rendezvous.

Tradition, rather than history, becomes the bearer of the past. It is a tradition, too, associated with place and naming. Certain names like Otsego "convey the idea of a spot," whose meaning has remained stable since before white history began in America. Just as the name Cooperstown carries with it the sense of historical founding, Otsego holds out a sense of timelessness and permanence. And it is with some irony that we read of the political struggle within the town itself between incorporation as the Village of Otsego or as the Village of Cooperstown.[23]

In effect, the victory of "Cooperstown" over "Otsego" creates a palimpsest, a rewriting of a historical text over a traditional myth, analogous to the founding of the town on the site of an original Indian resort. The legal act of incorporation suggests that legal authority has been substituted for the traditional authority of origins or priority held by the Indians. But the conflict between different conceptions of authority and the very different forms of representing that authority are never truly settled in Cooper's work. Historical fathers like Judge Temple, Colonel Munro, and Mark Heathcote inevitably find their authorities challenged and suffer some sort of defeat. Against these white fathers and their promise of patrimony, Cooper proposes an alternative paternal authority transmitted symbolically. In contrast to Judge Temple's legal authority in Templeton, we find Natty Bumppo and Chingachgook holding sway on the edge of the mythic Otsego Lake at the foot of Mount Vision. Colonel Munro, the defender of the historical Fort William Henry in the first half of *The Last of the Mohicans*, finds his counterpart in Tamenund, the ancient Indian patriarch whose words conclude the novel. The old testament patriarch in *The Prairie*, Ishmael Bush, is opposed by Le Balafré, the Indian father. Throughout Cooper's early works we find a doubling of fathers, each embodying a contrary form of authority. Each patri-

[23] See Cooper, *Chronicles*, pp. 64–65.

arch represents a different kind of origin and together they polarize the novels between history and myth, change and permanence, white and Indian.

Within his novels, the division between fathers creates narrative divisions as well. In the 1832 edition of *The Pioneers*, Cooper added a new introduction that places this novel even more surely within a framework of historical flux and mythic stasis. It is here that he makes his well-known distinction between "how much of [the novel's] contents is literal fact, and how much is intended to represent a general picture" (P, 6). Cooper continues the distinction between literal particularity and figural generality and broadens its bounds to include history and fiction: "This rigid adhesion to truth, an indispensable requisite in history and travels, destroys the charm of fiction, for all that is necessary to be conveyed to the mind by the latter had better be done by delineations of principles and of characters in their classes, than by a too fastidious attention to originals" (P, 6). Literal, historical truth involves the imitation, the representation, of "originals." Within this context we can see the subtitle of the novel—*A Descriptive Tale*—not as a generic classification but as an acknowledgment of its divided nature. *The Pioneers* is minutely *descriptive* of Templeton, and as such claims as its territory the truth of history and as its method the imitation of originals. But it is also a "tale," partaking of the "charm of fiction." If it begins in the representational world of the historical novel through its self-acknowledged autobiographical descriptions of the lives and mores of remembered people, it ends with the less clearly visualized romance of Leatherstocking and Chingachgook. Their world, like their hut, cannot be entered or described realistically at all because it is located in a place where deer and panthers still exist. Their world is presented as the territory of myth.

Although myth provides an alternative father in Cooper's early novels, these mythic origins seem at odds with the temporal flux of history, which marks only divergence from its origin. Arising from a violent revolutionary origin, the American empire seemed doomed to recurrent revolutions and disruptions because it destroyed its own foundation. Cooper's concerns are best visualized in Thomas Cole's famous series of paintings, *The Course of Empire*. Painted in 1836, the series depicts the classic rise and fall of a great nation. Taken together, these five paintings—comprising *The Sav-*

age State, The Pastoral State, The Culmination of Empire, Destruction, and *Desolation*—create the appearance of a huge imaginative sweep of history.[24] Cole, like Cooper, conflates the visual and temporal by using landscape as the marker of change. Using a large, jutting mountain and harbor as continuous points of reference, Cole would have us believe, again like Cooper, that history is a series of palimpsests, or, to take a modern analogy, transparencies that we put over unchanging nature to show the progress of modern civilization.

Both writer and painter, however, are faced with the problem of temporal continuity in their works. On closer examination of Cole's series it is not clear how we actually get from the "there" of a savage origin, to the "here" of civilization's culmination (if that is where we are), and then to the "there" of culture's desolation at the other end of history. That is, between each historical moment we must imagine more than the continuous passage of years; rather, arising in the darkness between paintings are complete paradigm shifts that demarcate the boundaries of temporal discontinuity. The savage and pastoral states actually mark two separate origins: the former, a Hobbesian political origin; the latter, a poetic source.

We recognize this discontinuity by Cole's use of point of view as a thematic reference. Safely distanced from the first scene, we note *The Savage State* evokes the idea of the sublime through a series of conflicts: between warring men, between the dark storm clouds and light, between sea and land. In the second scene, we again stand apart from the actions framed by nature, but this time the scene represents the picturesque rather than sublime. It is only in the third painting, *The Culmination of Empire,* that our point of view actually resides *within* the scene as we stand in the city and watch a religious procession pass before us. This change is crucial, for our perspective is now complicit in the action we behold. Rather than looking *into* a foreign culture, we now look *out* from civilization toward the sea; we can never lose this point of view again, even in *Desolation,* where there is no human presence in the landscape *except for our vision.* In other words, as we move from painting to

[24] On Cole's series and the relationship between history and point of view, see Ringe, *Pictorial Mode,* pp. 143–44, 148–49.

painting we are not observing a continuous temporal movement but the figurative diversion and displacement, the *troping*, of meaning. Therefore, what looks like history, complete with origin and presumably conclusion, turns out to be imaginative variations on the theme of discontinuity.

In Cooper's works, this problem of discontinuity manifests itself in the intersection of the visual and temporal. Judge William Cooper had looked over newly founded Cooperstown and was cheered to see "by what means the face of nature can be altered, and how in half the span of one man's life, towns, roads, and cheerful seats, with all the comforts of civilized life, can be substituted for the gloomy monotony of the barren desert."[25] But his son looked over the American scene and discovered that the process of founding *as substitution*, made possible by the Revolution and Constitution, generated the power of history to obliterate its own origins and thus make problematic the son's ability to inherit his patrimony. Like *The Course of Empire*, the succession of Indian (mythic), English (traditional), and American (legal) foundings in *The Pioneers* creates the sense of divergence rather than continuity.

For Cooper, then, the father stands as the nexus of conflict between the origin of the historical father's authority and the authority of some prior mythic origin. Cooper's fictional founding fathers, as was his own father, are associated with the disruptive forces of historical and revolutionary settlement and as such their authority—found in institutions, laws, and land—never has absolute priority. Democratized American society arising during the Revolution threatened the inheritance of this authority because of its insistence on change and its devaluation of the generational links of inheritance. Once the actual patrimonial transmission of goods and property is transformed solely into the symbolic ties of filial imitation, the children are released to speculate, but without ties to the past. Although the economic security of the family may be at question, the principal conflict for Cooper lies in history itself. As historian, the son must attempt to recreate the links severed by time and by the revolutionary origins of American democracy. But as a writer of romance, Cooper can imagine other origins

[25] William Cooper, *A Guide in the Wilderness* (1810; reprint, Dublin: Gilbert and Hodges, 1897), p. 2.

and a stable tradition passed on through an alternative form of representation. He can imagine mythic presence. Thus the novels themselves serve as disputed territory: Seeking to reconcile conflicting forms of authority and representation, they most often end with a repressive solution. As Tocqueville noted, the impact of democracy on American culture was to threaten the separation of fathers and sons, past and present, duty and freedom. Throughout his novels, Cooper sought to unite past and present by aligning myth and history as a means to his own power as author.

History and Myth in Cooper's Early Novels

In 1827, Thomas Cole painted two works based on chapter 26 of *The Last of the Mohicans*, which had been published the year before.[26] Both depict Cora Munro kneeling at the feet of the ancient Indian patriarch, Tamenund, attempting to save the life of her sister Alice. The two versions of this scene, in effect, create two different readings of the novel, a consequence, I would claim, of the uneasy alliance of two conflicting worlds the novel depicts. Cole's choice for a suitable scene for his painting suggests an attempt to locate a moment of crisis, a moment in which the always-present threat of violence is balanced by the judgment of Tamenund and "the inviolable laws of Indian hospitality."[27] Up to this time, the reader has experienced little justice in the massacre of Fort Henry's soldiers and the two captivities of Colonel Munro's daughters. Now the action becomes a series of rhetorical encounters among the main characters. In this very complex scene, the evil Magua argues over the possession of Cora, while Duncan Heyward and Hawkeye each tries to persuade Tamenund that he is the real "La Longue Carabine" (Hawkeye), and Uncas unveils himself as the descendant of the original race of Delawares, the last of the Mohicans.

In both versions of the scene, Cole renders the human activity almost insignificant as he dwarfs these main players and encircling Indians by the powerful presence of huge rocks in the foreground,

[26] These two paintings are reproduced in James Fenimore Cooper, *The Last of the Mohicans*, ed. James A. Sappenfield and E. N. Feltskog (Albany, N.Y.: State Univ. Press of New York, 1983), between pp. 336 and 337.

[27] Cooper, *Last of the Mohicans*, p. 317. (Hereafter cited in text as LM.)

a towering, jutting rock overhanging the scene, large mountains fading in the horizon, and an implied gorge over which this table of rock hangs. In one version the perspective places the viewer just outside the scene, which is partly framed, partly obscured by massive dark rocks on either side of the scene. Horizontally centered, we see Cora in miniature kneeling before Tamenund, but the size makes it impossible to detect any emotion except through the dramatic gesture of her figure. Just above them a rock perches precariously, a sign of balance, of precipitant danger, of judgment. The autumn foliage surrounding the scene reminds us of the passage of time and imminent death.

Cole's second painting places the viewer above and at a distance from the setting. No longer framed by rocks, the scene and characters appear even smaller and more insignificant in the context of nature. The precariousness of this world is emphasized here by the rock ledge on which the figures stand, dropping off suddenly into an unseen valley or gorge below. Another ledge, tilted uncertainly to the left in the foreground repeats this image of danger. But the Indians remain in the circle, seemingly unaware of the danger at their backs. Cora again kneels before a barely seen Tamenund. To the right of them we see a dense forest, again in autumnal colors, and above them rises a tower of rock, unmistakably phallic in appearance. In the background we again see a line of mountains gradually becoming obscured in the golden haze of the horizon. Perhaps the major difference here is not the scene, but the viewer's position: If in the first version we are onlookers, viewing through obscuring rocks, here we are literally up in the air without a solid footing, completely divorced from the activity below and threatened by our dangerous placement.

Before discussing the relationship between these paintings and the novel, I must pay some attention to the scene they represent. Seated at the center of the circle, Tamenund presents himself "with the dignity of a monarch, and the air of a father" (LM, 304), and it is as a father Cora addresses him: "Art thou not Tamenund—the father—the judge—I had almost said, the prophet—of this people?" (LM, 304). To free Alice, Cora tries to remind him that their own father (Colonel Munro who is standing in the background, a senile and exhausted old man) had once freed one of Tamenund's children. Failing there, she asks, "Is Tamenund a father?"—hoping to engage his sentiment as a parent to free "the daughter of an old and failing man"—and he responds, "Of a nation" (LM, 305). Again she has failed to persuade the patriarch, who has heard in her plea for mercy the implicit fear of miscegenation and the distaste of a white woman contemplating the union of the blonde Alice with Magua.

It is only with the appearance of Uncas, and the revelation of his true identity that we find the threat narrowly averted. As a member of the " 'unchanged' race," Uncas stands before Tamenund not only as the son of Chingachgook and descendant of the original tribe, but as the *original* Uncas, unchanged and present: "Yet is Uncas before him [Tamenund], as they went to battle, against palefaces! Uncas, the panther of his tribe, the eldest son of the Lenape, the wisest Sagamore of the Mohicans! Tell me, ye Delawares, has Tamenund been a sleeper for a hundred winters?" (LM, 310). For a brief moment time is reversed and Uncas the son almost becomes the father to this childlike chief. In this scene, order, justice, and balance are restored to the novel because there is no difference between the last of the Mohicans and the first. We seem to be in the mythic world of the Lenni Lenape, the original race of Indians. John Heckewelder, one of Cooper's principal sources of information about Indians, describes the significance of their name: "The name signifies '*orginal people*,' a race of human beings who are the same that they were in the beginning, *unchanged* and *unmixed*."[28] Whereas the Lenni Lenape see the whites as "a mixed race, and therefore a troublesome one," Uncas is all the more powerful because he is unmixed, unchanged, indeed original.[29]

Although we seem to have come far afield from the original discussion of this scene as it is represented by Cole, it will be helpful to consider its implications. First of all, it is a scene composed of carefully balanced oppositions. Beyond the obvious conflict between Uncas and Magua, we notice the odd competition between Hawkeye and Duncan Heyward and now the contrast between Cora's ineffectual suit to gain Alice's freedom and Uncas's revela-

[28] John Heckewelder, *History, Manners, and Customs of the Indian Nations Who Once Inhabited Pennsylvania and the Neighbouring States* (Philadelphia: Abraham Small, 1819), p. xi. This volume is a reprint published as volume 12 in the *Memoirs of the Historical Society of Pennsylvania* (Philadelphia, 1876).

[29] Ibid., p. 187.

tion. Herself a product of a mixed racial marriage, Cora cannot envision the same fate for her sister. But before we condemn Cooper for his simplistic answer to the problem of race, we should realize that in this context the key feature is not sexual miscegenation in itself, but the historical mixing and change it represents. That is, the underlying sexual fears represented here are intimately associated with a sense of temporal flux and historical change. Standing on this rock ledge, we have suddenly found ourselves before an unmediated origin, a moment in which no history is at work. As H. Daniel Peck has noted, the last half of the novel describes an unchanging, unified, mythic world.[30] The circled tribe, the patriarch, and the son exist within a world of balanced laws. Cora, as victim of the white history of slavery, is "mixed" and for that reason belongs to the European scheme of temporal progression and change: "The curse of my ancestors has fallen heavily on their child!" (LM, 305). In other words, Cora's sin can never be original; rather, it is measured by the distance from her historical origins. The curse is not simply her mixed heritage, but the fact of history itself.

One of the principal mythic elements in the second half of this novel involves the metamorphosis of the characters' identities. Hawkeye becomes a bear; Chingachgook, a beaver; David Gamut, a shaman figure; and Duncan Heyward, a "natural fool." The substitutions we see attempted in this scene are of a different sort, however. Heyward usurps Hawkeye's identity to preserve the scout from danger, just as Hawkeye offers himself as a sacrifice for Cora, who indeed has always sacrificed herself for her sister. Significantly these attempted self-sacrifices fail. But in what light are we to see them? Duncan and Hawkeye attempt to place themselves as surrogate victims in order to stop the revenge of the Delawares and Magua against their enemies. Seeking to displace the violence, these men are also attempting to render it beneficial in some way. In a novel so filled with images of revenge and reciprocal violence that its very structure is divided, these acts seek to restore order and unity in the face of potential chaos.

To use René Girard's term, we see here a moment of "sacrificial

[30] H. Daniel Peck, *A World by Itself: The Pastoral Moment in Cooper's Fiction* (New Haven: Yale Univ. Press, 1977), pp. 120–45.

crisis." For Girard, ritual sacrifice is meant to establish order, unify society, and prevent violence by finding a suitable victim on which to displace the violence. "In such cases," he claims, "society is seeking to deflect upon a relatively indifferent victim, a 'sacrificeable' victim, the violence that would otherwise be vented on its own members, the people it most desires to protect."[31] This process involves first a synecdochic substitution of a victim for the whole of the community, and then a metaphoric substitution "of a victim belonging to a predetermined sacrificial category for the original victim."[32] The original victim belongs inside the community; the "real" victim, outside. Girard's point is that ritual sacrifice is intended to substitute for reciprocal violence, for revenge, by locating a victim outside of the diadic revenge relationship. When Duncan Heyward attempts to take on Natty's identity, and when Natty in turn offers to sacrifice himself, both are seeking to redirect the implicit violence of vengeance and thereby to give it order. That the actions of both men are usurped by Uncas's revelation of his true identity, and that Uncas and Cora both become sacrificial victims, is surely ironic, but this is not to deny the importance of the underlying mythic order that each character attempts to recover.

When we return to Thomas Cole's paintings, these same images and conflicts stand out. In the first painting, we stand as observers of this scene. Encircled by the dark foreground, the mountainous background and this framework, the scene of Cora and Tamenund is carefully presented in direct, full light. We gaze into the middle distance, the space of history that, like the theater, is dramatically produced and framed by the natural setting. But in the second painting our eyes sweep across this scene, moving from the darkness in the right foreground to the brilliant light of the horizon receding in the left-hand background. It is the horizon that lures the eye, and it is the rocky phallic structure that reigns over this world. Here the world is more dangerous, seen by the positions of the human figures and by the viewer's own precarious position, but it is also of absolute forces: of light versus dark, the shaft of natural rock and the circle of human community. The second

[31] René Girard, *Violence and the Sacred* (Baltimore: Johns Hopkins Univ. Press, 1979), p. 4.

[32] Ibid., p. 102.

version is more elemental, more mythic, while the first version exists in the viewer's historical space.

The Last of the Mohicans is a novel created by division. Its two halves serve as mirrors: The first half portrays the white world in the wilderness; the second half, the Indians in nature. For this reason there is really no neutral ground to fight over, because each society inhabits a different world, run by different principles. As H. Daniel Peck has noticed, this "novel describes two complete and distinct journeys, each with its own objective. And these two objectives define and establish the polar values of Cooper's imaginative world."[33] In the first half of the novel, the white father's authority (located in his land—Fort William Henry) is threatened, a persistent theme in Cooper's early works. But whereas Peck sees the first journey as seeking civilization and the father, and the second seeking the primitive and "eternal feminine," it appears more likely that the figure of Tamenund who presides over the last half presents us not with the feminine but with an alternative vision of patriarchy. The complex judgment scene of potential sacrifice concluding the novel balances the ancient chief's mythic world against Colonel Munro's historical settlement that is beset by violence and revenge.

The search for Colonel Munro in the first half of *The Last of the Mohicans* is significant for several reasons. First, it places the journey of Alice, Cora, Uncas, Chingachgook, and Hawkeye in history.[34] As the novel's subtitle—*A Narrative of 1757*—makes clear, these characters progress toward a historical father and toward historical events whose violence scatters their little community, sending them into the landscape of myth. Although the first half is placed specifically in time and space (there are references to known geographical places such as Glenns Falls), the landscape itself does not provide sufficient "prospects" for a Thomas Cole. It is the "landscape of difficulty," described as suffocating, dense, and devious. History itself is presented in much the same terms. Soon after Colonel Munro and Fort Henry are betrayed by the English General Webb, Montcalm treacherously allows the massacre of the

33 Peck, *World*, p. 110.

34 Peck (*World*) claims that the world described in the first half of the novel is the world of the present. Given the novel's subtitle, and the historical event that climaxes the first half, I would argue that it is the world of white European history.

British forces, after having promised their safety and honor. And the massacre itself seems to have no source or origin; the violence occurs in random and pointless patterns that underscore its ferocity. Oddly enough, however, Cooper places these armies not in the wilderness, but describes them as if they were in Europe: "The hostile armies, which lay in the wilds of the Horican, passed the night of the ninth of August, 1757, much in the manner they would, had they encountered on the fairest field of Europe" (LM, 167). History again appears a palimpsest, a rewriting of European matters on American materials. Again there is no origin, no source of these events to be uncovered, only consequences to be put right or avenged.

As the literal, historical father, Colonel Munro presents an odd figure. When Hawkeye loses his direction on the approach to Fort Henry, we first see Colonel Munro, speaking "in the awful tones of parental agony," as he rescues his two daughters from the French and Indians surrounding them. But unlike George Washington in *The Spy* and even Judge Templeton in *The Pioneers*, the Colonel's public function as commander is superseded by his paternal concerns. We see him most clearly attended by his daughter Alice, sitting "upon his knee, parting the grey hairs on the forehead of the old man" (LM, 156). This domestic scene prepares us for Colonel Munro's eventual loss of authority and the impotence, even imbecility, that soon overtake him. Overwhelmed by the power of historical forces, this father is not only helpless in the wilderness but in his role as public father to his other children as well. Yet even in this he mirrors Tamenund, for the Indian patriarch is also too frail to protect his heir. But if Munro seems prematurely senile, Tamenund is ageless.

Although Tamenund clearly rules his world, both fathers remain impotent in the face of historical forces, for what seems clear by the ending of the novel is that history impinges on this mythic world, destroying the sources of its order and power. Reciprocal violence is the essence of history; revenge, attack, and counterattack establish the dichotomous relations between British and French, and this reciprocity spills over into the relations between Indians as well. Magua seeks revenge for his punishment under Colonel Munro; revenge is returned by others. While the Indian world is measured and defined by its circles—of the seasons, and circular construction of its community—European time progresses by the dialectic of war. In the final scene of the novel, we see another outsider, a soldier, who "finding his errand of peace frustrated by the fierce impetuosity of his allies, was content to become a silent and sad spectator of the fruits of the contest, that he had arrived too late to anticipate" (LM, 341). Time has been thrown out of balance by the violence here and seems unable to contain or to stop that violence from recurring. Ending the novel, we hear Tamenund acknowledge the absolute change that has occurred within the cycles of time: "The anger of the Manitto is not done. Why should Tamenund stay? The pale-faces are masters of the earth, and the time of the red-men has not yet come again. My day has been too long. In the morning I saw the sons of Unamis happy and strong; and yet, before the night has come, have I lived to see the last warrior of the wise race of the Mohicans!" (LM, 350). The influx of history ends the possibility of generational continuity; the sons and daughters of these fathers die not so much because of an *original* sin which must be visited on future generations, but as the result of a *historical* sin that interposes itself between origin and generation, one that threatens to cut off any relation between a father's original authority and its inheritance by the children.

Explicit in *The Last of the Mohicans* and, as we shall see, implicit in many of Cooper's early novels is the opposition of two forms of authority. On the one hand, we see the historical father whose authority is located in geography or property and which is often transmitted historically through law. But as a historical authority, it has no origin and thus provides no stable model for imitation or representation. Such instability gives rise to reciprocal violence, to opposing forces seeking to possess the land and its inherent authority. Contrasting this vision of historical authority, mythic authority, again represented by a father figure, relies on symbolic images rather than the actual transmission of goods or property to ensure its continuity. This authority is one of continuity, in which each representation implies the presence of its model. Any violence associated with this world is ritualistic and sacrificial rather than reciprocal. The problem facing Cooper, however, is that these forms of authority can find no common ground, and this novel provides no stable place outside of neutral ground to link history and myth, patrimonial authority and paternal authority.

The Last of the Mohicans reveals Cooper's divided conception of authority in its almost perfect symmetry. His earlier novel, *The Pioneers*, exhibits most clearly what D. H. Lawrence in his famous study of Cooper has called "the passionate love of America, for the soil of America."[35] Dispute over ownership and possession of this soil sets up three conflicting claims, each arising from a different conception of authority, and each embodied in a different father. Confronting Oliver Effingham are the claims of Natty Bumppo, of his father, Major Effingham, and of Judge Marmaduke Temple, his *father-in-law*. Chronologically, Natty has the priority of natural rights, for his was the first settlement in the area. Major Effingham presents the next claim; however, his rights were abrogated by the Revolution, and Oliver, like the young James Cooper, must struggle to regain his patrimony and reassume his name in the flux of history. Like William Cooper, Judge Temple possesses legal authority over the land, warranted and ratified by the Constitution, but his position as Templeton's founder, patriarch, and judge remain threatened by his antagonists. Oliver is torn between patrimony and paternity, between his material ties to a father and the symbolic values sustained by Leatherstocking. Together these three men represent the combined powers of natural origins, cultural continuity, and social order. But Cooper seems unable to forge a lasting link between them. The contrived ending of the novel reunites Oliver with his patrimony and his name, but it dispossesses Natty of both land and influence over Oliver. Nevertheless, Natty's exile, which removes the final obstacle to Marmaduke Temple's legal authority, does not erase doubts about the moral bases of the judge's claims.

Like many of the conflicts in Cooper's early novels, the source of Oliver's challenge to Judge Temple's ownership of the land is to be found in the American Revolution. The war's historical disruption separates the father's patrimony from the son, whose task it is to fulfill the father's will, regain his family name, and repossess the land. In the end, Cooper explains the conflict between Oliver and Judge Temple as a matter of misunderstood intentions. This explanation rescues the plot and redeems the Judge's character, but

[35] D. H. Lawrence, *Studies in Classic American Literature* (1923; reprint, New York: Viking, 1964), p. 51.

we should also remember that the Revolution's power has obscured the very notion of intentionality. Based as it is on the power of historical change, a power radiating from its revolutionary origins, this novel measures the distance from original intentions. Misunderstood, or misrepresented, intentions prove to be a common problem in Templeton. Each character, from Hiram Doolittle to Oliver Effingham to Natty Bumppo, masks his intentions, and the threat of violence arises from the ensuing confusions. Finally, however, the marriage of Oliver and Elizabeth promises to heal the Revolution's disruptions as the generations are given their property as the basis to form a new alliance.

But the struggle between Natty and Judge Temple denies reconciliation. Natty's claim for possession is based on priority and originality. The issue of originality is a crucial one for the novel, for it once again represents a seemingly irreconcilable dispute between two very different world views. If *The Last of the Mohicans* is a novel in search of fathers, then *The Pioneers*, as the subtitle tells us, seeks the mysterious "Sources of the Susquehanna." As David Quint has noted, the river as a source or fountainhead has been a significant figure for the topos of originality since the Renaissance.[36] The source of the river may be seen as the unchanging origin, existing outside of time, yet continuous with the historical flux of the river. The source is the Otsego, a lake whose Indian name reminds us of the number of origins contained in the novel. Leatherstocking's claim for possession based on temporal priority plays a significant role because the pursuit of the claim eventually leads him into conflict with Judge Temple's legal claims, and provides the dramatic struggle between the sources of their respective powers—myth and history.

Twice there is a direct conflict between the two men, both times precipitated by the killing of a deer. The second occurrence best represents the nature of their conflict and helps clarify the odd divisions in this novel between history and romance. In chapter 27 we see Leatherstocking and Indian John (Chingachgook) canoeing after a buck that has been chased by dogs into the lake. Despite a warning from Oliver that he is hunting the buck out of season,

[36] David Quint, *Origin and Originality in Renaissance Literature* (New Haven: Yale Univ. Press, 1983), p. 23.

Natty continues the chase, and finally, "bending low, passed his knife across the throat of the animal" (P, 299). Natty's first words reveal the underlying contest in this scene: "So much for Marmaduke Temple's law!" Paying no attention to Judge Temple's legal "season," Natty acts spontaneously to pursue and satisfy his hunting instinct. Contrary to Madison's injunction against self-judgment, Natty believes he is best qualified to judge his interests. That this is against the law seems not to mitigate a prior, natural claim for hunting. Moreover, the setting in the lake, the "source" and mythic origin of Natty's world, underscores Richard Slotkin's claim that Natty is actually enacting an Indian hunting myth in this gesture.[37]

The logic of Leatherstocking's sacrifice of the deer, however, seems obscure to the reader because its violence is unprepared for and apparently gratuitous. It may signify a link between Natty and some mythic experience, but it does not explain why this particular action directly confronts Judge Temple's legal authority. Natty's exclamation after the act suggests that it is not so much a "communion with the goddess of the world, the wilderness," but a ritualistic displacement of violence that he would have otherwise turned on Judge Temple as a representative of a repressive society.[38] Seen in Girard's terms of ritual sacrifice, this gesture creates order not because of its encounter with some prior natural power but because it enacts order by imitation of some original purifying act of violence. If, as we have already seen, ritual sacrifice involves a double substitution—first of a synecdochic substitution of a representative victim for the whole, and second of a "victim belonging to a predetermined sacrificial category for the original victim"—then we see the deer standing for Judge Temple, just as the Judge himself represents the townspeople of Templeton.[39] The violent death of the deer, then, exists as a part of some communal ordering mechanism that precedes the legal system of Templeton, a system growing out of a legal order empowered by the Constitution. We must not forget that Judge Temple's legal authority has its origins in the revolutionary period and it is revolution that war-

[37] Richard Slotkin, *Regeneration through Violence* (Middletown, Conn.: Wesleyan Univ. Press, 1973), pp. 489–91.

[38] Compare Slotkin, *Regeneration*, p. 490.

[39] Girard, *Violence*, p. 102.

rants his possession of Oliver's patrimony and his punishment of Natty Bumppo. Considered in the light of the ritual sacrifice, Natty belongs not to nature, but to some original order, some mythic presence.

By killing the deer, Natty preserves order in the community by metaphorically displacing his violence. But he himself is caught up in Judge Temple's machinery, whose laws are based on notions of public vengeance.[40] Whereas sacrifice involves a process of metaphoric displacement, Judge Temple's legal system works on the principle of metonymic reciprocal violence. His law does not displace violence but substitutes one form for another. Natty is guilty because he has broken the law, and he must be punished in some way. His accuser's motivation is less a desire for justice than a wish to seek revenge for Natty's mistreatment; justice *is* vengeance in this society. When asked his right to enter Natty's hut, Doolittle is described as "undergoing a violent struggle between his desire for vengeance and his love of legal fame" (P, 363). Within the novel, contests of skill gradually escalate into potentially violent confrontations, and the laws repeat that violence under socially warranted forms, rather than put an end to it. The contests, including the initial deer shooting and the turkey shoot, do not constitute a true ritual sacrifice because they are based on mimetic rivalry, which inevitably ends in reciprocal violence.[41] This society cannot transfer its violent tendencies into metaphoric categories, as Natty does by sacrificing the deer, but only through metonymic reciprocity of individuals.

The Pioneers and *The Last of the Mohicans* are novels divided into irreconcilable opposites, and the terms of the divisions are representative of Cooper's other early novels: *The Spy*, *The Pilot*, *The Prairie*, and *The Wept of Wish-ton-Wish*. On one hand, we have the families of history, associated with historical rebellion and disrup-

[40] For an excellent general discussion of law in American culture and literature, see Ferguson, *Law and Letters*, esp. 297–304. Ferguson's thesis is that "law is king in America." My point here and throughout is that law is only one of several competing forms of authority. See also Brook Thomas, "*The Pioneers*, or the Sources of American Legal History: A Critical Tale," *American Quarterly* 36 (1984): 86–111.

[41] Girard, *Violence*, p. 174. The only two scenes in the novel suggesting sacrificial rituals are the famous pigeon slaughter and the fishing episode. However, these are actually historical events associated with Cooper's own father and provide no displacement of violence in the novel.

tion, who find their claims to possession of inherited land challenged. Judge Temple and Colonel Munro are joined by Mark Heathcote, the Puritan regicide who flees first from England and then from the Massachusetts Bay Colony; Ishmael Bush, the Old Testament patriarch in *The Prairie*, is associated like Marmaduke Temple with the reciprocal violence of *lex talionis*—the law of retaliation. Because the origin of the historical fathers' claims resides in their own usurpation or departure from authority, the transmission of their powers—the perpetuation of parental authority and filial obedience—becomes the problematic concern for both fathers and children. The act of founding, with which all of these works are centrally concerned, because of its associations with historical violence and disruption, unleashes the forces of change and degeneration. Originality, signaled by the Indians' sense of ritual, is relativized by history.[42] Generation inevitably involves de-generation as each subsequent child and grandchild moves farther from the source of their authority and the origin of power.

The Wept of Wish-ton-Wish exemplifies how quickly communal authority and discipline decay under the influence of history. Its multigenerational form anticipates Cooper's later Anti-rent trilogy by depicting a community's changes through the course of history. Although Cooper generally found little sympathy for the Puritans, in this novel he accurately describes the generational strains and stresses at work within the Puritan psyche. As the community's founder and patriarch, Mark Heathcote is first associated with historical violence as he flees from England as one of the executioners of Charles II. Like the first generation Puritans, he inspires reverence from his children, but his son, Content, is unable to maintain the Puritan discipline and "did not leave the colony of his birth and the haunts of his youth, with the same unwavering obedience to the call of duty as the father."[43] In the two subsequent Indian attacks Content lives up to his name: Although he defends the land, he preserves little of the founder's strength.

Given its violent origins, historical founding always endangers its community with the threat of revenge, of inherited violence. Content's wife gives voice to the unspoken threat: "I fear some heavy

[42] See Michael Rogin's account of the misuse of paternal authority by Andrew Jackson in *Fathers and Children*, pp. 165–205.

[43] James Fenimore Cooper, *The Wept of Wish-ton-Wish* (New York: G. P. Putnam's Sons, 1895), p. 7.

judgment for the sins of the parents is likely to befall the children" (*Wept*, 44). And again the transmission of sins through generations falls to the force of history as this community entangles itself in cycles of violent engagement with the Indians. The concept of neutral ground gives this reciprocal violence a geographical point of reference and a site where the father's authority is constantly circumscribed and challenged by the forces of disruption. Historical founding generates the flow of attack and counterattack, and it is the lack of an original title, rather than actual possession of the land itself, that gives impetus for the initial attacks. Authority thus resides in the quality of the claim to possession, the type of authority, invoked by the father. In this case, Content Heathcote's wife expresses her fear in the religio-legalistic terms of "judgment," for Cooper describes the Puritan community as one committed to a code of law that ensures the escalation of cyclical violence.

Cooper contrasts the degeneration of white society with the Indians' ability to reproduce their power in each generation. In the novel's preface he pays particular attention to the theme of inheritance, when he asks whether the transmission of authority from a chief to his son is inherited or the product of the chief's influence. He concludes: "Let the principle of the descent of power be what it would . . . the child was seen to occupy the station formerly filled by the father" (*Wept*, vii). The Indians equate the formal transmission of authority with a magic, mythic replication of power and a fierce desire to live up to the father's glory. Cooper elides the problem of how the Indian sons come to occupy the fathers' position, for the principle of descent is disrupted by the incursion of the Europeans. When we first see Conanchet, the Indian hero of the novel, he is a youth seeking to revenge his father's death on the white settlers, thereby placing himself within the cycles of their reciprocal vengeance. In the final moral inversion, however, Conanchet rejects the reciprocity of violence by rescuing the Heathcote family, only to be treacherously murdered by the whites, with the assent of Content. Although a sacrifice to the whites, his death holds no ritual power; it promises not order but future violence. Beginning as rebels against tyranny, and having founded a society based on rebellion, this family eventually turns to Machiavellian expediency. In John P. McWilliams's words, "a dark and somber tone prevails, befitting a tale that has described the fall of a human patriarchy, with theocratic overtones, to a secular government in which power is divided among the vengeful."[44] McWilliams's description aptly defines the self-destructive qualities inherent in the founding of this community.

Linking this novel of Puritan founding with those coming chronologically later is the disruption implied in revolution. The Puritan revolution of 1642 thus becomes a type of the Revolutionary War, for its violence and displacement of authority shadows forth the historical disruption of 1776. Within the first founding of America are contained the seeds of its Revolutionary refounding, and perhaps of future revolutions. Historical founding reveals the relativity of its own originality; each generation must either complete the revolutionary impulse through imitation, or degenerate from its model. If the Revolutionary War is literally, as Cooper calls it in *Wyandotté*, "a family quarrel," then its origin lies in filial rebellion.

The disruptive forces of history present Cooper with the problem of literary representation. Marked by displacement and divisive conflict, history makes it impossible for Cooper to unify his own works. His early novels work themselves out in a series of unresolved battles between European and Indian, American and British, romance and history. Writing in *Notions of the Americans*, Cooper notes the problems in American literature in uniting history and romance:

> It certainly would be possible for an American to give a description of the manners of his own country, in a book that he might choose to call a romance, which should be read, because the world is curious on the subject, but which would certainly never be read for that merely indefinable poetical interest which attaches itself to a description of manners less bald and uniform. All the attempts to blend history with romance in America have been comparative failures, (and perhaps fortunately,) since the subjects are too familiar to be treated with the freedom that the imagination absolutely requires. Some of the descriptions of the progress of society on the borders, have had a rather better success, since there is a positive, though no very poetical, novelty in the subject; but, on the whole, the books which have been best received are those on

[44] John P. McWilliams, Jr., *Political Justice in a Republic: James Fenimore Cooper's America* (Berkeley: Univ. of California Press, 1972), p. 257.

> which the authors have trusted most to their own conceptions of character, and to qualities that are common to the rest of the world, and to human nature. (2: 146–47)

Although I would like to detect a pun in "familiar," such linguistic play would make an already confusing discussion impenetrable. Just as he dissociates literal description and general truth in *The Pioneers,* here Cooper suggests the irreconcilability of history ("a description of the manners of his own country") and romance. Because American manners are "less bold and uniform" and the historical subjects too "familiar," there is not the proper perspective or distance from which we can achieve the right "vision." I emphasize vision because, as H. Daniel Peck and others have pointed out, the search for the prospective vision above the neutral ground characterizes Cooper's representative heroes. Although this should not be taken as self-criticism entirely, Cooper's final acknowledgment that works involving general truth ("qualities common to the rest of the world, and to human nature") have been most successful suggests a change in his approach away from description and toward the source of general human truths. In short, his claim marks a conditional privileging of works most clearly associated with the romance of origins.

The novels of Cooper's first creative decade lend themselves to critical scrutiny because such divisions create a kind of critical neutral ground perfect for scholarly debates. In these early novels, disputes over the father's authority generate the divisions under discussion: patrimonial (historical) authority versus paternal (symbolic) authority, historical founding versus mythic originality. In his second decade (roughly from 1830 to 1839), however, Cooper sought to settle these divisions. *Homeward Bound* and *Home as Found* create very different problems for critics who find in them an attack on American society so consistent that it allows no critical ground. Now Cooper assumes the role of judgmental father and his novels serve as his patrimony.

The Effinghams and the Coopers

When James Cooper and his family left for Europe in 1826, he was toasted as perhaps the most celebrated author in America. Just seven years later, as he was preparing to return home in 1833, he wrote to Horatio Greenough as an exile: "I go home, if home I go, Master Greenough, to take a near view for myself, and to ascertain whether for the rest of my life I am to have a country or not" (*Letters*, 2: 268). Much had happened in those seven intervening years to poison Cooper's relations with his American audience. Criticism of his books, talk that he was losing ties to his native land, and more legal troubles gradually fueled his anger. For his part, Cooper decisively closed the initial phase of his life and career. In 1826, he finished the third book of his Leatherstocking series, *The Prairie*, managing in the process to kill off his popular hero, Natty Bumppo. That same year he also added his mother's family name, Fenimore, to his own, an act connecting him to an alternative heritage. In 1828, he published *Notions of the Americans*, which was to be his last positive assessment of America.

It has been said that Cooper's characters are observers but not interpreters.[45] This same distinction helps explain the nature of his personal and political transformations during his stay in Europe. His sociological study and defense of America, *Notions of the Americans*, is narrated by a European observer who ingenuously presents the external manners and mechanisms of the nation to his European friends. A decade later, however, Cooper's *The American Democrat* (1838) rejects observation in favor of historical interpretation and political judgment. If Cooper had earlier presented Natty Bumppo and Harvey Birch, the "Spy," as keen observers of nature and society, the Effinghams (heroes of *Homeward Bound* and *Home As Found*) act as satirists and cultural commentators. It seems that Europe provided Cooper a new perspective on America and its revolutionary origins—the perspective of history. As it had in his earlier novels, history in this middle period moves through the reciprocal violence of dialectical positions, the attack and counterattack over some unpossessed ideological territory. Missing, however, is the natural, mythic outlook of Mount Vision; lost is the sense of a stationary place, a reflective position from which one can safely observe the changes of time.

In addition to the new judgmental tone and increased emphasis on history, Cooper raised the status of his fathers from being embattled owners of ambiguously warranted claims to their new po-

[45] Peck, *World*, pp. 9–13.

sitions as embodiments of conservative cultural and political values. In his fiction and social criticism of the 1830s, the image of the father as the stabilizing origin of value becomes primary precisely because historical flux acquires even greater significance. In his earlier works, the white fathers had been attacked because their participation in revolutionary founding undercut any claim to original authority; now they assert legitimate authority but are battled by rebellious democratic mobs.

Much of this change marks Cooper's reconciliation with his father's combative spirit. Cooper's return to America touched off a series of controversies that ensured his isolation: battles with his Cooperstown neighbors over Three Mile Point, a piece of land willed by his father, but claimed by the townspeople; with journalists over libel; and arguments with critics over his novels and history of the United States Navy. Previously, the father had been the center of controversy; now it was the son who became embroiled in the endless cycles of legal violence and retaliation. More accurately, it was as son *and* father that Cooper returned to America. As a son, a "Cooper of Cooperstown," he made arrangements to purchase his old home in Cooperstown, sought to buy a portrait of his father to enshrine there, and fought for possession of his inheritance at Three Mile Point. When William Cooper's patrimony was called into question, his son carried on the father's litigious nature by quarreling with neighbors and countrymen. But as a father himself, Cooper set out not only to fulfill his father's "will," but to act as a literary patriarch by refounding his fictional settlement of Templeton.

Returning to the site of his success in *The Pioneers*, Cooper creates another historical palimpsest, a rewriting of new materials over old. He is not, however, substituting history for myth, but revising history. In *Home as Found*, whose working title was "Templeton in 1837," he makes direct references to the earliest settlement of Templeton and even to Natty Bumppo's prior claims, but this novel (the companion volume to *Homeward Bound*) is more a revision than it is sequel. The earlier work questioned all claims to original authority, but *Home as Found*'s argument hammers away at the community's backsliding from the founder's original intentions. The return of the Effinghams to Templeton marks Cooper's attempt to assert a new social order based on the father's authority, to "re-found" (as the title suggests) a stable community in America's democratic wilderness. But to ensure the transmission of values through history proved once again a difficult task.

* * *

It has been a critical tradition to consider *Homeward Bound* and *Home as Found* as thinly veiled autobiographies recounting Cooper's own quarrels with his countrymen, particularly the battle with his neighbors over the disputed ownership of Three Mile Point. In this reading, these two novels employ the Effinghams to recount Cooper's return to America, his growing disillusionment with its democratic culture, and his eventual, uneasy resettlement in Cooperstown. The Effingham sea adventures in *Homeward Bound*, their constant comparing of American and European societies, and finally their encounters with the American democrats over Fishing Point in *Home as Found* serve as transparent reworkings of Cooper's experiences and a convenient excuse for his criticism of American society.

Eric Sundquist's recent discussion of *Home as Found*, however, has raised the problem of who, or what, is actually being satirized in this novel. In his analysis, Sundquist argues that the "strangulated self-esteem of the Effingham's is perhaps just as much the object of Cooper's ridicule as the frenzied Templeton populace, though in an intensely covered and sublimated fashion."[46] The remainder of Sundquist's claim encapsulates the essential problems of the novel:

> What is generally brushed aside as one more piece of rather obtrusive machinery—the disclosure of the mysterious identity of Paul Effingham and his fairytale marriage to his cousin Eve—is the very heart of the book, not only because the resolution of the plot hinges on it, but because aristocratic incest and inbreeding is the last, and most extreme, bulwark against the chaos of mob rule which Cooper found threatening himself and his country.

What Sundquist finds paradoxical and self-defeating in this novel is that Cooper's satire seems as easily directed at the Effingham's

[46] Eric Sundquist, *Home as Found* (Baltimore: Johns Hopkins Univ. Press, 1978), p. 3.

as at their democratic neighbors: "The very imitation that the Effingham's despise in their countrymen is carried out with a vengeance in their own clan. . . . The Effingham's repetition, their echoing and plagiarizing, at once constitutes an inviolable authority and threatens to collapse into itself."[47] In the light of traditional views of the novel, Sundquist's analysis of *Home as Found* lays out the essential problem for modern readers: How are we to respond to the Effingham family, particularly the fathers, as a model of political and cultural authority? Moreover, given Cooper's difficulties aligning history and myth in his earlier novels, can he effect the transmission of his literary values?

As Sundquist suggests, imitation appears to be the principal issue at stake in *Home as Found*: Because Americans lack proper imitable models, because novelty is more important than tradition, and because its origins have been lost, Templeton society is blown whimsically about by the winds of public opinion. Parents name their children after characters from popular romances; "Bianca-Alzuma-Ann" becomes the empty imitation, the plagiarizing, of a tradition to which the people have no ties. Returning to the scene where the romance of Natty Bumppo's was defeated by history and law, *Home as Found* portrays the scout as it might a legendary hero. Natty remains without issue or mimetic authority, a figure quickly displaced by the changes in American society. However, if history is the force propelling Templeton and America, it is by its revolutionary origins without imitable models. Without ties to its mythic origins, and having turned its back on European conventions, America rushes about with pointless enthusiasm, substituting empty slogans for political principles and basing its imitations on romances rather than experience. Franklin's mimetic authority seems unworkable here, for real models are soon abandoned in favor of other imitations.

Cooper presents these social ills under the general heading of provincialism. Writing in his preface to *Home as Found*, he makes the novel's theme clear: "The governing social evil of America is provincialism; a misfortune that is perhaps inseparable from her situation. Without a social capital, with twenty or more communities divided by distance and political barriers, her people, who are

[47] Ibid., p. 39.

really more homogeneous than any other of the same numbers in the world perhaps, possess no standard for opinion, manners, social maxims, or even language."[48] In the novel, this lack of standards polarizes the characters who betray their provincialism by poor judgment. For example, Mr. Howells is the American anglophile who, having never been to England, imitates his own notions of English society and ignores those people like the Effinghams who try to correct his misconceptions. Mr. Wenham, on the other hand, is a chauvinist American who, equally ignorant of European customs, believes American culture must create itself *ab ovo*. Without a sense of distinction, imitation leads only to repetition, a point Cooper makes clear in his prefatory remarks on homogeneity: "Money produces money; knowledge is the parent of knowledge; and ignorance fortifies ignorance. In a word, like begets like" (HF, iv).

Home as Found presents the excesses of American border society much as Brackenridge had forty years before. In describing the social, linguistic, and legal confusions arising from misrepresentation, *Home as Found* and *Modern Chivalry* bear a striking resemblance. Class conflict, the heavy-handed satire, and mistaken or misrepresented identity recur in Cooper's novel in the same images of incipient populist violence, demagoguery, and epistemological uncertainty. Both novels recreate these unsettled conditions by moving from picaresque wandering to founding. Perhaps most striking is the way both works recast autobiographical events in oddly sublimated forms of self-representation.

The problem with Cooper's society, as with Brackenridge's, lies in the epistemological corruption of democratic ideals. What begins with American egalitarianism—the claim that "no one (not even an Effingham) is better than anyone else"—ends in a concept of social identity based solely on resemblance. The stifling identification of Steadfast Dodge and Aristabulus Bragg, the two representatives of democratic notions in the novels, with "the people" and their obedience to public opinion constantly pits them against the Effinghams, who locate their power in hierarchy. And at stake for the Effinghams, as for the elitist Captain Farrago of Bracken-

[48] James Fenimore Cooper, *Home as Found* (New York: G. P. Putnam's Sons, 1895), p. iv. (Hereafter cited in text as HF.)

ridge's novel, are the possibilities of social stability and temporal continuity based on class. Like Farrago, the Effinghams assume their personal interest to have virtual representative power.

Cooper's satire on provincial American society similarly takes as its source the American inability to distinguish between the "real" and the merely "represented." In *Homeward Bound,* Steadfast Dodge cannot tell the real Sir George Templemore (called for a time Mr. Sharp) from his ostentatious and offensive copy, whereas the Effinghams are immediately suspicious of the imposter because his actions belie his title. The "real" in this case is slowly discovered by reader and characters through observation and discriminating judgment of the two Templemores' actions. As in Cooper's other fiction, one's name is earned; Dodge's mistake is not to evaluate the name and title through experience. Having no experiential model of aristocratic behavior, Dodge bases his evaluation on names. The rustic Captain Truck plays Teague O'Regan's role when the hostess of a literary gathering confuses him for a famous writer as if she had "picked up some struggling porpoise, and converted him, by a touch of her magic wand, into a Boanerges of literature" (HF, 92). Such transformation is more than the consequence of social pretension, for it is also representative of the inherent instability of American notions of identity. The problem is not only that Americans cannot tell the difference between real and represented but that they make no distinction between the two: Resemblances in this country have the power to enact identity.

Cooper employs these confusions of identity for a conservative end by basing them on Shakespearean comedy. Full of mistaken identity and disguise, *Homeward Bound* and *Home as Found* employ their Shakespearean epigraphs as thematic signposts for the reader who might miss the references. Here the difference between Brackenridge and Cooper is instructive. Brackenridge's novel, based on the picaresque form of *Don Quixote,* thematizes its form by making instability and unsettlement the sources of humor and satire. Although reflecting some of these picaresque elements, the Effingham novels' ultimate models are Shakespeare's romantic comedies and romances in which alienation, tyranny, and usurpation result first in the overturning of convention and eventually in the renewal of social unity marked by the marriage of its principal characters. Transposed and transformed identities become the sources for a regenerate society, and marriage commemorates the new alliance of identities. What Sundquist calls the "fairytale marriage" of Eve and Paul Effingham is necessitated by Cooper's determined use of his literary model. Faced with the rebellion of American democrats, he imposes order and distinction on his novel through its final, ritualized marriage.

For Cooper, however, democratic tyranny presents a very different kind of danger and necessitates a reworking of the comedic form. The real threat to American society is homogeneity, the masking or suppressing of distinction and difference. What Tocqueville called the "equality of conditions" in America, Cooper presents as the repetition of empty likenesses. However, the return of the Effinghams to Templeton polarizes this homogeneous society by exposing its contradictions. What begins in *Homeward Bound* as a comic mirroring and confusion of identities gradually develops into a tense confrontation of polar opposites in *Home as Found*. This growing estrangement of the Effinghams from their American neighbors is more than a matter of taste, or class, or politics; rather, it restates the epistemological issues of identity and difference in social terms. Perhaps most confusing about these novels are the proliferation of doubles (the two Sir George Templemores), mirrors (the "twinned" John and Edward Effingham), and symmetrical opposites (Mr. Blunt and Mr. Sharp). On the one hand, any sense of distinction continually threatens to collapse into homogeneous, democratic sameness; on the other, we see the movement toward polar opposition and potential reciprocal violence.

In this world poised between absolute difference and entropic sameness, we again see Girard's "sacrificial crisis." In Girard's definition, when a culture begins to lose its traditional rituals, it goes through a "crisis of distinctions—that is, a crisis affecting the cultural order. This cultural order is nothing more than a regulated system of distinctions in which the differences between individuals are used to establish their 'identity' and their mutual relationships."[49] Having lost ritual's ability to demarcate the ultimate difference between sacred and profane, a culture goes through a se-

[49] Girard, *Violence*, p. 49.

ries of critical stages, first creating symmetrical doubles who are twins or mirrors, and then projecting this doubleness onto an "other" who becomes the sacrificial victim. Thus the absence of difference, what Cooper calls homogeneity, characterizes a culture's loss of conventions and leads to a doubling of identities in which this lack of distinction threatens to break out in reciprocal violence. People's fears are thus projected onto, or mirrored in, their symmetrical doubles. Brackenridge terms this same confusion "self-love," but it involves a similar slippage of the borders of identity caused by the reordering of social categories and rituals. As Girard says, "If violence is a great leveler of men and everybody becomes the double, or 'twin,' of his antagonist, it seems to follow that all the doubles are identical and that any one can at any given moment become the double of all the others; that is, the sole object of universal obsession and hatred."[50]

Girard's concept of the sacrificial crisis helps to order the confusion of identity and difference in *Homeward Bound* and *Home as Found*. The crisis involves democracy's leveling of differences and the Effinghams' attempts to maintain them. There can be two Sir George Templemores because democratic society, based as it is on imitation of names, maintains no standards for judging *difference*. John and Edward Effingham seem to add to the confusion because they appear to be physical and social twins.[51] But if John and Edward appear identical to their Templeton neighbors (and to the readers at times), they are in fact quite different. What appears to be *their* homogeneity is actually a set of finally perceived differences. The necessity of judging such differences explains the novel's endless comparing and contrasting of coastlines, social customs, clothes, and personalities. What the reader finds unbearably long-winded at times is precisely the novel's point: To be able to judge difference is, at least in Cooper's eyes, a bulwark against the homogeneity of America's slide into democratic chaos—its sacrificial crisis. Sundquist has fallen into the democratic trap when he sees no difference between the proliferation of American common names and the continuation of the Effingham surname in the mar-

[50] Ibid., p. 79.

[51] Girard, *Violence*, pp. 62–63, explains that such "twins offer a symbolic representation . . . of the symmetrical conflict and identity crisis that characterizes the sacrificial crisis."

riage of Paul and Eve. The former entails the loss of distinction in arbitrary imitation, but the latter surely involves the transmission of cultural values and their ability to represent standards of difference. The Effinghams are not the objects of Cooper's satire, even though their willfully anachronistic beliefs appear to modern readers as absurd as Farrago's.

Girard's work presents a valuable perspective on the apparent confusions and contradictions in Cooper's novels, for both writers are concerned with examining the basis of social order. For Cooper, America's sacrificial crisis arises from its democratic ideology; the absence of imitable models, the leveling of social distinctions, and the disdain for the past, negate the transmission of cultural rituals that might insure stability. In their critique of America's fluid, volatile frontier society the Effingham novels establish Cooper's negative argument. Their positive argument, however, works to undo the sacrificial crisis by invoking paternal authority as a means to restoring social ritual in the filial obedience of children and the father's continued protection of their futures.

* * *

The concept of sacrificial crisis helps explain why *Homeward Bound* and *Home as Found* seem barely able to keep their polar terms from collapsing, for within the novels distinction is constantly threatened by homogeneity and sameness. One of the most curious and revealing "doublings," however, is the way these two novels seem to mirror each other. Cooper himself intended them as a single volume meant, as he tells the reader in the preface to *Homeward Bound*, to "exhibit the present state of society in the United States" in much the same way that *The Pioneers* is "descriptive."[52] But this novel soon grew into two large volumes, the first of which (*Homeward Bound*) barely transports the characters from the English harbor to New York. For this reason, critics have focused almost exclusively on *Home as Found*, assuming that what Cooper himself calls the "diversion from the author's design" (HB, iii) did not alter his intention to write a satiric description of American society. *Homeward Bound* subordinates its social criticism to the novel's romantic adventures as the *Montauk* is first pursued by an English

[52] James Fenimore Cooper, *Homeward Bound* (New York: G. P. Putnam's Sons, 1895), p. iii. (Hereafter cited in text as HB.)

warship, then driven by a violent storm to the coast of Africa, and finally rescued from Arab bandits. This "diversion" seems more a diverting entertainment than part of Cooper's intended design to represent (and correct) the customs of American society.

But *Homeward Bound* is a diversion also in the sense that it is a trope or *turn* away from one level of meaning to another. Just as *Last of the Mohicans* works by parallel readings of white and Indian cultures, the obvious differences between *Home as Found* as an autobiographical novel of manners and *Homeward Bound* as a fictional romance are meliorated by their structural and thematic parallels. Thus the doubling and polarization of American society detailed in these novels becomes the organizational strategy for their pairing. Both novels begin with comparisons (between England and America in *Homeward Bound* and between Eve Effingham and Grace Van Cortlandt in *Home as Found*); have as their central actions attacks on revered property (Captain Truck's ship the *Montauk* in *Homeward Bound* and Fishing Point in *Home as Found*); and even parallel characters (Steadfast Dodge in *Homeward Bound* is replaced by Aristabulus Bragg in *Home as Found*). Taken together, these parallels suggest Cooper is rewriting the same novel, once as romance and again as novel of manners, employing in the process first the conventions of his sea tales and then his descriptive fiction.

Like Cooper's other novels of the sea, *Homeward Bound* is an adventure of escape, disguise, and testing. *The Pilot* and *The Red Rover* are typical Cooper sea romances, whose titles are taken from their disguised heroes. In *Homeward Bound*, Paul Blunt, Mr. Sharp, and the false Sir George Templemore carry on their separate deceptions. The theme of disguise in Cooper's nautical tales arises from their adventure plots; the freedom of the sea, the absence of legal or social conventions, warrants the assumptions of new identities and unleashes the possibility of adventure and violence. Before the *Montauk* leaves its English harbor and the legal jurisdiction of that country, the novel employs the conventional forms of Cooper's descriptive fiction by describing characters through detailed observation of manners. Once out into the open sea and away from the harbor, however, the novel begins its transformation into romance. Signaling the change from realism to romance is chapter 5's epigraph from *Twelfth Night* which suggests the *Montauk* has emerged into a new reality: " 'What country, friends, is this?' / 'Illyria, lady.' " Freed from generic constraints of Cooper's descriptive fiction, the ship is driven by a violent storm to the coast of Africa where it is attacked by Arab bandits. The vivid account of the ship's rescue by its passengers and crew comes straight out of Cooper's best adventure tales. As the novel's subtitle, *The Chase*, suggests, what is important here is movement, exertion, and performance. Once the adventure is done, the descriptive, realistic novel reasserts itself in the form of the elaborate funeral ritual and accounting to British justice that conclude *Homeward Bound*.

In contrast, Cooper's working title for *Home as Found*, "Templeton in 1837," emphasizes the historical sensibility in the second volume.[53] From this perspective, the division between these two novels suggests Cooper's continuing dissociation of his mythic or metaphoric impulse from his concern for historical accuracy and didacticism. Whereas in *The Last of the Mohicans* history gives way to the visionary prospect of myth, in 1838 Cooper begins with romance and ends with the historical moment. Instead of the mythic ceremonies of the Leatherstocking novels, *Home as Found* ends with the establishment of a new social order seen in the social rituals of Eve and Paul Effingham's wedding. In its historical specificity and autobiographical subtext, *Home as Found* belongs to the whole series of historical writings published by Cooper in the late 1830s: *The American Democrat* and *The Chronicles of Cooperstown*, both published in 1838 (significantly in Cooperstown), and *The History of the Navy*, published the following year.

However, the diversion of Cooper's original intention into *Homeward Bound* and the recasting of his realistic design into a romance adventure plot also throw new light on the supposed autobiographical transparency of Cooper's novel. Most striking about the autobiographical details of *Home as Found* is the degree to which they *do not* correspond to the facts of Cooper's real battle over Three Mile Point and the slight role the fictionalized account plays in the novel.[54] The affair itself takes up less than two chapters (chapters 15 and 16) and the protracted legal battle that Cooper

[53] See Cooper, *Letters*, 3: 269. In a letter to his publisher, Cooper emphasized the divided nature of his novel when he called it "half sea half shore" (*Letters*, 3: 295), even before he decided to write it as two separate novels.

[54] For details of Cooper's battle over Three Mile Point see McWilliams, *Political Justice*, pp. 223–26, 403–4.

experienced in the actual controversy is transformed in the novel into a complete victory for the Effinghams. The truth of the Effingham claim becomes self-evident:

> As soon as the truth became generally known in reference to the real ownership, and the public came to ascertain that instead of hitherto possessing a right, it had, in fact, been merely enjoying a favor, those who had committed themselves by their arrogant assumption of facts, and their indecent outrages, fell back on their self-love, and began to find excuses for their conduct in that of the other party. (HF, 239)

Rather than serving to characterize the stubborn irrationality of public opinion, the fictional account resorts to didactic mis-representation of the events in order to support the Effinghams', and Cooper's, claim for truth. Far from being transparent, these events seem oddly repressed and opaque.

It is in *Homeward Bound*, not *Home as Found*, that Cooper expresses the violent anger he felt over the Three Mile Point affair. That is, in the battle of passengers and crew of the *Montauk* with the North African bandits over possession of the ship, the scene directly paralleling the Fishing Point scenes in *Home as Found*, Cooper effects, as Stephen Railton has pointed out, "an imaginative transmutation of the struggle over a piece of land in Cooperstown."[55] What had been a case of petty bickering over legal interpretation becomes a heroic fight over a possession that will insure the future safety of the characters. The Effinghams experience a real battle in *Homeward Bound*, one that involves the sacrifice of lives. Whereas the original battle, as Cooper writes, had originated when some people went to Three Mile Point "and cut down a tree that had a peculiar association with my father" (*Letters* 4: 271), the parallel scene in *Homeward Bound* occurs as the captain and crew attempt to replace the mast lost in the violent storm while battling the Arabs.[56] And despite the transformation of the legal and class struggles over Fishing Point into the romantic conflict between

55 Railton, *Fenimore Cooper*, p. 174.

56 Here the transformation of Cooper's tree into the *Montauk*'s mast retains a symbolic tie to the family, but the father's phallus becomes the mother's nourishment: The "spar," Captain Truck claims, is more important "than our mother's milk in infancy" (HB, 257).

Christian and infidel, both battles end with a reasonable acknowledgment of defeat by the townspeople/Arabs. "Unused to frays so desperate" (HB, 377), the Arab leader retreats with his men, signaling his admiration of the *Montauk*'s defenders. What requires just two chapters and no bullets in *Home as Found* takes up nearly a third of *Homeward Bound* and saves that novel from the tedium of long-winded cultural comparisons.

In effect, Cooper has rewritten his autobiography using two entirely different forms of representation. Just as Brackenridge had turned his experience of the Whiskey Rebellion into the metonymic narrative of his *Incidents of the Insurrection* and into the metaphoric allegory of *Modern Chivalry*, Cooper maintains a divided vision of his experience in regaining Three Mile Point. These two versions of self-representation suggest a great deal about Cooper's psychic conflict but perhaps they tell us as much about his skeptical audience. Sublimating personal antagonisms into romantic sea adventures proved more advantageous than his direct attack on American society. The troping or turn of *Homeward Bound* diverts metonymic realism into metaphoric representation, extending like *Modern Chivalry* into allegory. For example, the description of the *Montauk*, beached on Africa's coast, resonates with symbolic potential:

> The solitary and gloomy grandeur of the coast, the sublime sterility,—for even naked sands may become sublime by their vastness,—the heavy moanings of the ocean on the beach, and the entire spectacle of the solitude, blended as it was with the associations of Africa, time, and the changes of history, united to produce sensations of pleasing melancholy. The spectacle of the ship, bringing with it the images of civilization, as it lay helpless and deserted on the sand, too, heightened all. (HB, 210)

The pronomial confusion concluding this passage transmutes this adventure tale into an allegory of decaying European civilization. It is a sublime prospect which envisions the desolate "changes of history." What had begun as a simple journey back to America becomes here a meditation on history's flux. The description takes what had been the novel's explicit account of European conventions in 1837 and creates a symbolic perspective from which to view them. Rather than *being* history, as we assume *Home as Found* to be, *Homeward Bound* serves as history's metaphor.[57]

Homeward Bound remains, however, as Cooper had admitted, a "diversion." Despite its ability to recast Cooper's personal battles in powerful symbolic terms implicating a disastrous decay of Western civilization, this adventure novel is brought back to its intended course of satire and social criticism. Thus, if *Homeward Bound* reveals a turn toward metaphoric representation, then its companion volume, *Home as Found*, provides the literal, stable background against which the first novel's deviance can be measured. No longer are competing authorities and their forms of representation held in ambiguous suspension as they had been in *The Pioneers* or *The Last of the Mohicans*. Now we see history supersede romance, bringing with it all of its attendant problems—the absence of origins, the danger of rebellion, the threat of violence. But while Cooper chooses to privilege history over romance, he does so from a new critical, judgmental position. His role as historian is not just as a chronicler of events, an observer of history; now he seeks to redress change and assert historical connections.

We can measure something of this new stance in the angry, disillusioned tone he takes in his writings of the late 1830s. Heating since the beginning of the decade, Cooper's anger at American democracy was brought to a boil by the events surrounding Three Mile Point and spilled over into his Effingham novels and *The American Democrat*. It is *The American Democrat* that provides the intellectual argument for *Homeward Bound* and *Home as Found*, and it serves as a good indicator of how far Cooper's conservative reaction has brought him since his balanced praise of American institutions and culture in *Notions of the Americans*, written just ten years before.

In *Notions of the Americans*, Cooper had treated the United States' Constitution as empowering the communal identity of the people:

57 The traditional association of the Effingham novels with transparent autobiography or clumsy personal attacks must also take into account Cooper's self-satire. Steadfast Dodge, the democratic "people's man" of *Homeward Bound*, also appears to be an oddly refracted image of Cooper himself. A citizen of "Dodgetown," Dodge is also a keeper of journals, like Cooper, and a registrar of American "notions" on his trips. As he recounts his misadventures and misunderstandings in Europe, Dodge sounds suspiciously like Cooper, whose faux pas in European society were well-known.

"The very word *constitution* implies the control of all those interests which distinguish an identified community. . . . Americans now became one people in their institutions, as well as their origin and in their feelings" (2: 200–201). *The American Democrat*, however, conceives a different origin. Beginning with the same linguistic emphasis, Cooper diverges from his earlier conception of the Constitution as a symbolic and legal document, by replacing it with a legalistic, Lockean conception: "The word constitution," he claims, implies "a social compact, fundamental and predominant."[58] As he continues, his intent to dissociate the people from the document becomes clear: "The constitution of the United States was framed by the states then in existence, as communities, and not by the body of the people of the Union, or by the body of the people of the states" (AD, 14). What Cooper has done here is to deny "the people" any original or originating power by first transforming them into a legal fiction, a mere phrase, and then by having the Constitution owe its own originality to another legal fiction, the states as represented by their delegates. "We the *people*," becomes in his view, merely "We the *constituencies* of the several states" (AD, 15).

In other words, the greatest departure from his "notion" of the Americans is his new belief that all power is represented power, that the true issue at stake for American democracy is that of representation. "The leading distinctive principle of this country," to put it in his own plain words, "is connected with the fact that all political power is strictly a trust, granted by the constituent to the representative" (AD, 21). From this claim follows each of Cooper's complaints about American democracy: the power of public opinion, the dissociation of the children from their inherited rights, and the threat of demagogues. And at each step of his argument, Cooper defines representation as an impersonal, legal fiction whose general application overrides any particular constituent's motivation. If "a representative is a substitute" (AD, 106), then it is a "besetting vice of democracies to *substitute* public opinion for the law" (AD, 64). In other words, the problem with public opinion is not that it is untrue but that it is a form of misrepresentation because it metonymically substitutes personal interests for the law.

[58] James Fenimore Cooper, *The American Democrat* (New York: Alfred Knopf, 1931), p. 12. (Hereafter cited as AD in text.)

Cooper's suppression of metonymic representation becomes even clearer in a further contrast with *Notions of the Americans.* When discussing the issue of representation in the earlier work, Cooper had spoken sanguinely, almost romantically, of the American representative as "commonly a plain, though always a respectable yeoman, and not infrequently a mechanic" (2: 28). In *The American Democrat,* however, Cooper retreats to a position Brackenridge would have found acceptable: "A system must be radically wrong, when the keeper of a tavern, or of a grocery, through his facilities in humoring one of the worst of our vices, can command more votes than a man of the highest attainments, or of the highest character" (AD, 135).

Among its other conservative goals, *The American Democrat* seeks to define the position, responsibilities, and character of the ideal representative. Between the representative and constituents Cooper interposes the Constitution, which he uses to separate the elected from the electors. By keeping the legislator, executive, or judge free from the harmful influence of public opinion, Cooper seeks to preserve the representative's authority and autonomy. After his election the representative remains independent from the people's direct power: "The legislator, by the nature of his trust, having full power to enact and to repeal, knows no other control than his conscience. The expressed compact between the representative and constituent, gives to the first an absolute discretionary power, subject to this great rule, and, by the implied, no instructions can ever weaken this high obligation, since it is clearly a governing condition of the bargain between them" (AD, 102). In effect, Cooper returns to the conservative Federalist concept of virtual representation. Just as the representative has the same relation to both majority and minority parties of his constituency, and acts equally for both, "he has the same relations to the entire country, as to his own immediate constituents, else would legislation be reduced to a mere contest of local interests, without a regard to justice or to general principles" (AD, 102–3). Notice here that Cooper circumvents the "contest of local interests," the reciprocal conflict of political parties, by granting the representative a transcendent position. Although he later makes clear that local residence is a necessary part of American representation, Cooper maintains that American government is based on "a compact between states," which obviates any personal ties between representative and people.

Opposed to the representative, who obviously must maintain a moral as well as legal independence, is the demagogue. If the representative ideally maintains a virtual relation to the principles of government, that is, becomes a synecdoche for the government, then the demagogue is one who feigns metonymic association. "The peculiar office of the demagogue," Cooper writes in the chapter preceding his discussion of representation, "is to advance his own interests, by affecting a deep devotion to the interests of the people" (AD, 92). Cooper continues: "The demagogue always puts the people before the constitution and the laws, in face of the obvious truth that the people have placed the constitution and the laws before themselves" (AD, 92). By flattering the people's belief in their supposed power, the demagogue substitutes himself for the laws, transforming their desire for self-importance into his own personal power.

Among its other issues, *Home as Found* can be seen as a fictional amplification of Cooper's critique of representation in *The American Democrat.* The principal conflicts in the novel arise not because the people willfully neglect the law—they legitimately believe that Fishing Point is theirs—but because Aristabulus Bragg, the representative agent of the Effinghams to the people of Templeton, does not fulfill his obligations. For example, commissioned to order young people off the Effingham property, Bragg (who recognizes "these apprentices were not voters, but then some of them speedily would be" [HF, 157]) resorts to persuasion rather than command, a rhetorical turn reflecting his confusion over the location of authority in this society. Bragg never achieves the independence of thought or judgment that his position as mediator permits. Bragg and his counterpart, Steadfast Dodge, illustrate *The American Democrat*'s assertion that democracy collapses when it fails to maintain a distinction between representative and constituency.

Oddly enough, the only act of true representation in the novel comes not during the Fishing Point controversy but during the protracted negotiations between Paul and Eve Effingham over his proposal of marriage. Edward Effingham ratifies the connection between the two twice, once when he conveniently steps out of the bushes to end Paul's clumsy proposal and then again when he warrants the engagement between the two. In the latter scene, Edward has taken upon himself the role of "negotiator" for Eve concerning the matter of engagement. We see in the following scene the culmination of Cooper's positive argument in this novel as Edward Effingham restores public ritual by substituting legal for cultural tradition:

> "You [Eve] have nothing to do, if I have said too much, but to refuse to ratify the treaty made by your negotiator."
>
> "You propose an impossibility," said Eve, taking the hand again that she had so lately relinquished, and pressing it warmly against her own; "the negotiator is too much revered, has too strong a right to command, and is too much confided in, to be thus dishonored. Father, I will, I do, ratify all you have, all you can promise on my behalf."
>
> "Even if I annul the treaty, darling?"
>
> "Even in that case, father. I will marry none without your consent, and have so absolute confidence in your tender care of me, that I do not even hesitate to say I will marry him to whom you contract me." (HF, 383)

Transforming the engagement into a legal treaty, Edward Effingham makes himself the independent representative who has at heart only the happiness of his constituent. In this case, the marriage provides a political solution to the novel's unwieldy plot, for Edward is portrayed as the ideal representative, one to whom Eve accedes the independence of judgment and the power of paternal authority.

If the reader stops at this point, perhaps overcome by Cooper's rather heavy-handed machinations, the "fairytale," as Eric Sundquist calls it, seems complete. But we must not forget the chaotic world in which this wedding will take place. If Edward is to be the representative, the independent judge of stable political principles, what is his real power in an American society already described as mutable, deceptive, and rebellious? This troubling question seems to have flickered across Eve's mind too, for she adds a final twist (albeit with "childish playfulness") that presents a new problem to this ending. Eve willingly obeys her father-representative, but what of her new husband? Speaking of her betrothed, Paul Effingham, whose real identity remains at this point unknown, she says, "You forget that you yourself have been instrumental in transferring my duty and obedience to another. What if this sea-monster should prove a tyrant, throw off the mask, and show himself in his real colors? Are you prepared, then, thoughtless precipitant parent . . . to preach obedience where obedience would then be due?" (HF, 384). Eve's question, unnecessary for the novel as romance, gets to the heart of its central problem: rebellion. If there is to be an absolute distinction between governed and governors, constituency and representative, particularly if the governors have paternal power, then how far can that authority extend before it becomes a tyranny that must be checked?

At this point the dialogue is interrupted, but we are left with disturbing questions about the legitimacy of rebellion in any conceivable situation. Significantly, the backdrop of Eve's question is Templeton's celebration of Independence Day. The citizens not only celebrate the Revolution but use it as a model for their own rebellion against the Effinghams. It might appear that once again the Revolution's legacy is the perpetuation of reciprocal, legalistic violence and that rebellion is the necessary but unsettling consequence of American democracy and independence. But Cooper's relentless attack on "the people" includes a reinterpretation of the Revolution which appropriates its authority and returns it to the father.

In order to understand Cooper's privileging of paternal authority at the end of *Home as Found*, we must turn back to the parallel scene in *Homeward Bound*, in which the Effinghams discuss the Revolution in terms of parental control and filial responsibility. This issue arises in an exchange between Eve and Paul: Responding to Eve's belief that his criticism of America brands him a foreigner, Paul asks, "Do you admit that an American can be no American, unless blind to the faults of the country, however great?" Eve's response foreshadows her later exchange with Edward Effingham: "Would it be generous for a child to turn upon a parent that all others assail?" In return, however, Paul suggests a different tack to the argument: "It is the duty of the parent to educate and correct the child, but it is the duty of the citizen to reform and improve the character of his country" (HB, 419).

Following this rather opaque discussion of filial duties and paternal responsibility, John Effingham restates the same issues in terms of the American Revolution. It is here that Cooper makes his most daring, if desperate, assertion. John Effingham's argument begins with the claim that the rebellion of the American colonists was against Parliament and not the king, who had, he claims, "a common parental regard for all his subjects" (HB, 420). He continues:

> Parliament . . . ruled the colonies absolutely and legally, if you please, under the Stuarts; but the English rebelled against these Stuarts, dethroned them, and gave the crown to an entirely new family,—one with only a remote alliance with the reigning branch. Not satisfied with this, the king was curtailed in his authority; the prince, who might with some justice be supposed to feel a common interest in all his subjects, became a mere machine in the hands of a body who represented little more than themselves, in fact, or a mere fragment of the empire, even in theory; transferring the control of the colonial interest from the sovereign himself to a portion of his people, and that, too, a small portion. This was no longer a government of a prince who felt a parental concern for all his subjects, but a government of a *clique* of his subjects, who felt a selfish concern only for their own interests. (HB, 421)

John Effingham's attempt to preserve the idea of patriarchal sovereignty presents the Revolution in new light. He concludes: "This revolt was against a usurper, and not against the legitimate monarch, or against the sovereign himself" (HB, 422).

After finishing his tortuous argument, we must understand it as a failed attempt to rescue the Revolution from the chaos of historical disruption and the conditional authority of the United States' constitutional origins. Rather than breaking ties to traditional authority, the Revolution in fact reestablishes direct lines of historically transmitted values. And most importantly for Cooper, these values are embodied in the king's paternal authority. No longer seen as a tyrannic father, the king becomes the benevolent parent whose power itself has been usurped by "a body who represented little more than themselves." If we extend this political interpretation to Templeton in 1837, we conclude that the true danger to society comes not from Edward Effingham but from the false representatives, the oligarchy of demagogues who threaten his position and possessions. The Fourth of July celebration provides an ironic backdrop to the proposal of Paul to Eve, for not only are the people *not* independent, there is actually no legitimate revolution to celebrate. To rebel against the English rebellion merely reasserts a dependence on traditional paternal authority. In other words, rather than *diverting* or disrupting history, the Revolution realigns America and England, preserving their historical continuity, and the idea of paternal authority.

A strained need to fix and stabilize lies behind this twisted logic. Before presenting his interpretation, John Effingham has cautioned his listeners "to forget professions and names . . . and to look only at [the] facts and things" of history (HB, 420). His advice echoes Cooper's warning in the conclusion of *The American Democrat* that "men are the constant dupe of names, while their happiness and well-being mainly depend on things. The highest proof a community can give of its fitness for self government, is its readiness to distinguish between the two" (AD, 182). Unlike Captain Farrago who had attempted to fix language referentiality with "things," Cooper turns to history as a means to uncover these things apart from the fluctuations of names. The habit of Templeton's citizens to name their children Bianca-Alzuma-Ann exhibits the empty repetition of names that have no model nor have reference to common experience. Their names are not earned experientially like Hawkeye's; having their origin in popular conceptions of literary romance, they are empty imitations of a culture to which the people have no ties. But it would be a mistake to consider the metamorphosis of Paul's names—from Blunt to Powis to Assheton and finally to Effingham—to be imitations of the same kind. Just the opposite: The profusion of his names is not empty of referential significance but, rather, frees him from the burden of a self-created identity and exchanges an English patronym for an identity embracing both paternal and maternal families and histories. Like Cooper's assumption of the metronymic Fenimore in 1826, the association of multiple surnames with Paul Effingham at once grants him a historically transmitted identity, one with ties to both England and America, and establishes the familial and social bonds which stand as the real "things" of social reality.

Rather than marring the novel with a fairytale, incestuous marriage of cousins, the union of Paul and Eve achieves Cooper's goal of a resurrected paternal authority—and with a vengeance. The most unnatural thing about the novel is that it presents the children with two interchangeable fathers as a guarantee for stability and paternal guidance. What Cooper hopes to do here is preserve the symbolic power of paternal authority, the basis of his utopian political system, by asserting a patrimonial inheritance. In *Nature*, published two years earlier, Emerson had complained that "old words are perverted to stand for things which are not; a paper currency is employed, when there is no bullion in the vaults."[59] Cooper, however, seeks to preserve the old names by ensuring a continuity of inheritance, both as father and historian.

It is in history that one locates and preserves the stable "thing" and Cooper is the historian who attempts to preserve it against the democratic forces of mutability and change. His return to history from a diversion in myth and romance is expressed in these two novels, as well as by his cultural criticism in *The American Democrat* and his two works of history, *The Chronicles of Cooperstown* and *History of the Navy*, all published in 1838–1839. In each case Cooper's sense of himself as historian is allied with his desire to stabilize the present by locating principles of order within its origins. His *Chronicles* is a book of "firsts": the first view of the area, the original charter, first buildings, doctors, lawyers, even the "first adult who died a natural death in the village" (CC, 38). In other words, as historian, Cooper's role is to recount the series of *original* moments, but their originality comes not from their existence as completed historical events but from the necessary continuity that flows from them. Each first earns its originality precisely from the repetition of similar occurrences. The significance of originality, therefore, lies in the present, or rather in the historian's ability to restore the past to the present. Thus history involves the repetition of the past, rather than the symbolization of events. The importance of the first doctor or the first death is established relative to those who come after and is dependent on the descendant's ability to insure the continuity of the imitated or repeated events. The authority of origins is therefore conditioned by the present, and is mediated by the historian in whose mind that authority is maintained.

[59] Ralph Waldo Emerson, *Nature*, ed. Robert E. Spiller and Alfred R. Ferguson (Cambridge, Mass.: Harvard Univ. Press, 1971), p. 20.

It is this role of historian, the writer who allows the authority of origins to continue by representing it, that informs Cooper's method in *Home as Found* and provides the connecting ties between the Templeton of Judge Temple and that of Edward Effingham. If *The Pioneers* presents the difficulty of locating authorizing origins on which to found a new world, *Home as Found* attempts to "re-found" Templeton in such a way as to avoid the historical disruption of rebellion *and* to insure the continuity of history that authorizes its own past. The title of *Home as Found* therefore unites the process of discovery and of this act's intimate ties of founding. Moreover, the potential rebellion of the townspeople against the legitimate claims of the Effinghams endangers those rights and Cooper himself precisely because it calls into question the power of present owners to re-possess and therefore re-present the past. By threatening Templeton in 1837, they challenge the original settlement and the patrimonial authority and intention of Judge Temple as well. The marriage of Paul and Eve will ensure that once again "like begets like," will ensure the continuity of history. Such an act is a willful rewriting of history, but as historian, Cooper *can* rewrite the Revolution, uncover the true meaning of the Constitution, and save Templeton's present and past.

Together *Homeward Bound* and *Home as Found* serve as a rewriting, an encapsulation really, of America's founding as a means to provide a paradigmatic social institution. The voyage across the Atlantic, the return to Templeton, and the reestablishment of the family in the center of the town, in addition to reappropriating the original property, recapitulate America's history; more accurately, this return creates a new past on which to found a new nation. For in this version America has not sundered itself politically or culturally from its European origins. Cooper effects something of a magical circumvention of the American Revolution through John Effingham's recasting of events; by placing the cause of the Revolution on the English oligarchy instead of the king, Cooper bridges the king's paternal authority and the American people, while simultaneously suggesting the evil consequences of the rebellious acts of Templeton's citizens against their patriarch, Edward Effingham. Preserving the king's authority from willful misuse is only the first step in doubling the power of the fathers in Edward and John Effingham. The marriage of Eve and Paul thus completes this desire to resurrect the power of the father and the promise to unify cultural history and national differences through their marriage.

Cooper's concern with hereditary transmission indicates the wider dislocation and disintegration of the family in Jacksonian America. As David Rothman has pointed out, the family began to lose its position to artificial institutions such as almshouses and asylums meant to replace the regularity and discipline missing from homes.[60] In addition, the age of adolescence was gradually lengthening as the romantic innocence of youth became the presiding myth. Cooper has taken the opposite approach from Benjamin Franklin: Whereas Franklin had attempted to imbue social institutions with a kind of paternal benevolence, Cooper seeks to instill the image of the father with institutional force. However, to transform Edward Effingham into both executive and representative is to preempt the legal authority warranting the institutions of government. Moreover, to present the family as the governing social institution is also to permit the inevitable recurrence of filial disobedience whose force is increased by the metaphorical association of institution with family.

In *Home as Found*, Cooper attempts to rewrite America's history and to replace popular sovereignty with a naive notion of benevolent, paternal tyranny. With the absence of original authority, the task of the historian is the continual refounding of the republic, the ceremonial repetition of original acts. Thus Cooper the son repeats the father's original founding of Cooperstown by returning from England, and even repeats his father's act of encoding that founding in a work of history. As a writer Cooper repeats his own imaginative founding of Templeton by reestablishing the family and its underlying political principles.

Writing in the introduction to *The Chronicles of Cooperstown*, Cooper places himself as the necessary link between past and present. "If those who come after the compilers of the 'Chronicles of Cooperstown,' " he writes, "should do as much in their generation, they who inhabit the place a century hence, will, beyond question, be ready to ackowledge [*sic*] that in one essential duty they were

[60] David Rothman, *The Discovery of the Asylum* (Boston: Little, Brown, 1971), pp. 65–78.

not forgotten by their predecessors" (CC, 4). The curious construction of "not forgetting" the future telescopes both past and future, history and prophecy within the historian's role. It is necessary to "re-found" Cooperstown and Templeton in order to insure both the origins of their authority and the continuation of that authority through history. But those origins remain constantly endangered by the instability of the democratic present.

CHAPTER FIVE

Ralph Waldo Emerson and the American Representative

Representation in Jacksonian America

No American writer seems farther from James Fenimore Cooper's conservative social vision than Ralph Waldo Emerson. If Cooper was the defender of social distinction and filial piety, Emerson has long been labeled a social radical and the decrier of pious retrospection. At the very moment Cooper was fighting to regain his father's property at Cooperstown, Emerson was complaining of an age that "builds the sepulchres of the fathers." Emerson, scholars repeat, is the poet, the preacher of inner divinity, the believer in self-reliance, universal principles, absolute freedom; Cooper remains the novelist, the rational critic of democracy's excesses, the son of the founding father. Such distinctions obscure their common problems.

On 12 September 1835, Emerson presented his "Historical Discourse at Concord" commemorating the bicentennial of Concord's incorporation. In almost exactly a year from this moment *Nature* would be advertised for sale, but Emerson was already deep in the intellectual and spiritual ferment that would produce his most radical work. Here, however, his avowed purpose, much like Cooper's intention in chronicling Cooperstown's history, was to "review the deeds of our fathers, and pass that just verdict on them we expect from posterity on our own."[1] Emerson's aim is retrospective; his oration presents Concord as the positive exemplum of America's achievements from its founding through the Revolution. Like Cooper, Emerson felt the intimate ties between history and autobiography and earlier this same year he had come to live in Concord, returned to his ancestral home where his grandfather had preached and lived.

The scene of the oration exemplifies the peculiarities of Emerson's public role, for it combines his talents as writer and speaker, his ambitions to lead, and his personal motives to reestablish a place in this town and align himself with its long history. Everywhere in the old meetinghouse Emerson could see reminders of Concord's origin as he paid homage to the past. The ancient Reverend Ezra Ripley, now eighty-five years old, read scriptures and the assembled town sang a psalm, as a participant later described, "from the New England version of the psalms made by Eliot, Mather, and others, in 1639."[2] Also present at the scene were ten surviving veterans of the famous 1775 battle at the Concord Bridge. Surrounded by the weight of the past, Emerson could look out and see direct lineal descendants of the town's first settlers, and he significantly includes himself among them by his ties to Peter Bulkeley: "If the name Bulkeley is wanting, the honor you have done me this day, in making me your organ, testifies your persevering kindness to his blood" (W, 11: 30).[3] Emerson consecrates the

[1] *The Complete Works of Ralph Waldo Emerson*, ed. Edward W. Emerson, Centenary Edition (Boston: Houghton Mifflin, 1903–1904), 11: 29. (Hereafter cited in text as W.) Citations from the first four volumes of Emerson's works will be from the more recent *Collected Works of Ralph Waldo Emerson*, ed. Alfred R. Ferguson et al. (Cambridge, Mass.: Harvard University Press, 1971). (Hereafter cited in text as CW.)

[2] This description comes from Edward Emerson's notes to the Centenary Edition of his father's works (W, 11: 552–55). He is quoting here from an eyewitness account.

[3] Edward Emerson's note to this passage explains his father's comment:

> Mr. Emerson's right of descent to speak as representative of Peter Bulkeley, who was the spiritual arm of the settlement, as Simon Willard was its sword-arm, may here be shown: Rev. Joseph Emerson of Mendon (son of Thomas of Ipswich, the first of the name in this country) married Elizabeth, daughter of Rev. Edward Bulkeley, who succeeded his father, the Rev. Peter Bulkeley, as minister of Concord. Edward the son of Joseph of Mendon and Elizabeth Bulkeley, was father of Rev. Joseph Emerson of Malden, who was father of Rev. William Emerson of Concord, who was father of Rev. William Emerson of Harvard and Boston, the father of Ralph Waldo Emerson. (W, 11: 555)

origins of his community, announces his historical ties to Concord's founding, and speaks as the "organ," the representative, of its citizens. Two days after the address he drove to Plymouth, married Lydia Jackson, and returned her to his Concord home.

For both Cooper and Emerson, local history becomes the paradigmatic repository of American history, personal success is endowed with national virtues. And the secret of national identity resides, as Emerson says, in "the two great epochs of public principle, the Planting, and the Revolution of the colony" (W, 11: 85). In the opening pages of the "Historical Discourse," Emerson narrates the settlement of Concord by the Puritans, their relations with the Indians, the subdividing of the land, and finally the imposition of taxes. Oddly enough, it is here that Emerson pauses for emphasis: "Fellow citizens, this first recorded political act of our fathers, this tax assessed on its inhabitants by a town, is the most important event in their civil history, implying, as it does, the exercise of a sovereign power, and connected with all the immunities and powers of a corporate town in Massachusetts" (W, 11: 42). The key to Concord's future success lies in its peculiar "immunities and powers," granted, as Emerson quotes, by the General Court: "The freemen of every town shall have power to dispose of their own lands, and woods, and choose their own particular officers" (W, 11: 44). In other words, the origin of Concord's political identity, characterized by the exercise of sovereign power, is to be found in the possession of its own "nature" and in its particular form of local representation. Continuing, he describes his ideal community and model state: democratic in spirit, questioning of authority, bound by an "internal constitution."

> I esteem it the happiness of this country that its settlers, whilst they were exploring their granted and natural rights and determining the power of the magistrate, were united by personal affection. Members of a church before whose searching covenant all rank was abolished, they stood in awe of each other, as religious men. . . . For the first time, men examined the powers of the chief whom they loved and revered. For the first time, the ideal social compact was real. The bands of love and reverence held fast the little state, whilst they untied the great cords of authority to examine their soundness and learn

> on what wheels they ran. They were to settle the internal constitutions of the towns, and, at the same time, their power in the commonwealth. The Governor conspires with them in limiting his claims to their obedience, and values much more their love than his chartered authority. (W, 11: 45)

In its form of representation and careful examination of the "cords of authority," Concord becomes the prototype of the United States. Because of its location as the first inland town in the colony, too distant from Boston's authority, Concord began to accomplish its political business through town meetings, the form of government Emerson calls "the great secret of political science . . . how to give every individual his fair weight in the government, without any disorder from numbers" (W, 11: 46–47). But if the town meeting foreshadowed American democracy, it also embodied its attendant problems: "In this open democracy, every opinion had utterance; every objection, . . . its entire weight. The moderator was the passive mouth-piece, and the vote of the town, like the vane on the turret overhead, free for every wind to turn, and always turned by the last and strongest breath" (W, 11: 47). Continuing, Emerson recalls events from the town records as he begins to balance the power of the democratic principle against its resulting "meanness and private pique": "If the good counsel prevailed, the sneaking counsel did not fail to be suggested; freedom and virtue, if they triumphed, triumphed in a fair field" (W, 11: 48–49). Emerson does not hammer away at his democratic audience as Cooper might, but he too is aware of democracy's excesses and failings. If Concord's power arises from its sovereign authority to elect representatives, then this power leads to the same cacophony of competing voices we have heard in Brackenridge, Brown, and Cooper. Moreover, the rise of democracy leaves its chosen representative a mere "passive mouth-piece," a phrase which must mean much to Emerson who had been chosen the community's "organ" at this celebration.

Emerson's "Historical Discourse" provides an odd yet useful perspective on his better-known works of this period—*Nature*, "The American Scholar," and "Self-Reliance." "The American Scholar" has been called America's literary declaration of independence; this earlier oration seems more an assertion of historical necessity and dependence. Perhaps more important than any political theory of representation that it details, the oration tells us a great deal about the public imperatives acting on Emerson. Standing in the old meetinghouse, itself shored up to support the great weight of the audience, he found himself a representative called upon to shore up tradition rather than to tear down its decaying supports. He effects no "original relation" with history as he will soon seek with the universe in *Nature*. Instead, his public role as representative of the people seems more compelled than compelling. Emerson's ambitions to lead, like Father Abraham's, are here self-defeating.

Emerson's oration replays a now-familiar scene in America's political drama. A writer with public ambitions, an ex-minister who wishes to guide and instruct his audience, Emerson prefigures his own American Scholar, whose duty it is "to cheer, to raise, and to guide men by showing them facts amidst appearances" (CW, 1: 62). The question of *duty* is key here, for Emerson's performance exhibits the ambiguities inherent in the search for authority. With a moral duty to move and educate the people, his authority nevertheless comes from the people who have made him their "organ" and representative. However, like Father Abraham they grant him only his public office, not the moral principles by which he must act or those which he tried so hard to express. In other words, there are two forms of duty here, two kinds of imperatives, each with a separate form of authority: the public conventions of his position as representative of the people and the "private virtues" which arise, as Emerson says of the Scholar, "out of his own constitution." The next two decades of intellectual work were spent trying to reconcile the constraints of public duty and the dictates of moral authority.

On this day in September Emerson tempered his call for liberation with a reverence for the past and suppressed his personal ambitions for the sake of public harmony and historical continuity. His was a complex ambition, divided between a desire to be a popular public figure who is "borne forward . . . by the weight of thousands" (W, 11: 86) and a reticence to expose himself before others. As a lecturer of nearly fifteen hundred such public engagements from Maine to Ohio, Emerson would continue to exercise his desire to lead and instruct. But he would also ask himself, "Were it not a heroic adventure in me to insist on being a popular speaker & run full tilt against Fortune who with such beautiful consistency shows evermore her back?"[4] Emerson desired to represent the people, yet be more than their popular, passive representative.

When Emerson made the concept of the representative the subject of a book years later, this dichotomy reappears as he divides the nineteenth century between two representatives: Napoleon and Goethe. Bonaparte is the "representative of the popular external life and aims" of this century; Goethe, "its poet." With this gesture Emerson also creates an apparent opposition between material and intellectual activity by dissociating the man of letters, the poet, from the practical and political events of the world. It would seem the writer and the political leader can find no common ground in Emerson's scheme of things. But like his other polarities, this opposition arises from a unifying principle. Here the common point of reference lies in this volume's subject: Napoleon and Goethe, the man of the world and the writer, are both "representative," a term that bridges political and literary issues by engaging the concept of representation. Within the relationships between these two men, Emerson suggests we may discover a fundamental and originating source of representation manifested in a multiplicity of forms, including politics and poetry.

Emerson's division between Napoleon and Goethe might just as easily apply to the two representatives of American antebellum culture: Andrew Jackson and Emerson himself. A discussion of the "Historical Discourse" must include its political context, for much of what Emerson was to write here and in the next few years implicitly attacks what has been called the "persuasion" of Jacksonian democracy. Although statistics carry more explanatory weight about the conditions of the nation during the 1820s, 1830s, and 1840s, Jackson's "persuasion," the careful use of key concepts and rhetorical phrases, became the vehicle for his power.[5] To focus on

[4] *The Journals and Miscellaneous Notebooks of Ralph Waldo Emerson* ed. William G. Gilman et al., 16 vols. (Cambridge, Mass.: Harvard Univ. Press, 1960–1982), 6: 315. (Hereafter cited in text as JMN.)

[5] One of the best discussions of Jacksonian America and its "persuasion" remains Marvin Meyers's *The Jacksonian Persuasion*, 2nd ed. (Stanford: Stanford Univ. Press, 1960). See also Edward Pessen, *Jacksonian America*, rev. ed. (Homewood, Ill.: Dorsey Press, 1978).

style is not to insist on its unchanging, monolithic quality but to define the battleground as language itself. The contest between Jackson and Emerson was over the authority to define the meanings of the key terms—words like *democracy*, *power*, and *representative*—and therefore to control the reality they both describe and enact.

Democracy, as Alexis de Tocqueville noted, was the sacred word of the period. Even before Jackson's election of 1828, this word had acquired the aura of sanctity and liberty, of both political and moral ideals, never imagined by the founders. For Tocqueville and most Americans, the word connoted "the equality of conditions" to be found throughout American society.[6] Egalitarian sentiment seemed to be the spring that drove the busy machine of America. The sentiment of democracy, however, obscured the fact that inequality, not equality, was the rule: The rulers were the wealthy, not the common man or woman. Slavery, poverty, and political oppression existed at the heart of society. Even an embattled aristocrat like Fenimore Cooper could tell you that America was a dangerous place to live. But the victory still belonged to democracy, for if the reality of a truly democratic society had not triumphed, its rhetoric had.

One consequence of this rhetoric was that the balance between aristocrat and democrat sought by the Constitution threatened to dissolve in the corrosive language of the new politicians. The rhetoric of Jacksonian democracy pushed the people in two directions: toward the autonomy of radical individualism and toward the tyranny of public opinion. Implying a lack of a hierarchical or centralized authority, democratic rhetoric allowed (or forced) an individual, in Brackenridge's phrase, to create his own constitution. "Every new man," he wrote in the early part of the century, "must have a new constitution; for he will wish to suit himself; and he will have no doubt but that he can make one, that will at least have in it what he wants."[7]

To Tocqueville, this situation meant that "the individual is the best and only judge of his own interest and that society has no right to direct his behavior unless it feels harmed by him or unless

[6] Tocqueville, *Democracy*, p. 9.
[7] Brackenridge, *Modern Chivalry*, p. 676.

it needs his concurrence."[8] *Interest* is the operative word here, for as Madison explained in the *Federalist* No. 10, "No man is allowed to be a judge in his own cause; because his *interest* would certainly bias his judgment and, not improbably, corrupt his integrity" (my emphasis).[9] By the 1830s, Madison's argument for a representative government seems to have been superseded by the new rhetoric of democracy. The tendency of Americans to guard their independence, to judge their own interest, and to resist authority splintered parties into associations, and associations into rebels. As we will see, the key move in Emerson's concept of moral authority is to redefine the *self* in ways to make judging self-interest a spiritual duty.

The converse of this disintegrating force was the equally powerful authority of public opinion. Tocqueville accounted for this paradox by stating that equality leads the individual to trust his equals—the public. Consequently, "the majority of the United States takes over the business of supplying the individual with a quantity of ready-made opinions and so relieves him of the necessity of forming his own."[10] More precisely, the American is, in Marvin Meyers's words, the "masterless man." "Free to invent a fresh world," this citizen "finds all the important value answers (and many petty ones) given in familiar, comfortable form by his own self-image magnified to authoritative dimension by the majority."[11] Meyers's explanation makes projection the mechanism of conformity: The individual finds in the majority the image of his own interests. For Emerson, the problem became how to define self-interest apart from the coercive rhetoric of the majority and the equally dangerous power of what Brackenridge called self-love.

Another effect of the rhetoric was to increase the importance of the speaker's personality as a sign of sincerity. As the national stakes grew larger, politicians like Daniel Webster wagered their characters in order to heal political inconsistencies. Personality rather than principle became the criterion for judging the qualifications of political figures. Describing the contrast between Americans and their leaders, Tocqueville wrote, "good qualities [are]

[8] Tocqueville, *Democracy*, p. 66.
[9] Hamilton, Madison, and Jay, *Federalist*, p. 46.
[10] Tocqueville, *Democracy*, p. 435.
[11] Meyers, *Jacksonian Persuasion*, p. 55.

common among the governed but rare among the rulers."[12] Great political parties, he states, are attached to "ideas rather than to personalities," but America had no great parties so the people depended on individuals rather than principles for guidance. Describing the enormous popularity of Andrew Jackson, Tocqueville found that "General Jackson's power is constantly increasing, but that of the President grows less."[13] Charismatic authority arising from personality negates the codified rules constituting an office, displacing the criteria for judging a representative's performance from his duties to his character. Thus contemplating the future election with apprehension, Emerson writes, "We shall all feel dirty if Jackson is reelected" (JMN 4: 57).

Between Washington's presidency and Jackson's, the eighteenth century's use of conventionalized codes of public performance to realize one's status and nature gave way to the belief in an authentic self that erased the distinction between public and private lives. Public personality, the authentic unity of psychological impulse and appearance, rather than public performance, which replaces the idea of a true self for the sincerity of correct actions, became the criterion for judging political figures. Washington represented public virtue, but Jackson seemed to consider only private ambition. Emerson declared in "Politics," and muttered throughout his journals, parties have been "corrupted by personality" (CW, 3: 200). As it requires identification rather than obedience, this authority of personality subverts individual freedom. To paraphrase Richard Sennett, Americans in the Age of Jackson found leaders whom they wanted to believe in, rather than had to obey.[14] In his journal, under the heading "GREATNESS," Emerson quotes, "political eminence is like a pyramid none get to the top but reptiles or eagles" (JMN, 6: 193). In this case, it appeared as though the reptiles had arrived before the eagles, or, looking back on the founders, that the eagles had since departed.

In his style and preferences, Emerson remained, as Perry Miller called him, "the child of Boston," in his distaste for the low, vulgar, and popular.[15] "Popularity is for dolls," Emerson writes in his jour-

[12] Tocquevlle, *Democracy*, p. 197.
[13] Ibid., p. 394.
[14] Sennett, *Fall*, p. 210.
[15] Perry Miller, "Emersonian Genius and the American Democracy," in *Emerson:*

nal; "a hero cannot be popular" (JMN, 7: 178). The authority of personality, however, was both personally aversive and politically dangerous. While Jacksonian politicians usurped belief by conventional rhetoric, Emerson had no theory of public performance with which to oppose them. Because authority is "an act mediated by the public philosophy," that is, one dependent on the cultural and linguistic conventions that constitute the meaning of any command, it does not easily fit into his radically anticonventional conception of self and society.[16] In other words, his epistemological position, which includes the abandonment of Lockean sensationalism, implies a simultaneous rejection of Locke's contractualism.

Almost exactly two years after his "Historical Discourse at Concord," Emerson gave his famous "American Scholar" speech at Harvard. What connected these two lectures were his continuing ambitions and the persistent success of Jacksonian politicians at getting "the hurrah on their side" (JMN, 12: 123) by substituting personality for morality. In the 1835 address, Emerson had privileged "private virtue" over public ambition: "The merits of those . . . who are borne forwards, as it were, by the weight of thousands whom they lead, sheds a perfume less sweet than do the sacrifices of private virtue" (W, 11: 86). In 1837, however, Emerson attempted to combine the powerful democratic rhetoric of heroic leadership with an intellectually grounded argument for "private virtue" in order to redirect American democracy to spiritual ends.

The Scholar's Autonomy

Imbued with the rich religious tones intimating America's corporate election, the Jacksonian persuasion preached the powers of independence, virtue, democracy, divinity. Surprisingly, these are also the terms of Emerson's rhetoric, a vocabulary powered by the urgency of his imperative demands.[17] Nevertheless, although we often hear him utter words like *power*, *will*, *freedom*, *greatness*, we

---

A Collection of Critical Essays, ed. Milton Konvitz and Stephen Whicher (Englewood Cliffs, N.J.: Prentice-Hall, 1962), p. 72.

[16] A. Robert Caponigri, "Individual, Civil Society, and State in American Transcendentalism," in *Critical Essays on American Transcendentalism*, ed. Philip F. Gura and Joel Myerson (Boston: G. K. Hall, 1984), p. 547.

[17] On the basis of Emerson's rhetoric, see Julie Ellison, *Emerson's Romantic Style* (Princeton: Princeton Univ. Press, 1984), esp. pp. 3–14, 26–28.

must not assume too much of their conventional meanings, for he redefines them according to new principles. The contract we bring to most discursive situations, the agreement to assume certain conventions about consensually achieved definitions, logical structures, and even intentions, is not binding when we read an essay like "The American Scholar." Rather, Emerson seeks to appropriate and then transform the consensual into the private.

In the following passage from "The American Scholar," Emerson appropriates the conventional notion of the scholar as an ineffectual parasite and infuses it with the powerful rhetoric of heroism to make this figure compete with the political leaders in the society. He does so by emptying his terms of their conventional, institutionalized definitions and redefining the intellectual basis of the scholar's vocation.

> In self-trust, all the virtues are comprehended. Free should the scholar be,—free and brave. Free even to the definition of freedom, "*without any hindrance that does not arise out of his own constitution.*" Brave; for fear is a thing which a scholar by his very function puts behind him. Fear always springs from ignorance. . . . So is the danger a danger still: so is the fear worse. Manlike let him turn and face it. Let him look into its eye and search its nature, inspect its origin,—see the whelping of this lion,—which lies no great way back; he will then find himself a perfect comprehension of its nature and extent; he will have made his hands meet on the other side, and can henceforth defy it, and pass on superior. The world is his who can see through its pretension. (CW, 1: 63–64, my emphasis)

Emerson here defines two preconditions for the scholar's success: bravery and freedom. Associating fear with ignorance, he then makes them both a function of the past by placing this fear "behind" the scholar and then exhorting him to turn around to "inspect its origin." Bravery consequently involves an act of revision when the scholar makes the world ("its nature") transparent by looking "through its pretension." We are immediately put in mind of *Nature*'s insistent use of transparency as a metaphor for revelation, but here the revelation comes when the scholar looks into fear's "eye" and discovers, again as in *Nature*, that it is also "I": "He will then find *himself* a perfect *comprehension* of its nature and extent." What Emerson defines here is the scholar's great power of "comprehension," which, as its etymology implies, involves the process of seizing and taking up the world and discovering in it himself. Moreover, he puns on the fact that "comprehension" is also a rhetorical trope equivalent to synecdoche, which allows a term for the part to stand for, or comprehend, the whole.[18] The scholar comprehends his own fear and danger and thus proves "superior." The scholar's bravery, in other words, manifests itself when he repossesses the world through the troping powers of his perception. The scholar can affect the world through his intellect: "Not he is great who can alter matter, but he who can alter my state of mind" (CW, 1: 64). With the pun on "state," combined with his earlier play on "constitution," Emerson turns each scholar into a politically sovereign microcosm.

While the rhetorical force of Emerson's language exemplifies his call for bravery, the lecture setting, as in his earlier address at Concord, meliorates his cry for freedom. His claims are liberating, but his tone is demanding and imperative, even authoritarian. Like Franklin before him, Emerson preaches the necessity of independence yet assumes the mantle of authority, a position he can hold only by radically redefining the conditions of freedom. Before Emerson, the value America placed on individual independence had always been mitigated by the demand for corporate success. In *The Autobiography*, Franklin equated the freedom of independence with rationality and self-control. He believed that loosening constraints on an individual within a mobile society will eventually aid that society. Independence becomes the means for personal success, but social progress—the increasingly rational organization of men and women—becomes the motive and the end. If our internal drives and passions, arising spontaneously, appear to determine our behavior, then logic, reason, and disciplined judgment work to free us from involuntary controls. At the same time, those internal motives (greed, ambition, vanity, lust) externally subject us to those who control the means to fulfilling our desires. Credit becomes the key metaphor to explain our moral obligations to repay "errata," for our debts mark our moments of failed self-govern-

[18] The *OED* (1971 ed.) quotes *Chambers Cyclopedia*: "whereby the name of a whole is put for a part; or that of a part for a whole." In logic, comprehension is defined as "the sum of attributes comprehended in a notion or concept; intension."

ance, and such reciprocal transactions become the quantifiable, logical bonds of duty forming the network of society.

Franklin's dualistic conception of independence is powered by our ability to internalize authority. Beginning with external standards and models, we eventually incorporate them as our own form of self-government. As he records in *The Autobiography*, the freedom derived from rational self-control gradually dissolves the bonds of subordination for child and apprentice, replacing them with the voluntary associations of the Junto, the lending library, and other consensual organizations. Franklin's equation of independence with rationality requires a stable, ego-centered concept of self and the positivist's belief that identity resides in particulars rather than in types. Franklin was a practical man, concerned more with the consequences of independence than with its metaphysical basis. Emerson, however, was the philosopher of moral principles and spiritual origins; his task was to delineate the laws by which we *must* act to be free and moral.

Like Franklin, Emerson begins by severing one's internal self from external constraint. In his "Historical Discourse," Emerson had distinguished a public "space in the world's history" from the "sacrifices of private virtue" (W, 11: 86), but here he uses the concept of political sovereignty to define the border of one's internally constituted identity: "Man shall treat man as a sovereign state with a sovereign state" (CW, 1: 68). This definition preserves an autonomous individual's right and responsibility to resist subjection to the will of someone or something external. Obviously, this right rejects externally imposed authority, the imperialistic claims upon the self by others. Authority, as A. Robert Caponigri has stated, "is the complete annihilation of his [the Transcendentalist's] self-dependency, for in the view of the transcendentalist principle authority is the complete other, with which there can be no compromise or conciliation. Authority is the ideally unmediated will of the other and carries with it no warranty from the univeral mind."[19] Created in this opposition is the apparent conflict between public duty and private virtue, outer and inner, other and self (or "Not me" and "Me").

"The American Scholar" reverses Franklin's terms through its

[19] Caponigri, "Individual," pp. 548–49.

particular definition of freedom: "without any hindrance that does not arise out of his own constitution." Whereas Franklin's self gradually gains independence by learning the laws of society, Emerson's self *originates in independence* while remaining prey to the powers of social subjugation. His definition raises two problems: (1) how an individual derives the laws of his or her own constitution without recourse to external standards; and (2) how personal identity may be defined in relation to those laws. In other words, an autonomous self, if we are to take the concept to its logical limits, must originate its laws of action internally and use them to "legislate" its behavior and nature. Acts are thus *constituted* in that they are derived from self-created principles, but the origin of those principles remains hazy. To reverse Kant's famous phrase, for Emerson "can implies ought."[20]

Emerson's concept of autonomy or self-reliance requires both a negative and a positive argument, each depending on a special understanding of the self. The essay "Self-Reliance," for example, expends much of its rhetorical energy by telling us what *not* to do. If self-reliance negates establishing an identity based on conformity (we *are* because of an association with a family, nation, or religion), or based on consistency (we *are* because we imitate our past actions and believe we will do the same tomorrow), then the real problem it raises is not what we mean by reliance, but on what form of "self" we will rely. Once we have rejected all external supports and conventional definitions of self, we are left with "the resolution of all into the ever blessed ONE. Self-existence is the attribute of the Supreme Cause, and it constitutes the measure of good by the degree in which it enters into all lower forms" (CW, 2: 40). Moral good for Franklin was measurable by society's progress. Here, we infer just the opposite: Society depends on the degree to which an individual locates the original authority, "the Supreme Cause," within himself.

Emerson also breaks with Franklin over the concept of imitation, for it is now the tool of conformity. Emerson's claim that "imitation is suicide" accurately describes imitation's consequences: Custom externalizes identity and abrogates one's inner constitution by sub-

[20] In "The Divinity School Address," Emerson claims, "When he says, 'I ought,' . . . then deep melodies wander through his soul from Supreme Wisdom" (CW, 2: 79).

jecting the self to conventions. The experiential, processional self is stabilized by its projection onto the objects of perception, but it loses its origins, mistaking them for those representations. Custom is the castoff husk of creation, an exhausted trace of action, and the empty form of originality. Following custom, we imitate the pastness of an act, mistaking the consequences for the inspiration, and give up our sense of a creative self for mere imitation of others: "The sacredness which attaches to the act of creation,—the act of thought,—is instantly transferred to the record. . . . Instantly, the book becomes noxious. The guide is a tyrant. We sought a brother, and lo, a governor" (CW, 1: 56). To imitate is not only to warrant the authority of a reified past, but to identify with it as a determined and determining power, even as we perceive ourselves determined by history and culture. "What is imitation," Emerson asks in "Self-Reliance," "but the travelling of the mind?" (CW, 2: 47), meaning that mere imitation diverts the mind away from itself towards external representative objects.

Conformity and imitation comprise two key elements of Emerson's negative argument for autonomy. More important is his negative definition of freedom: "*without* any *hindrance* that does *not* arise out of his own constitution." We should pay careful attention to Emerson's argument here, for it places definite restrictions on his concept of autonomy, restrictions necessary to link the universal moral principles of Spirit with the Scholar's practical acts. The Scholar's internal constitution legislates the limits of his freedom, without appending his Bill of Rights. The Scholar's freedom is inextricably bound to his duties; the Scholar must be "free and brave" because each free act implies a necessity to act morally, that is, according to the moral dictates of his constitution. For this reason, Emerson finds it necessary to outline a list of the Scholar's duties, which arise, significantly, from the same source as his freedom: "They may all be comprised in self-trust. The office of the scholar is to cheer, to raise, and to guide men by showing them facts amidst appearances" (CW, 1: 62). In other words, the Scholar's freedom, arising from self-reliance, is indistinguishable from his duty to be self-reliant. His freedom and his duty are the same; his imperative is to be autonomous. Unlike Franklin's concept of independence, Emerson's self-reliance becomes the principal end for the Scholar rather than the means.

Absolute authority corresponds to autonomy when the scholar obeys the imperatives arising from an internal constitution.[21] "Every man," he tells us, "discriminates between the voluntary acts of his mind, and his involuntary perceptions, and knows that to his involuntary perceptions a perfect faith is due. He may err in the expression of them, but he knows that these things are so, like day and night, not to be disputed. My wilful actions and acquisitions are but roving" (CW, 2: 37). The irrational and involuntary—the "necessary"—belong to the workings of intuitional Reason; the voluntary, to understanding. Autonomy, in other words, springs from its own necessity, or, as he says in "Self-Reliance," "that source, at once the essence of genius, or virtue, and of life, which we call Spontaneity or Instinct" (CW, 2: 37). To speak of autonomy as a characteristic is misleading, for, like all workings of Reason, it is an act of self-creation. Terms like *self-reliance* and *self-possession* are therefore misleadingly ontological; they imply *something* that can be owned, a piece of property. Autonomy, as Emerson says of the soul, "*becomes*" and must be described in terms of process: "Why then do we prate of self-reliance? Inasmuch as the soul is present, there will be power not confident but agent. To talk of reliance, is a poor external way of speaking. Speak rather of that which relies, because it works and is" (CW, 2: 40).

Emerson's Scholar is free by necessity, a paradox that has led to a number of misconceptions concerning the concept of self-reliance. A comparison with Kant's concept of autonomy will help dispel claims of Emerson's egocentrism or "imperial self."[22] Kant distinguishes between heteronomy and autonomy: The former involves a subjection to external causes, while the latter acts according to self-derived universals. Heteronomy is based on what Kant calls a "hypothetical imperative," an attempt to rationalize an action according to external causes. A hypothetical imperative can

[21] See David Van Leer, *Emerson's Epistemology* (New York: Cambridge Univ. Press, 1986), pp. 91–95, esp. p. 95: "[Virtue] is intransitive and categorical, with a moral force deriving not from external circumstances or consequences but from its own innate lawfulness."

[22] Quentin Anderson, for example, speaks of Emerson's "affirmation of an imperial separateness and timelessness." See *The Imperial Self* (New York: Alfred Knopf, 1971), p. 58. My discussion of Kant's concept of autonomy has benefited from Sir David Ross's *Kant's Ethical Theory* (Oxford: Clarendon Press, 1954) and Robert Paul Wolff's *The Autonomy of Reason* (New York: Harper and Row, 1973).

be expressed as a conditional statement; for example, "I should not lie if I wish to keep my reputation," or, "If you want to avoid a spanking, take a bath." Autonomy, on the other hand, "is that property of the will by which it is a law to itself independently of any property of objections of volition."[23] It has no origin other than the categorical imperative: "I can act only on that maxim which I can at the same time will as a universal law." "Ought," as in "I *ought* to tell the truth," becomes categorical when I conceive the moral law within me and freely bind myself to it, knowing that it must equally apply to all human beings. Created by my own "constitution," the moral law must also be freely conceived by all other humans. Being autonomous, my existence is my own end, a fact true for all others. Therefore, as Kant finally concludes, autonomy leads to this practical imperative: "So act as to treat humanity, whether in your own person or in that of any other, never as a means only but in every case as an end also."[24]

Autonomy is the principal quality of the American Scholar, "the soul, free, sovereign, and active" (CW, 1:56). This virtue embraces the other qualities which together comprised the Emersonian "Great Man." As we have seen in the Scholar, politics is not a means for the Great Man, but a consequence of these qualities. Man Thinking presents the mind engaged in acts of pure intellect, unclosed by the particular thought of some thing. Man Thinking exists autonomously in the universality of the act, never in the particularity of a thought's creation. In "Self-Reliance," Emerson describes the curious division of the self that occurs in the loss of autonomy. The "alienated majesty" we perceive as a mirroring of our original thoughts in others suggests how far we project ourselves from our origins. Describing the intellectual déjà vu experience of encountering the uncannily familiar person or idea, he finds it analogous to alienation: "Ordinarily every body in society reminds of somewhat else or some other person. Character, reality, reminds you of nothing else; it takes place of the whole creation" (CW, 2:35). This claim forces us to see that to be "*re*-minded" involves the *re-cognition*, the re-production, of memory, never the original *cognition* of Reason. The autonomous self can never be

23 Immanuel Kant, *Foundations of the Metaphysics of Morals*, trans. Lewis White Beck (New York: Liberal Arts Press, 1959), Ak. 440 (p. 59).

24 Ibid., Ak. 429 (p. 47).

past, but arises at every instant out of the spontaneous universality of the act.

The Scholar, Man Thinking, possesses not only himself in the act of thinking, but "must sometimes return from his own labor to embrace all the other laborers" (CW, 1: 53). Whereas others are "metamorphosed into a thing, into many things"—"the priest becomes a form; the attorney a statute book; the mechanic, a machine; the sailor, the rope of a ship"—the Scholar contains them, remains whole and all encompassing because of his autonomy. To use perhaps the most important of Emerson's images, the Scholar exists as the circumference of the circle, embracing all others in the universality of his position.[25] Images of encircling, embracing, and "comprehension" abound in "The American Scholar," suggesting the Scholar's ability to unite and understand. From this position, the Scholar negates both conventional preconditions of Franklinesque autonomy: He reverses the common notion of public and private, and destroys our conventional understanding of the self as a stable, consistent, and imitable being. At the same time, the Emersonian self arises from its incarnation within an infinite procession of selves, each original and divine. The whole notion of self is a fiction of provisional selves created in the process of finding objects for its contemplation or cognition. "Self-existence," as I have already quoted, "is the attribute of the Supreme Cause" (CW, 2: 40).

The Scholar "comprehends," that is, encircles, perceives and tropes when he acts by universal principle.

> He is one who raises himself from private considerations, and breathes and lives on public and illustrious thoughts. He is the world's eye. He is the world's heart. He is to resist the vulgar prosperity that retrogrades ever to barbarism, by preserving and communicating heroic sentiments, noble biographies, melodious verse, and the conclusions of history. Whatsoever oracles the human heart in all emergencies, in all solemn hours has uttered as its commentary on the world of actions,—these he shall receive and impart. And whatsoever new verdict Rea-

[25] I am borrowing here Hazard Adams's distinction between the center and circumference in symbolism. See *The Philosophy of the Literary Symbolic* (Tallahassee: Univ. of Florida Press, 1984), pp. 19–23.

> son from her inviolable seat pronounces on the passing men and events to-day,—this he shall hear and promulgate (CW, 1: 62–63).

As this passage presents him, the Scholar is the Great Man, who is not only the "hero of metaphor" (to borrow Emerson's phrase effectively employed by Eric Cheyfitz), but one whose power is metaphoric. Emerson's use of the two metaphors—"He is the world's eye. He is the world's heart"—illustrates the Scholar's reliance on the power and autonomy of metaphor. His power exists by transforming the material world, nature and culture, from the literal (i.e., the particular and material) incongruity of the image to its figural (the typological and spiritual) significance. He maintains his autonomy in our metaphoric perception of him. We recognize in him the ability to translate action into universal principles. Emerson's metaphors, like the famous transparent eyeball, are less concerned with their representative ability than their own power of translation.

Emerson radically reshapes not only the meaning of autonomy, but the very conditions of its meaning, in order to create a new position from which to view political matters. Opposed to Jacksonian demagogues, his doctrine of the Great Man is meant to possess their powers. If the demagogues command sympathy from the voters for their heroic military feats, Emerson calls "self-trust . . . the essence of heroism," transforming it from a call to obedience to popular leaders to an act of rebellion as it "works in contradiction to the voice of mankind" (CW, 2: 149). When the leaders proclaim the power of democracy, Emerson rebuts that true democracy is not "that ill thing vain & loud, but the spirit of love for the General good whose name this assumes" (JMN, 5: 302), meaning by "General" a universal equality. Redefining the independence of "self-trust" from the possession of a material self, defined by imitation of custom, to the decentered, liberated self, bound to the universal interest, Emerson attempted to fit democracy to his ideals.

The magnet and mirror symbolized for Emerson the two poles of the age (JMN, 11: 230–31). The Great Man is the magnet; the demagogue, the mirror in whom the people see their own image. Mere personality is the ignis fatuus of men created by the projection of their fantasies and desires onto the image of a charismatic figure. The hero and man of action like Jackson became the object of worship; personality, not principle, evoked the people's trust and admiration. By separating the idea of heroism from its incarnations in individuals, Emerson sought to distract the people from the "small sort" of popular men in America "who never saw a grander arch than their own eyebrow" (JMN, 13: 438). Years before this remark, Emerson had written, "Reverence men, & not Plato & Caesar. Wherever there is sense reflexion, courage, admit it to the same honour—embrace it,—. If you cannot get the habit of seeing qualities except in the great,—if any thing new should spring up, it will be lost to you" (JMN, 4: 38).

Although self-reliance provides Emerson with the means to redefine independence by universalizing the idea of constitution, it also undermines the basis of America's representative government. "The root & seed of democracy," he writes in his journal, "is the doctrine Judge for yourself. Reverence yourself" (JMN, 4: 342). Not only does this formulation presume to make the self worthy of reverence, but it also contradicts James Madison's explicit injunction that "no man is allowed to judge in his own cause." When Emerson transforms each individual into a sovereign state, he includes the executive and judicial branches of government, but he later provides an ambiguous place for the legislative when he claims that "the poet is representative."

The Poet as Representative

In 1838, as he was making his most controversial statements before the conservative audiences of Harvard and Dartmouth, Emerson was annoyed at Harriet Martineau's descriptions of him in her book, *Retrospect of Western Travel.* She had taken away, he claimed, "my privacy & thrust me before my time (if ever there be a time) into the arena of gladiators, to be stared at."[26] This confession reveals his barely concealed ambition, the self-conscious sense of mission, and the concomitant fear of and desire for martrydom before a hostile, pagan audience. Although antiauthoritarian, Emerson

[26] *The Correspondence of Emerson and Carlyle,* ed. Joseph Slater (New York: Columbia Univ. Press, 1964), p. 185.

nevertheless exaggerates his own public role and contemplates a greater future even as he fears its consequences.

In his effort to lead America toward spiritual success, Emerson discovered that his enemy was the other America, the sensual, material America of Andrew Jackson and Martin Van Buren. Writing to Carlyle, he again expresses his hopes and self-doubt: "My whole philosophy—which is very real—teaches acquiesence and optimism. Only when I see how much work is to be done, what room for a poet—for any spiritualist—in this great, intelligent, sensual, and avarice America, I lament my fumbling figures and stammering tongue."[27] Distressed at his own deficiencies, Emerson here presents the poet as a true savior of America and remedy for Jacksonian materialism. "The poet would be a great man," he writes in his journal, "his power is intellectual." Continuing, Emerson inflates the power of the poet above the leaders of nations: "Instantly he seizes these hollow puppets of Caesar, of Tamerlane, of Boadicea, of Belisarius, & inflates them with his own vital air. If he can verily ascend to grandeur,—if his soul is great, behold his puppets attest his might, they are no more puppets, but instead vehicles of the wind of God. . . . If he sing a true ode, then he is Caesar & not the player of Caesar" (JMN, 7: 188). Emerson here sounds much like Charles Brockden Brown praising the rhapsodist, without the final ironic undercutting.

According to most critics and scholars, the poet stands as Emerson's true hero, successor to the American Scholar. Joel Porte associates Emerson's poet with Christ, "whose *logos* breaks our chains."[28] According to Richard Lee Francis, "It is the poet who represents the final realization of Emerson's vocational quest, the fullest embodiment of all the previous roles of naturalist, moralist, and scholar."[29] At the same time, however, both critics are puzzled why Emerson placed his definitive statement on the poet in *Essays: Second Series* because this volume's darker tone belies the optimism and quasi-divine status of the poet. Porte sees "The Poet" as belonging to the sunnier philosophy of the first volume of essays and

[27] Ibid., p. 304.

[28] Joel Porte, *Representative Man: Ralph Waldo Emerson in his Time* (New York: Oxford Univ. Press, 1979), p. 177.

[29] Richard Lee Francis, "The Poet and Experience," in *Emerson Centenary Essays*, ed. Joel Myerson (Carbondale, Ill.: Southern Illinois Univ. Press, 1982), p. 94.

Francis places it as a positive complement to the frightening vision of "Experience."

Their views are supported by passages scattered throughout Emerson's writings that claim a kind of natural authority for the poet. For example, in "The Method of Nature," Emerson states, "It was always the theory of literature that the word of the poet was authoritative and final. He was supposed to be the mouth of a divine wisdom" (CW, 1: 201). The poet as well provides the highest public service: "Poets should be lawgivers; that is, the boldest lyric inspiration should not chide and insult but should announce and lead the civil code and the day's work" (CW, 2: 218). In "The Poet" he declares, "The poets are thus liberating gods" (CW, 3: 18). And we should remember his earlier claim to the future Lydia Emerson, "I am born a poet, of a low class without doubt yet a poet."[30]

Nevertheless, despite this evidence, there is a stronger counter-argument to Emerson's deification of the poet. We must remember his final comment about the poet's former status as the "mouth of a divine wisdom": "If the theory has receded out of modern criticism, it is because we have not had poets" (CW, 1: 201). In other words, Emerson's rather abstract theory of poetic divinity finds no corresponding practitioner. The problem here is not simply the disparity between theory and practice or the present state of American culture (although that is certainly part of the problem). Rather, as Emerson says in "The Poet," the "breadth of the problem is great, *for the poet is representative*" (CW, 3: 4; my emphasis). We have assumed the divinity of the Emersonian poet for so long that we overlook the possibility of a problem in his representative "office." Specifically, throughout the 1840s Emerson increasingly circumscribes the poet's role and such heroic rhetoric acquires a somber undertone, for now the poet has a public office. The poet becomes "representative" by acquiring that office, but it is one that limits his powers. Emerson's essay "The Poet" reveals the basic difference between the Scholar's autonomy and the Poet's representativeness.

"The Poet" begins by setting apart the men of Spirit from those who consider the world through taste, historical evidence, and experience:

[30] *The Letters of Ralph Waldo Emerson*, ed. Ralph L. Rusk, 6 vols. (New York: Columbia Univ. Press, 1939), 1: 435.

> For we are not pans and barrows, nor even porters of the fire and torch-bearers, but children of the fire, made of it, and only the same divinity transmuted, and at two or three removes, when we know least about it. And this hidden truth, that the fountains whence all this river of Time, and its creatures, floweth, are intrinsically ideal and beautiful, draws us to the consideration of nature and the functions of the Poet, or the man of Beauty, to the means and materials he uses, and the general aspect of the art in the present time. (CW, 3: 3–4)

We have the inspired Emerson here, the writer who can convince us of our divinity and abrogated power. But the next sentence brings us back to earth with a characteristic Emersonian puzzle: "The breadth of the *problem* is great, for the poet is representative." If the poet is divine and the man of beauty, then what is the problem? Looking back for the referent of "problem," we find that it could be any one of Emerson's ostensible subjects: nature, the Poet's function, his means and material, or (and we suspect this to be the case) the "general aspect of art in the present time." We must then ask, What does he mean in stating the cause: "for the poet is representative"? By "for" does he mean "because" or "as" or "since," that is, is he seeking a causal connection or simply a loose linguistic tie? Finally the most important problem for the reader, because of the syntactical pressure placed on this word, is what Emerson means by "representative." The passage's logical and syntactical dislocation is also characteristic of Emerson, for with it he creates the counterargument, the sense of doubt that revises the preceding description of the divine poet.

Emerson continues the idea of the representative by describing the three children of the Universe, calling them "cause, operation, and effect; or more poetically, Jove, Pluto, Neptune; or, theologically, the Father, the Spirit, and the Son; but which we will call here, the Knower, the Doer, and the Sayer. These stand respectively for the love of truth, for the love of good, and the love of beauty." "The poet," he finally declares, "is the sayer, the namer, and represents beauty. He is a sovereign, and stands on the center. For the world is not painted, or adorned, but is from the beginning beautiful; and God has not made some beautiful things, but Beauty is the creator of the universe. Therefore the poet is not any permissive potentate, but is emperor in his own right" (CW, 3: 5).

Keeping in mind the Scholar's intimate relation to the "Supreme Cause," we note here the poet's office is allied with "effect." And the terms of this office remain obscure: By representing beauty, does the poet *stand for* the love of beauty as a substitute or model, or does he *act for* beauty by re-presenting it?

We should remember Hannah Pitkin's definition of representation as simply a "*re-presentation,* a making present again," or in my previous definition, it is the making of something figurally present that is literally absent. A person can represent a group of voters; a flag can symbolically represent a country; "Words," as Emerson says in *Nature,* "are signs of natural facts" (CW, 1: 17) within a system of signs. In calling the poet a representative and thereby part of the problem, Emerson focuses a whole series of interrelated problems concerning the origin of his authority and the terms of his office, that is, the nature of representation.

Modern theories of literary representation, as well as the frequent critiques of those theories, most often equate representation with the problems associated with mimesis. Mimetic theories rely on a descriptive correspondence between a thing and its representation, a condition of substitution as when a person "stands for" a group of people or a word stands for an object. However, representation involves not only conditions of mimetic correspondence, of "standing for," but also of agency as a representative "acts for" his constituency and thereby performs the office of representative. Conventional theories of realism posit a direct albeit hazy correspondence between a text and the external world; words stand, or are substitutes, for real objects and they create a text that describes the world. This type of "descriptive representation," to use Hannah Pitkin's term, creates a static, mirroring relation between representation and represented, a relation measurable by the accuracy of correspondence.

Such correspondence theories of "standing for" have rightfully been charged with a naive conception of language, for words are not reliable substitutes for real objects, events, or states. However, too little has been said about a theory of representation involving agency or "acting for." Using language as their paradigm, critiques of mimetic representation have assumed that representations have an arbitrary relation to what they represent, but if we use political representation as the controlling paradigm, then the representation is also a representative, an *agent* conceived and instructed by a constituting subject, a "constituency." As Hannah Pitkin says:

> When the representative is likened to a descriptive representation or a symbol, he is usually seen as an inanimate object and not in terms of any activity; he represents by what he is or how he is regarded. He does not represent by doing anything at all; so it makes no sense to talk about his role or his duties or whether he has performed them. On the other hand, this conception of representing as "standing for" brings with it another notion—the making or creation of representations or symbols; and that *is* a kind of activity.[31]

Representation seen as agency, or "acting for," exists within perception's epistemological conditions and potentially avoids the philosophical problems of mimesis. The difference between a substitute and agent is that an agent requires a "constitution," that is, a set of rules or principles that define and delimit the agent's powers and activities and by which the represented object may be figurally present in some determinate degree. An agent is representative because his identity as agent has been constituted in the process of election (or s-election). Agency may involve a certain degree of description (as voters look for identifying characteristics of class or ideology in their representative), but it does not seek correspondence. The agent's encoded ties, the laws governing his activities, become the terms of his representativeness. To consider representation as a form of agency is to render it essentially nonmimetic, for it is not the accuracy in representing that is important, but the terms by which the constituency determines the representative's actions.

Emerson's nonmimetic theory of the representative and representation rests on the epistemology of his theory of symbols. He can call the Poet a "representative" only by outlining the symbolic terms of the Poet's office. By placing the power for knowing the world within a constituent self who *conceives* that world (I place emphasis on the creative act) in the act of perception, Emerson establishes the basis for considering representation a matter of agency and the representative as a particular type of agent. Writ-

[31] Pitkin, *Concept*, p. 113.

ing in the introductory essay to *Representative Men*, "The Uses of Great Men," he claims, "The constituency determines the votes of the representative. He is not only representative but participant. Like can only be known by like" (CW, 4: 7). In other words, the principal epistemological issues here are how we know or recognize the representative, how his performance and identity are in turn determined by the constituency (or constitutive subject), and, most importantly, how the relationship between the representative and constituency is constituted. We can say that the representative (whether person or object) becomes an Emersonian symbol created by the intellectual "comprehension," to use Emerson's term, of a constituent subject, and the representative acts as the subject's agent. Therefore, what allows Emerson to bridge politics and literature—to claim "the poet is representative"—is the nonmimetic nature of his symbolism. But we must keep in mind that the poet's representativeness is also the "problem."

Returning to the Poet, we see more clearly his role as representative. As "the sayer, the namer," the Poet re-presents Beauty by calling it into existence. He has the power of expression to make nature and heroic actions visible to all ages and generations of humankind. As he speaks originally (in the essay the term is "primarily"), the poet does not imitate nature or beauty but fulfills his "office" by affirming "the beauty of things, which becomes a new, and higher beauty, when expressed" (CW, 3: 8). The material he uses is nature; the means, its symbolic potential: "Nature offers all her creatures to him as a picture-language. Being used as a type, a second wonderful value appears in the object, far better than its old value, as the carpenter's stretched cord, if you hold your ear close enough, is musical in the breeze. . . . Things admit of being used as symbols, because nature is a symbol, in the whole, and in every part." The poet is "an utterer of the necessary and causal" because "the beautiful rests on the foundations of the necessary" in that Spirit is the necessary first cause. The poet is a representative in that he acts as an agent of Spirit.

Given these powers, what is the "problem" of the poet's office as a representative? First of all, his principal problem is that he has an "office," a conditioned ground determining his powers. Like any representative, the poet is constrained and limited by relational and conditional terms of his activity. He is the universe's

"Son," but he lives in a world of effect rather than cause or operation. Thus, oddly enough like Cooper's sons, his role is to mediate consequences. I stress this point in order to distinguish the poet from Emerson's Great Man. Although he claims, "The poet *would* be a great man" (JMN, 7: 188; my emphasis), representation is very different from greatness or heroism; the representative is such because he can be put to use as a mediator, agent, or trustee, rather than exist as a model or metaphor. Emerson acknowledges the limitations of the representative in the beginning of "Nominalist and Realist": "I cannot often enough say, that a man is only a relative and representative nature. Each is a hint of truth, but far enough from being that truth, which yet he quite newly and inevitably suggests to us" (CW, 3: 133). Acting within a role circumscribed by its defining conventions, the representative is confined even as he acts. Although "words are also actions," the poet's expression of these words institutionalize his power.

Rather than maintaining the autonomy of the metaphoric Great Man, the representative, as we saw with Brackenridge, exists in a metonymic relation of the part to the whole, and his identity is derived from the larger term, the concept of the constituency he represents. He loses the scholar's "comprehension," that is, the power to replace the whole by his part. Because his place and significance are determined by the object or group to which he refers, he has no autonomy but is always *signifying* something. The conditional nature of the representative's office, conditioned both by its represented object and its constituted powers, therefore obscures the poet's authority. If Spirit alone is "necessary," then the poet lacks the freedom of self-trust: He does not spin the laws from his own constitution but is *constituted* by his spiritual office.

Emerson consistently reminds us of the determined and limited position of the representative poet. In his journal (in a passage later used in "Shakespeare; or, the Poet"), he writes, "All originality is relative. Every thinker is representative. Locke thinks for thousands just as much as Clay or Cushing at Washington vote for thousands. Show me the constituency & the invisible channels by which the senator is made aware of their wishes & it will bereave his fine attitude & resistance of something of its impressiveness" (JMN, 8: 67). This passage's political implications deserve more attention, but for the moment it serves to emphasize the diminished status of the poet as representative. As Emerson repeats in "The Uses of Great Men": "The constituency determines the vote of the representative. He is not only representative, but participant" (CW, 4: 7).

If we compare the Poet with the American Scholar, we can better see the problem of the poet's position. Man Thinking maintains and enacts the autonomy of self-trust, encompassing himself and all others in the universality of his act. In "Circles," Emerson explains that the "key to every man is his thought," and it is the scholar's ability to exist on the circumference of the circle, growing and progressing as thought's circle grows, that keeps him free. But the Poet "stands on the centre" (CW, 3: 5); his power is not in thought but in expression. His ability to pronounce the world into existence using nature and language as his vocabulary is great, but the Scholar then comprehends and transmutes that world. The poet may be "sovereign," as he is called, but it is the uniqueness of a point at the center of the divine circle whose circumference is nowhere and its center everywhere. He is still determined and confined by his central position, no matter how great his powers of expression. Everything he calls into being is a "representation," a repetition that becomes the "externization of the soul" (CW, 3: 9). The poet's place, therefore, is at "the secret of the world, where Being passes into Appearance, and Unity into Variety" (CW, 3: 9). It is true, according to Emerson, that poets are "liberating gods," but they themselves are Promethean figures; with the power to liberate others, they are confined and unable to free themselves.

Thus "The Poet" does belong to the following essay, "Experience," for it demarcates its own experiential limits, even the limitations of Emerson himself. My point here is not to claim the Poet's impotence but to recognize that he serves a purpose in Emerson's intellectual scheme by having an office. Neither a Great Man nor a completely free and divine creature, the Poet does present a valuable achievement for Emerson because as representative he combines both political and poetic arguments in his power of symbolic representation. And it is the pragmatic use of the symbol that allows Emerson to consolidate political and poetical representation.

The purpose of "The Poet," therefore, is not to inflate the figure of the Great Man and float him above the masses, but to make him representative, as he "stands among partial men for the complete man" (CW, 3: 4), and thereby to attach his powers to all people. The essential link is that "every man is so far a poet as to be susceptible of these enchantments of nature: for all men have thoughts whereof the universe is the celebration. I find that the fascination resides in the symbol. . . . It is nature the symbol, nature certifying the supernatural, body overflowed by life, which he worships, with coarse, but sincere rites" (CW, 3: 9–10). Finally, Emerson finds his example, but his choice purposely combines the political with the symbolic:

> The inwardness, and mystery, of this attachment, drive men of every class to the use of emblems. The schools of poets, and philosophers, are not more intoxicated with their symbols, than the populace with theirs. In our political parties, compute the power of badges and emblems. See the huge wooden ball rolled by successive ardent crowds from Baltimore to Bunker hill! In the political processions, Lowell goes in a loom, and Lynn in a shoe, and Salem in a ship. Witness the cider-barrel, the log-cabin, the hickory-stick, the palmetto, and all cognizances of party. . . . The people fancy they hate poetry, and they are all poets and mystics! (CW, 3: 10)

In short, "we are symbols and inhabit symbols" (CW, 3: 12). The simplicity of this assertion belies its powerful political consequences. Not only does Emerson make clear that all representatives are merely symbols, but he transforms each person into both representative and constituent, thereby making the self both constitutive subject and instrumental object in its figural perception.[32]

However, these examples also constitute a critique of the modern use of symbols: If men and women are poets, they are not necessarily good poets. These political emblems may stand as expressions of the people, but they also exhibit the meanest and most material use of symbols, for, as they exist as the reified consciousness (or even unconscious desires) of the voters, they exemplify the alienation of the people from their own symbolic perception. Without an awareness that the power of these symbols lies not

[32] In *Seeing and Being* (Middletown, Conn.: Wesleyan Univ. Press, 1981), pp. 91–118, Carolyn Porter provides a useful discussion of what she calls the "plight" of the participant observer. Her thesis works best to describe the Poet, but the Scholar retains his autonomy within Emerson's scheme of things.

in their objectified status as signs but rather only as the concepts signified by them, the voters, in essence, see only themselves. They are "intoxicated" by their own symbols, which have become grotesque objects detached from Spirit. These emblems, which significantly are also economic signs, mimetically reproduce a static and inert world. To complete Emerson's warning from "The Poet": "But we sympathize with the symbols, and, being infatuated with the *economical uses* of things, we do not know that they are thoughts" (CW, 3: 12; my emphasis). Contained within this description are Emerson's means to express the bonds between politics, economics, and poetry as well as analysis of the failure of American perception. At stake is the ability to dislodge Americans from their materialistic vision of the world toward a fluid, semiotic perception of unity.

The electoral metaphor by which Emerson equates poetry and politics presents a calculated attack on the issue of democratic representation by presenting it as a cognitive and constitutive act, rather than as a mere legal fact. First of all, in his formulation of the issue of representation, Emerson anwers the troublesome question concerning the relationship between American representatives and their constituency. Whom we elect as representatives, how we judge their qualifications, and how we define their ties to us become, in his terms, a matter first of recognizing their status as representatives, that is, as symbols, and then putting them to use. Rejecting the obsolescent Federalist description of the representative as a member of the best bred and educated, Emerson seems to claim that we share a basic identity with him ("Like can only be known by like"). In so doing, he once again appropriates the popular democratic notion of descriptive representation (we know our representatives because they are our neighbors who look and sound like us) and rephrases it in spiritual terms.

Emerson's distaste for such demagogic, mimetic representation is well-known. A demagogue creates his appeal by mirroring the voter's desire for power through the theatrical and illusory promise of *presence* in his representative role. He claims to identify himself with each voter in turn for the voter's complete sympathy, thereby eliding the epistemological and ontological divisions existing in the act of representation and promising to achieve a perfect mimetic correspondence. Emerson's antimimetic strategy appropriates the popular belief in actual representation, a belief that requires only the illusory identification between representative and constituent, in order to redefine it in terms that retain authority within the constituent's emblematic perception. Jacksonian demagogues were able to insinuate themselves into office because they abrogated the voters' constitutions. By subverting this naive mimetic notion of representation as standing-for, Emerson hopes to replace it with a nonmimetic theory of agency. Our identification with a representative would be based on spiritual principles rather than popular slogans and banners.

Emerson's denomination of Americans as "poets and mystics" characterizes their habits of perception. Distinguishing "betwixt the poet and the mystic," he states, "the last nails a symbol to one sense, which was a true sense for a moment, but soon becomes old and false" (CW, 3: 20). The poet, on the other hand, "did not stop at the color, or the form, but read their meaning; neither may he rest in this meaning, but he makes the same objects exponents of his new thought." In other words, the mystic believes in one-to-one correspondence between thoughts and natural objects—he believes in *mimesis*. It is the mistake, we learn, "of an accidental and individual symbol for an universal one" (CW, 3: 20). Such use of symbols leads to naive allegory and eventually the displacement of authority from thought to symbol. Recognizing this mistake, the poet conforms nature to his thought, acknowledging in this act that thoughts are original and necessary, "symbols are fluxional; all language vehicular" (CW, 3: 20). The poetic use of symbols reveals that they are equally referential to Spirit, constituting an *expressive* theory of literature, in which the poet is the sayer, the *agent* of the Divine. The poet "perceives the thoughts' independence of the symbol, the stability of the thought, the accidency and fugacity of the symbol" (CW, 3: 12). In Emersonian semiotics, the signifiers are arbitrary, but the signified is necessary, transcendental, and determining.[33]

Now we can see more clearly how the poets can be "liberating gods" as well as the more limited "representatives." They liberate us by revealing the world to be at once determined and arbitrary.

[33] Barbara Packer discusses the fluid quality of the symbol and its consequences for Emerson's poet in *Emerson's Fall* (New York: Continuum Press, 1982), pp. 193–195.

By sharing the poet's perception of the accidental nature of symbols, by becoming poets ourselves, we return to their necessary origin and first cause. Poets represent beauty as they find natural symbols with which to express this originality. Still, the danger remains that the poet will become entangled in the symbols, reifying himself, and the reader will mistake the fluxional symbols for Spirit's imperative principles. "The history of hierarchies," Emerson explains, "seems to show, that all religious error consisted in making the symbol too stark and solid, and, at last, nothing but an excess of the organ of language" (CW, 3: 20). The concept of the representative, therefore, is less concerned with greatness than with the power and consequences of symbolic representation. With this theory in mind, we can now turn to Emerson's *Representative Men.*

Emerson and *Representative Men*

Thomas Carlyle, Emerson's friend and sometime rival, had urged him in 1845 to "take an American Hero, one whom you really love; and give us a History of him."[34] In fact, Emerson had already been thinking and gathering notes on a similar subject for a decade, and he was soon to begin his series of lectures on "Representative Men."[35] The subject of these lectures arose from his determination to delineate the office of the representative and to create a unified theory of representation that bridges cultural and political matters.[36]

[34] *Correspondence of Emerson and Carlyle*, p. 381. Emerson had already given a series of lectures on biographies of historical figures, including Michelangelo, Martin Luther, John Milton, George Fox, and Edmund Burke. See *The Early Lectures of Ralph Waldo Emerson*, ed. Stephen Whicher and Robert Spiller, 3 vols. (Cambridge, Mass.: Harvard Univ. Press, 1964), 1: 93–201.

[35] Perhaps to maintain his independence from Carlyle's own work in *Heroes and Hero-Worship* (published in 1841), Emerson studiously avoided any direct references to the "hero." See Kenneth Marc Harris, *Carlyle and Emerson* (Cambridge, Mass.: Harvard Univ. Press, 1978), pp. 44–55, for the ambivalences of their relationship.

[36] Most scholars have wrongly associated the representative with the Emersonian Great Man. In *American Renaissance* (New York: Oxford Univ. Press, 1941), p. 632, F. O. Matthiessen claims the representative exists as kind of Swedenborgian correspondent symbol, revealing "no individual [is] great except through the general." Following him, John O. McCormick attributes Emerson's concept of the representative to Garth Sampson, Coleridge, and especially Victor Cousin. See "Emerson's Theory of Greatness," *New England Quarterly* 26 (1953): 291–314.

Moreover, *Representative Men* reveals Emerson's attempt to develop the public consequences of his philosophy by outlining the conditions of social power. In America, the middling sort—or worse, the demagogues—filled the political offices. In his journals, Emerson ironically commented on the loss of representative power: "The King, or political head, was awful in the eyes of men; would still be so, if the man who really represented the laws & genius & future of this nation sat in the seat. But now we put ignoble obscure persons without character or representative power of any kind, there, & get a figure aweful—to office seekers" (JMN, 14: 398). In late 1844, as he was drafting his lectures, Emerson wrote to Carlyle in a mood of personal insecurity, skepticism, and frustrated ambition: "I am only a sort of lieutenant here in the deplorable absence of captains & write the laws ill as thinking it a better homage than universal silence."[37] Notice here the pun on "lieutenant," one who holds another's place—a representative. These lectures, and their final published version, must be seen as a response to the lack of representative Americans—or to the failure of American representation.

Most striking in this volume is Emerson's historical approach to the concept of representation. In earlier essays his method either avoids the problem of history as a determination of genius or abstractly addresses the idea of history. In *Representative Men*, he places his portraits within the confines of temporality, partly as a consequence of his belief that history is "the group of the types of representative men of any age at only the distance of convenient vision" (JMN, 10: 289). In contrast to this historical view, however, he also claims that in reading the biographies of great men like Luther or Bonaparte we see "this particular man represented the idea of Man. And so far as we accord with his judgment, we take the picture for a standard man" (JMN, 4: 256). In *Representative Men*, Emerson chooses both aspects of the representative—the representative as symbolizing a historical period or an ahistorical idea of Man—in order to set out the resistance of history to the repre-

[37] *Correspondence of Emerson and Carlyle*, pp. 372–73. In an interesting note on their relationship, Emerson would later inscribe Carlyle's copy of *Society and Solitude*, "To the General in Chief from his Lieutenant," marking another place where he associates the representative with diminished power.

sentative, or rather, the difficulty of transcending history by any representative.

The sense of practicality expressed in the first of this volume's essays, "The Uses of Great Men," concedes the diminished status of his metaphoric hero.[38] The essay introduces the succeeding portraits by defining the terms of our relation and ties to the Great Man, or, in other words, making him represent us. Beginning the essay with a concession to our reverence for such heroes—"It is natural to believe in great men" (CW, 4: 3)—Emerson moves toward a surprising warning that the term *great men* itself "is injurious" (CW, 4: 17). As Perry Miller has commented on Emerson's representatives, "in the most American of fashions, [he] put them to work."[39] Emerson describes two types of service, direct and indirect. Rejecting the direct service of a teacher or institution, Emerson turns to indirect: "Men have a pictorial or representative quality, and serve us in the intellect. Behmen and Swedenborg saw that things were representative. Men are also representative; first of things, and secondly, of ideas" (CW, 4: 6).

Here Emerson's earlier discussion of the Poet's power of representation comes into play, but now he describes it in terms of the representative's relation to us:

> We speak now only of our acquaintance with them in their own sphere, and the way in which they seem to fascinate and draw to them some genius who occupies himself with one thing all his life long. The possibility of interpretation lies in the identity of the observer with the observed. Each material thing has its celestial side; has its translation through human-

[38] In *Myth and Literature in the American Renaissance* (Bloomington, Ind.: Indiana University Press, 1978), Robert Richardson, Jr., makes what has become a common claim about the Representative Man: "*Representative Men* illustrates Emerson's conviction . . . that 'the gods of fable are the shining moments of great men.' " I argue that Emerson presents a less exalted notion of the representative. Richardson's reading arises from the presupposition that in this volume, "Emerson was to make a serious effort at reconciling his recognition of greatness with his fervent democratic idealism." While I agree that *Representative Men* proposes an accommodation to social necessity, Emerson's intellectual scheme at this point in his career seems more a prototype of pragmatism than a form of idealism. On this aspect of Emerson, see A. J. Cascardi, "Emerson on Nature: Philosophy beyond Kant," *ESQ: A Journal of the American Renaissance* 30 (1984): 201–10.

[39] Miller, "Emersonian Genius," p. 82.

> ity into the spiritual and necessary sphere, where it plays a part as indestructible as any other. . . . But also the constituency determines the vote of the representative. He is not only representative but participant. Like can only be known by like. The reason why he knows about them, is that he is of them: he has just come out of nature, or from being a part of the thing. . . . Man made of the dust of the world does not forget his origin. (CW, 4: 7)

Emerson's theory of symbolic correspondence works here to subsume natural history and politics within the general problem of perception. On the one hand, scientific discoveries occur from an essential epistemological link between naturalist and physical object ("the identity of the observer with the observed"). However, this connection is determined by the metaphoric substitution carefully concealed within their identification: "*Like* can only be known by *like*." There can be no "original relation" between subject and object, observer and observed, "Me" and "Not me," in this argument because each term is derived indirectly, that is, through its representation. In other words, both subject and object are "like" but never identical.

Let me clarify this with a comparison to the argument of *Nature*. In that earlier essay, he argues for the role of nature as a phenomenal representation of Spirit. The essay's strategy is to take us from an initial perception of nature as an ontologically solid object of economic and aesthetic consumption, through its status as a sign or symbol, and finally to concern itself with the signified—Spirit. Nature and those other forms of the "Not me" have a necessary place, for they are also potential representations of the "Me" that allow it to become self-aware. However, in the course of this essay, as we achieve an "original relation" with Spirit through Reason's direct apprehension, as nature becomes transparent, representation becomes presentation. There can be no comparison, no "like" at this moment. If nature's opacity is allied to its representative form as the "Not Me," then transparency suggests the intuited state of being and vision—for they are here the same—that no longer requires representation or comparison.

Seen from a political point of view, the claim that "like can only be known by like" reminds us of an earlier passage from the journals: "All originality is relative. Every thinker is representative. Locke thinks for thousands just as much as Clay or Cushing at Washington vote for thousands. Show me the constituency & the invisible channels by which the senator is made aware of their wishes & it will bereave his fine attitude & resistance of something of its impressiveness" (JMN, 8: 67). At first this statement sounds oddly enough like the popular belief in mimetic representation: We vote for those who look or sound like us, or who are identifiable by some empirical tie to a geographical place or class association. But representation replaces the physical object with the conceptual sign, an act in which the intellect actually *conceives* of the identity between the two. The act of seeing the fitness between representation and represented object allies the naturalist and others, including the poet and voter. This is the class of those who live to the "beauty of the symbol; as the poet and artist, and naturalist, and man of science" (CW, 2: 132).

The representative, therefore, actually serves us in two ways. He re-presents the material world in the "necessary sphere" of the intellect by translating it into ideas. By locating the moral and physical laws to which material objects conform, he effects their metamorphosis from accidental and arbitrary signifiers to the determined laws of the signified—Spirit. However, the representative himself exists as a symbol as he represents each individual. We translate his actions into moral principles, making the discoveries of the scientists to correspond to our recognition of intellectual laws. "This class serve us," Emerson says, "so that they have the perception of identity and the perception of reaction" (CW, 4: 11). As representatives, men "are helpful through the intellect" by offering new perceptions of the world; however, "true genius will not impoverish, but will liberate, and add new senses" (CW, 4: 8, 11). Much like Emerson's earlier characterization of the poet, the representative *leads* in a temporal sense because he is the first to perceive universals and, in his words and actions, represents or expresses these ideas to others. As William Scheick has pointed out, in this section he is associated imagistically not only with explorers but also with cartographers.[40] The representative leads us

[40] William Scheick, *The Slender Human Word* (Knoxville: The Univ. of Tennessee Press, 1978), pp. 80–81.

and thereby leaves a trail, which is the institutionalized monument of his discovery.

There remains a danger in the perception of identity. In every act of perceiving identity we must overcome the basic quality of difference, serving as a kind of alloy to the cognitive act. This danger can be called misrepresentation, or the mistaking of the representative for the idea he represents: "The dominion of Aristotle, the Ptolemaic astronomy, the credit of Luther; of Bacon; of Locke; in religion, the history of hierarchies, of saints, and the sects which have taken the name of each founder, are in point. Alas, every man is such a victim" (CW, 4: 11). Although representatives can liberate us, we enslave ourselves when we worship their images or we confuse their personalities with their power.

Emerson responds to the failure of American representatives by inscribing a figure who does away with himself in the act of representation: "But I find him greater, when he can abolish himself and all heroes, by letting in this element of reason, irrespective of persons, this subtilizer and irresistible upward force, into our thought, destroying individualism;—the power so great, that the potentate is nothing. Then he is a monarch who gives a constitution to his people" (CW, 4: 14). He stands as representative when he bridges the world and Spirit. In so doing he ceases to be a static symbol, and we, as his constituents, cease to regard him as the signified, now only as the signifier. Or, as Emerson finally says at the end of his introduction, the "opake self becomes transparent with the light of the First Cause" (CW, 4: 20). We are the figural constituents for we create the representative through our intellect, trusting our own constitutions which create the rules of perception and action.

"Uses of Great Men" presents us with the light by which to read the subsequent biographies. Bridging the political and the poetic, this essay rephrases Emerson's concept of greatness in pragmatic terms. The entire volume serves as a philosophical extension of Emerson's theory of representation first presented in *Nature*, but with the emphasis now placed on the act of representation itself and its historical transformation. Fourteen years before *Representative Men*, Emerson made his most radical statement about the presence of Spirit, of which nature is a symbol. The succeeding years of tragedy and review revised not his belief in Spirit, but turned his attention to the acts of representation that mediate between Spirit and the intellect. His biographies of representatives, therefore, are analyses of the relational ties between these worlds, the bonds that make historical figures representative.

In *Representative Men*, the succession of portraits of Plato, Swedenborg, Montaigne, Shakespeare, Napoleon, and Goethe outlines a particular history of western civilization. Lacking any overt historical ties between these figures, Emerson establishes one term of their representativeness by the degree to which they are tied to their ages. When Carlyle wrote of his heroes, he claimed, they "are originally of one stuff; that only by the world's reception of them, and the shapes they assume, are they so immeasurably diverse."[41] Representatives, however, achieve a portion of their status and identity through their ages. With Spirit on one hand, and the world on the other, each figure is drawn toward both the liberation of Spirit and the bonds of the material world. To use Emerson's polarity, they struggle between the freedom of the intellect and the fate of the world and history.

The portrait in "Plato; or, the Philosopher" reveals the unconditional representative and resembles most strongly the American Scholar. Throughout *Representative Men*, Emerson appropriates the vocabulary of economics to distinguish those representatives who consume and those who produce. The metaphors describing Plato are those of consumption: "Plato . . . consumed his own times. What is a great man, but one of great affinities, who takes up into himself all arts, sciences, all knowables, as his food?" (CW, 4: 24). His devouring intellect effects the world's transmutation into the immutable ideas that his idealist offspring—Swedenborg, Kant, and Emerson himself—will then take up into themselves. The key to this essay, and the dichotomy which informs the entire volume, is Emerson's definition of Philosophy:

> Philosophy is the account which the human mind gives to itself of the constitution of the world. Two cardinal facts lie forever at the base; the One; and the two. 1. Unity or Identity; and, 2. Variety. We unite all things by perceiving the law which pervades them, by perceiving the superficial differ-

[41] Thomas Carlyle, *On Heroes, Hero-Worship, and the Heroic in History*, ed. Carl Niemeyer (Lincoln, Nebr.: Univ. of Nebraska Press, 1966), p. 43.

ences, and the profound resemblances. But every mental act,—this very perception of identity or oneness, recognizes the difference of things. Oneness and Otherness. It is impossible to speak, or to think without embracing both. (CW, 4: 27–28)

Plato's is the "balanced soul" that, Janus-faced, perceives both unity and variety. Unity "is the course or gravitation of mind"; variety, "the power of nature. Nature is the manifold. The unity absorbs and melts or reduces" (CW, 4: 29). Dialectic involves the discrimination of variety from identity, or false from true; Plato absorbed the manifold qualities of nature, transforming them into the unity of intellect and Idea. Analogously, monarchy is the rule of unity, democracy exalts variety as it seeks the otherness of the individual. As the mediating term between these polarities, representation creates variety, but it can only be known by the essential unifying identity between the represented object and its representation. The representations may be arbitrary in their material forms, but the signified coheres to them by necessity.

Plato, therefore, resembles the poet in that he is aware that "all things are symbolical" (CW, 4: 38). He "is clothed with the powers of a poet, . . . and (though I doubt he wanted the decisive gift of lyric expression,) mainly is not a poet because he chose to use the poetic gift to an ulterior purpose" (CW, 4: 25). This purpose is the ascension toward the Whole, Unity, or Identity, whereas the poet descends from perception of Identity to the task of expressing it in the multiplicity of nature and language. He exists as "the world's interpreter" (CW, 4: 34), interpreting its variety by translating it into his vision of unity. But Plato's desire to dispose of nature in favor of his eternal Ideas mistakes nature's diversity for weakness: "This is the ambition of Individualism. But the mouthful proves too large. Boa Constrictor has good will to eat it, but he is foiled. He falls abroad in the attempt; and biting gets strangled: the bitten world holds the biter fast by his own teeth. There he perishes, Unconquered Nature lives on and forgets him. So it fares with all: so must it fare with Plato" (CW, 4: 43). Nothing reveals Emerson's revision so much as this reading of Plato. *Nature*'s "noble doubt" of idealism that prepares the way for Spirit here revenges itself on Emerson. In his hubris, the philosopher cannot shake free of the world; each cognitive act ("the biter") devolves into its institutionalized memory ("the bitten world"). The representative cannot consume his own representative nature.

Plato presents the highest form of intellectual activity as he strives for Unity, escaping the world of variety and materialism. The subsequent biographies mark the declension of this power, the increasing subjugation of the representative to the world. In *Representative Men*, Emerson previews the vital conflict between individual and event, Power and Fate, Unity and Variety. As he recorded in a journal, and later made the cornerstone of his essay "Fate," "the secret of the world is the tie of person and event. Person makes event, & event person" (JMN, 11: 216). The role of his representatives, and of the concept of representation, is to determine the ties between self and world. The history of the symbol narrates its ever-increasing opacity: Beginning as a transparent referent of Unity and Spirit, the symbol becomes reified nature, consumed by the materialistic nineteenth century.

If Plato is the world's consumer, Swedenborg is its producer. He belongs to the class of poets "who, from the intellectual kingdom, feed the thought and imagination with ideas and pictures which raise men out of the world of corn and money, and console them for the shortcomings of the day, and the meanness of labour and traffic" (CW, 4: 53). The relationship between Plato and Swedenborg corresponds closely to the distinction between the American Scholar and Poet: Through his power of expression, the Poet calls the world into existence; the Scholar takes up that world into the necessary plane of the intellect. The two are complementary, but Emerson privileges knowledge over expression, for the Scholar is he who continually ascends. Plato stands on the circle's circumference, absorbing the symbols that Swedenborg, at the center, creates. As Emerson declares in "Uses of Great Men": "The centripetence augments the centrifugence. We balance one man with his opposite, and the health of the state depends on the see-saw" (CW, 4: 16). The continual outward movement toward the philosopher-scholar is augmented—that is, increased and complemented—by a contrary collapse toward the poet's centrality. The constant movement of the "see-saw" (or the biter and the bitten) enacts the perceptual activity of vision and memory, thought and expression. To place the distinction in aesthetic terms, "Art expresses the one or the same by the different. Thought seeks to know unity in unity; poetry to show it by variety, that is, always by an object or symbol" (CW, 4: 32).

As both poet and naturalist, Swedenborg belongs to the class described in "Prudence" of those who "live to the beauty of the symbol." In his transformation from naturalist to mystic, that is, in his incremental development as a cataloguer of nature through his doctrines of representation and correspondence, and finally to his description of the moral laws lying behind nature, Swedenborg "saw the poetic construction of things and the primary relation of mind to matter" (CW, 4: 80). Unlike Plato's idealism, Swedenborg's theories maintain the necessary *correspondence* between nature and Spirit, positing that we may know spiritual and moral truths through the study of nature. Having early on influenced the young Emerson, Swedenborg continued to exemplify intellect's power to find the essential ties between nature and Spirit. But Swedenborg's economy, dependent as it is on the production of symbols, remains a closed system: It "wants central spontaneity; it is dynamic not vital, and lacks power to generate life" (CW, 4: 74). Because his symbols refer only to individual theological concepts—"a horse signifies carnal understanding; a tree perception; the moon, faith"—there exists a mistaken belief in their power rather than in the power of the signified. "The slippery Proteus," as Emerson cautions us, "is not so easily caught. In nature, each individual symbol plays innumerable parts, as each particle of matter circulates in turn through every system. The central identity enables any one symbol to express successively all the qualities and shades of real being" (CW, 4: 68). Symbols are not mimetic, because they do not refer to single objects or ideas; rather, they express identity as the intellect conceives them to express its thoughts within a symbolic vocabulary.

Emerson's philosophy depends on its ability to convince us of the vital circulation, the eternal movement between Unity and variety. As the skeptic, Montaigne avoids the closure of thought in certainty, jeering at "all that is stable and good" (CW, 4: 90). "The philosophy we want," Emerson reiterates, "is one of fluxions and mobility" (CW, 4: 91). Since Stephen Whicher's book, *Freedom and Fate*, Emerson's portrait of Montaigne has come to be taken as a self-portrait, a picture like Dorian Gray's that takes on the darker hues of Emerson's increasing doubt. Caught between heads and tails—"Infinite and Finite; Relative and Absolute; Apparent and Real" (CW, 4: 85)—the skeptic chooses neither. The "right ground of the skeptic," as Emerson calls it, is actually no ground at all, but rather the momentary stance of doubt itself: "this of consideration, of selfcontaining, not at all of unbelief, not at all of universal denying, nor of universal doubting, doubting even that he doubts" (CW, 4: 90). The power of the skeptic lies in his interrogation of customs and rejection of materialist interpretations of the world. He scorns both the evils of society and its reformers. He represents those who learn "to look for the permanent in the mutable and fleeting" (CW, 4: 105).

Montaigne is not so much the ideal intellectual as one, like Plato and Swedenborg, who finds a philosophy to resist the human tendency toward materialism. "Skepticism is the attitude assumed by the student in relation to the particulars which society adores, but which he sees to be reverend only in their tendency and spirit" (CW, 4: 97). The scholar's perception of Unity belies society's belief in variety, making him, like Emerson himself, "a bad citizen." The representativeness of Montaigne and that of the first two figures arises from his representation of the best tendency of the age, his ability to elevate it and himself out of the material world.

In the following essay, "Shakespeare; or, the Poet," we find the relationship between spirit and world has tipped from cooperation to tyranny. Like "The Poet," this essay delimits the high cost of being representative.[42] Behind the essay's cool detachment lies Emerson's claim that Shakespeare is "perfect representation" as he suffers the "spirit of the hour to pass unobstructed through the mind" (CW, 4: 122, 110). The entire essay argues that "what is best written or done by genius in the world was no man's work, but came by wide social labour, when a thousand wrought like one, sharing the same impulse" (CW, 4: 114–15). The public, according to Emerson, demanded stage plays and Shakespeare obliged their vulgar tastes. Borrowing from his progenitors, he constructed his plays, and achieved popularity (unlike Montaigne) by re-present-

[42] See Sanford Marovitz, "Emerson's Shakespeare: From Scorn to Apotheosis," in *Emerson Centenary Essays*, ed. Joel Myerson (Carbondale, Ill.: Southern Illinois Univ. Press, 1982), pp. 122–55, for a discussion of Emerson's composition of this essay. I would reverse the emphasis of this title, from deification to doubt.

ing them. As pure representation, the poet becomes the organ of social expression without original thought.

To appreciate the derogatory tone of "Shakespeare," one need only compare it to Emerson's lectures on the poet, given on 10 and 17 December 1835. In those earlier lectures, Emerson had granted Shakespeare the power of his great men. Through his control over language and natural symbols, that Shakespeare embodies "the power of subordinating nature for the purpose of expression beyond all poets."[43] More important, however, Emerson, writing with the same liberating rhetoric of *Nature*, avoids any taint of society. As he wrote in his working notes, "So far from Shak[e]s[peare] sacrificing his own taste to the corrupt taste of the times, as is always said, he seems never to consult any taste but his own."[44] The gulf between the two Shakespeares, the self-reliant poet and the representative, reveals the social fate of Emerson's poet.

One finds in Shakespeare a poet who has the expressive power to represent the thoughts of the world in symbols, but not the intellectual power to contemplate the origins of the symbols themselves. Like other great poets, Shakespeare "saw the splendor of meaning that plays over the invisible world; knew that a tree had another use than for apples, and corn another than for meal, and the ball of the earth, than for tillage and roads: that these things bore a second and finer harvest to the mind, being emblems of its thoughts, and conveying in all their natural history a certain mute commentary on human life." Shakespeare, however, betrayed these symbols in the sensuality of the theater: "He rested in their beauty; and never took the step which seemed inevitable to such a genius, namely to explore the virtue which resides in these symbols and imparts this power,—What is that which they themselves say?" (CW, 4: 123–24). Using his "genius for the public amusement" (CW, 4: 125) implies the limits of such poetic representation. The degradation of the symbol from its correspondence to moral laws to its alienation on the stage marks the turning point in the history of representation and leaves Emerson despairing: "The world still wants its poet-priest" (CW, 4: 125).

In the final two chapters, Emerson turns to his own century, and

43 Emerson, *Early Lectures*, 1: 292.

44 Ibid., 1: 510.

divides his attention between Napoleon, "the man of the world," and Goethe, "its poet" (CW, 4: 156). These two representatives complete the diminishment of the powers of the representative, chronicling the containment of Napoleon's "external life and aims" as well as Goethe's inner power. For Emerson, Napoleon is not the great military leader or hero; rather he is both the "incarnate democrat" and the representative of the middle class, "the class of business-men in America, in England, in France, and throughout Europe; the class of industry and skill" (CW, 4: 129–30).[45] Befitting the material terms of his representation, Napoleon is both master and servant of his age: "A man of Napoleon's stamp," Emerson claims (using the metaphor that best expresses the emperor's mutual power of expression and tendency toward impression), "almost ceases to have a private speech and opinion" (CW, 4: 131). To illustrate the relationship between Napoleon and his followers, Emerson returns to Swedenborg's theory of correspondence:

> It is Swedenborg's theory that every organ is made up of homogeneous particles, or, as it is sometimes expressed, every whole is made of similars; that is, the lungs are composed of infinitely small lungs, the liver, of infinitely small livers, the kidney, of little kidneys, &c. Following this analogy, if any man is found to carry with him the power and affection of vast numbers, if Napoleon is France, if Napoleon is Europe, it is because the people whom he sways are little Napoleons. (CW, 4: 129)

If at first Napoleon sounds like Shakespeare as he expresses the "tone of thought and belief, the aims of masses of active and cultivated men," we soon realize that his is the mob's voice and he becomes, in his own words, "the creature of circumstances" (CW, 4: 129, 133).

At first Napoleon seems out of place among the writers and thinkers of history, but the theory of symbolic correspondence de-

[45] In the "Historical Introduction" to the fourth volume of Emerson's *Collected Works*, Wallace E. Williams has noted that the lecture on Napoleon was the first and most important of the series: "It is Napoleon rather than Plato or Shakespeare who precipitates both [the volume's] thesis and structure" (CW, 4: xxvii). See also my article, "Emerson, Napoleon, and the Concept of the Representative," *ESQ: A Journal of the American Renaissance* 31 (1985): 230–42.

scribes that relation through which the emperor derives his representative quality. The power of his representation grows out of his peculiar identification with his people, the "little Napoleons." As Emerson tells us in "Uses of Great Men," "Like can only be known by like," and the people sympathize with Napoleon, they follow him into battle, because they recognize themselves in him. At the same time, like the representatives of popular democracy, his position depends on his mimetic representation, his mirroring of the people. Because of the intimacy of the relationship, evoked by the metaphor of the stamp, the emperor himself is helplessly chained to the citizens in this bond of power. The concept of correspondence, in which "every whole is made of similars," accurately describes this relation as a kind of trope—synecdoche, in which the part resembles the whole. As an extreme form of metonymy, a synecdoche of this type describes the part and whole as formally identical. The identity of the part (Napoleon) can only be known as it refers to the whole (the people). Hence, Napoleon's identity and "real strength lay in [his countrymen's] conviction that he was their representative" (CW, 4: 139). Although he may appear to have the self-reliant autonomy of the Great Man, in fact Napoleon's office is created by the people.

Swedenborgian correspondence also illuminates Napoleon's association with the industrial class and Emerson's critique of its values. The economic subtext that runs throughout *Representative Men* surfaces in this essay to become not only an explicit criticism of middle-class materialism, but also places this habit of material expression within the scheme of symbolic representation. In the course of these essays, Emerson marks the evolution of economics from the simple food consumption and production of Plato and Swedenborg, through the economics of trade in Montaigne, to the industrialization of the nineteenth century. Like "a young Ohio or New York" (CW, 4: 139), Napoleon has the energy and disdain for conventions to compete for monopoly of the marketplace. He belongs to "the throng who fill the markets, shops, counting-houses, manufactories, ships, of the modern world, aiming to be rich" (CW, 4: 144). But the metaphor of the stamp with which Emerson characterizes the relationship between Napoleon and his followers represents the mode of capitalist production. First of all, the metaphor suggests the reification of the self into objects to be manipulated and consumed. The people see themselves mirrored in Napoleon, while he is, Emerson reminds us, "a worker . . . in buildings, in money and in troops" (CW, 4: 132). He turns his countrymen into objects, but they are objects stamped with his own image. He can never be original or autonomous, like the Emersonian Scholar, for his power resides in his eternally reproducible and mimetic image which is stamped on each citizen and each French coin. He turns out self-copies to be consumed by the masses of little Napoleons.

The point here is that Napoleon and the class he represents know only "the economic uses of things," failing to remember that because these objects are symbols, "they are [also] thoughts" (CW, 3: 12). Through Napoleon, Emerson criticizes the class of "common sense" who "live to the utility of the symbol; esteeming health and wealth a final good" (CW, 2: 132). He attacks them and their economic materialism by revealing their shallow epistemological roots. He critiques Napoleon as both object and subject of middle-class, common-sense symbolic perception which turns ideas into things. Napoleon reifies his followers, turning them first into soldiers and then corpses; they, in turn, reify him as the heroic embodiment of themselves and their desires. The danger of Napoleon that occasions Emerson's harsh attack on him as "a rogue" does not end with Napoleon's exile and death but remains within the middle class as a materialistic mode of perception, chaining the French and Americans to material ends, to the money and productions of capitalism.

To this point we can see *Representative Men* as a philosophical extension of Emerson's interest in representation most clearly expressed in *Nature*. Through the succession of biographies, beginning with Plato and ending with Goethe, Emerson delineates the history of representation: how these men have stood metonymically as agents within their ages. Increasingly, Emerson shows, even the great men are being tied to the material advances of their societies while forgetting their spiritual origins. In fact, one ought to approach this volume as *Nature* read backwards; instead of beginning with commodity and ending in idealism and Spirit, it begins with Plato's idealism and progresses toward Napoleon's use of the world as commodity. Thus with *Nature* in mind, we discover in each succeeding portrait the increasing opacity of the world, that is, its loss of symbolic possibilities and spiritual correspondence and the growing materialism of its representatives. Plato's idealism, Swedenborg's theory of symbolic correspondence, even Montaigne's skepticism, maintain the attachment between world and Spirit, always privileging Unity above variety. Shakespeare, however, most purely speaks for his age and becomes the "perfect representation." Finally, Napoleon exhibits the nineteenth century's closure of perception, its loss of symbolic awareness, and its reification of thought in capitalism.

Goethe, the literary complement to Napoleon, shares the emperor's "impatience and reaction of nature against the *morgue* of conventions" (CW, 4: 166). Yet if Goethe, like Napoleon, lacks the transparency of the First Cause, his writings remain translucent, for Emerson can see the blurred outlines of Spirit behind them. Like Plato, "he detected the Genius of life, the old cunning Proteus," constantly slipping from Unity to variety. Goethe converts Swedenborg's theory of correspondence to teach us "that every part of a plant is only a transformed leaf to meet a new condition." Moreover, unlike Napoleon, he was aware that the "striving after imitative expression . . . is mere stenography" (CW, 4: 158). However, Goethe most clearly represents the nineteenth-century writers and scholars in that he lacks the American talent for adventure and English practicality. Instead, like Emerson himself as he wrote *Nature*, he "never rests in a superficial performance, but asks steadily, to *what end*?" (CW, 4: 162). In reminding us of his representatives, Emerson keeps us in constant view of the spiritual ends of the scholar.

Behind this apparent praise, however, lies the dilemma of intellectuals in the modern world. We can hear Emerson, frustrated with his own weakness, railing against the conditions placed on him by society to its own endangerment: "Society has really no graver interest than the wellbeing of the literary class. . . . Still the writer does not stand with us on any commanding ground. I think this to be his own fault" (CW, 4: 155). Once sacred to society, the scholar is "no longer the lawgiver, but the sycophant, ducking to the giddy opinion of a reckless public." The choices open to the man of letters are those we have already seen in America: subservience or impotent reaction. On the one hand, he may "sustain with shameless advocacy some bad government," or he "must bark all the year round in opposition" (CW, 4: 155). Neither alternative frees the scholar nor allows him to free others.

Thus Emerson's true complaint of Goethe is that "this man was entirely at home and happy in his century and the world" (CW, 4: 165). He "is the type of culture, the amateur of all arts and sciences and events; artistic, but not artist; spiritual, but not spiritualist" (CW, 4: 163). In the end, Emerson judges Goethe's interests to be mere dalliance: He "was the philosopher of . . . multiplicity" (CW, 4: 156). If Plato achieves the balance of Unity and variety, East and West, Goethe "has not worshipped the highest unity; he is incapable of selfsurrender to the moral sentiment" (CW, 4: 163). Read diachronically, *Representative Men* has the ever-darkening tone of tragedy as the circles of history and necessity tighten around the scholar.

This initial reading supports the traditional view of Emerson's career, first put forward by Stephen Whicher, as bending to accommodation and necessity. For Whicher, Montaigne represents the questioning soul who sees the truth of both statement and counterstatement, reflecting Emerson's own vibrating dualism and sense of the unceasing character of the Protean dialectic. However, if the constantly diminishing power of these figures diachronically traces historical necessity, a synchronic reading reveals another pattern. In other words, as they express the intellectual conflicts and components of Emerson himself, they become representative of his inner biography. As Henry Nash Smith commented on the earlier generalized figures like the Transcendentalist, these Representative Men are "in some sense Emerson, and all of them are what Emerson strove toward as an ethical ideal."[46] In these portraits, Emerson remaps territory he had explored from his earliest years. Filling his journals with their quotations and with his own commentary, they had been his guide into spiritual territory. Plato and Swedenborg provided earlier philosophical directions toward idealism; in fact, Emerson's son, Edward, saw the greatest resemblance between his father and the description of Plato. Yet in a sense all these figures come to resemble their creator, for they provide not so much ideas as the vocabulary for Emerson to write his

[46] Henry Nash Smith, "Emerson's Problem of Vocation," in *Emerson: A Collection of Critical Essays*, ed. Milton Konvitz and Stephen Whicher (Englewood, Cliffs, N.J.: Prentice-Hall, 1962), pp. 64–65.

intellectual autobiography. Something of this sense of intellectual worth—of valuing but in the same judgment also devaluing—occurs in "Uses of Great Men": "For a time our teachers serve us personally, as metres or milestones of progress. Once they were angels of knowledge, and their figures touched the sky. Then we drew near, saw their means, culture, and limits; and they yielded their place to other geniuses" (CW, 4: 19).

In recalling the facets of Emerson's life, the biographies are revisionary not retrospective. Like Plato, Emerson absorbs these figures as food for his own thought. The structuring of these portraits reflexively reenacts the tensions and diversity of Emerson's intellect. He follows his essay on Swedenborg, in whom he had earlier believed, with the skepticism of Montaigne, modifying and alloying his youthful optimism with the wisdom of experience. But Swedenborg's theory of correspondence then provides the basis for his criticism of Napoleon. The complex system of interconnections created by this structuring causes unity to arise from unlimited diversity. Separately, these portraits present individual aspects of the poet, his vision, symbolism, powers of expression. Suspended together by Emerson's intellect, they represent the whole scholar who can discover and map the necessary relations between them, ties that correspond to the scholar's inner laws. Emerson himself acts as the magnet to order the relationships according to their relative merits.

Composing *Representative Men*, then, was an act of rewriting and editing the past according to Emerson's experience. Like Franklin's *Autobiography*, it marks an attempt to model by "recollecting" the self's development. Whereas Franklin institutionalized the self within the nation's bureaucracy, Emerson's autobiographical act recreates an impersonal, progressive self. We can see here the Scholar's autobiographical impulse to "comprehend" his influences in the grouping of these biographies. Jotting notes for his series of lectures, Emerson clearly shows that the figures were arranged to reflect and balance one another: "Plato philosopher, Swedenborg mystic, affirmer, Montaigne skeptic, Shakspeare poet, Napoleon practical *will make my circle*" (JMN, 9: 223; my emphasis). Pairings of essays like "Swedenborg" and "Montaigne" are subsumed within the "circle" of the entire work, which becomes the encompassing intellect. In "Uses of Great Men," Emerson again uses his circle metaphor to suggest the way this structure would create its own energy: "The centripetence augments the centrifugence. We balance one man with his opposite, and the health of the state depends on the see-saw" (CW, 4: 16). The eternal epistemological movement of Proteus—from the "see" of Unity to the "saw" of variety—reminds us of the provisional nature of the self balanced on the fulcrum of perception.

In a playful mood as *Representative Men* was nearing completion, Emerson listed the names of his historical representatives alongside a list of corresponding Concord residents, associating himself with Goethe.[47] As he had fifteen years previously in his "Historical Discourse at Concord," Emerson interweaves public history and local history, dissolving the distinction between biography and autobiography. He was later to say of Theodore Parker, "Every man's biography is at his own expense. We furnish not only the facts but the report. I mean that all biography is autobiography" (W, 11: 285). In line with his implicit autobiographical intention, the "I" is experiential rather than axiomatic.[48] The reader is made dependent on Emerson's judgment; he sees through Emerson's eyes. In this work Emerson extends what Franklin realized almost a century before: In a nation devoted to the reverence of the individual, self-representation becomes a necessary step towards freedom. He thus invests history with the laws of self-representation, the principles by which poetry and politics must act according to our inner constitutions. We can see *Representative Men* not as a capitulation to personal tragedy, social power, or historical necessity but as a work of reconsideration and reaffirmation in the face of public and private disillusionment.

* * *

This pattern of skepticism yielding to reaffirmation continued to be tested by the increasingly gloomy events of the pre-Civil War days. In 1850, soon after the publication of *Representative Men*, the Fugitive Slave Law provoked bitter comments from Emerson on American representatives. Betrayed by Daniel Webster, on whom

[47] See JMN, 11: 173: Emerson's comparisons include Plato and Bronson Alcott, Swedenborg and Jones Very, Shakespeare and Charles King Newcomb, Montaigne and Ellery Channing, Napoleon and Henry Thoreau.

[48] Lawrence Buell, *Literary Transcendentalism* (Ithaca: Cornell Univ. Press, 1973), pp. 279, 296.

he had once planned to lecture, Emerson now reaffirmed the representative's determined status as he claims Webster "truly represents the American people just as they are, with their vast material interests, materialized intellect and low morals" (JMN, 11: 385). Emerson's angry rejection can only be attributed to the intensity of his earlier expectations. The political conflicts during the 1850s, the inexorable slide toward war, only exacerbated his disgust with Americans and their representatives, making him question even his idealism: "When judges do not judge; when governors do not govern; when Presidents do not preside, but sell themselves to somebody who bargains to make them Presidents again; when the People do not elect, but suffer a Caucus to take from them the trouble of electing, &, worst of all, when Representatives do not represent, what matters how good or wise the theory may be" (JMN, 14: 421–22). If Emerson had heard George Bancroft's eulogy of Andrew Jackson as "the representative, for his generation, of the American mind," it must have been with a bitter nod of assent.[49] Emerson could no longer ignore the disparity between the idea of democracy and its facts.

Perhaps the final irony in Emerson's search for true representatives and representation can be seen by looking briefly at two who arose late in his career: John Brown and Abraham Lincoln. The irony is that neither man could lead America out of the miasma of war or reconstruction: When Emerson lectured on these two men, Brown was condemned to death, Lincoln was already dead. Giving his speeches on John Brown, Emerson revived his vocabulary, calling Brown "a representative of the American Republic" (W, 11: 259). But the terms of Brown's representation are his expression of America's achievements and possibilities. In his first lecture, Emerson traced Brown's ancestry from the Pilgrims' landing, through the Revolutionary War, into the War of 1812, in short, through the mythic events of American history. In his idealism and ability to see "how deceptive the forms are," Brown has the symbolizing vision to escape the materialism of American society. Finally, in his second address, Emerson transforms Brown into a type of Leatherstocking: "He learned the manners of animals and knew the secret signals by which animals communicate. He made

[49] Quoted in Meyers, *Jacksonian Persuasion*, p. 4.

his hard bed on the mountains with them" (W, 11: 261). Yet as a shepherd, rather than hunter, he remains a Christ-like figure already condemned to suffer for America's sins.

In John Brown, Emerson found an idealist who could act according to his inner moral principles; in Lincoln he found a "man of the people" who elevated them as he represented. Ironically, Emerson came to this judgment after he had previously been unimpressed with Lincoln.[50] Like John Brown, Lincoln was purely American, born and raised in the mythic wilderness. Lincoln becomes in Emerson's vision the representative of the middle class standing in opposition to Napoleon's materialism: "This middle-class country had got a middle-class president at last. Yes in manners and sympathies but not in powers, for his powers were superior. This man grew according to the need. His mind mastered the problem of the day; and as the problem grew, so did his comprehension of it. Rarely was the man so fitted to the event" (W, 11: 311–12). The allusion to "Fate" in this passage reveals Lincoln's intellectual power of "comprehension," that is, his ability to contain the world and transform it in his mind. In one final passage, the idealistic figure of the earlier Emerson is once again briefly embodied in Lincoln: "He stood a heroic figure in the centre of a heroic epoch. He is the true history of the American people in his time. Step by step he walked before them; slow with their slowness, quickening his march by theirs, the true representative of his country, the pulse of twenty millions throbbing in his heart, the thought of their minds articulated by his tongue" (W, 11: 313). Always leading, never led, he symbolizes the best of an age, incorporates a people within him, expressing their best thoughts. In this remarkable description, Emerson himself participates in Lincoln's greatness, mediates between it and the people, and, for the last time, becomes the representative he sought to define.

[50] See Ralph Rusk, *The Life of Ralph Waldo Emerson* (New York: Columbia Univ. Press, 1949), pp. 414–15, for Emerson's initial dislike of Lincoln.

CHAPTER SIX

Herman Melville: The Authority of Confidence

It is perhaps only a literary critic's wishful thinking that Herman Melville's transcendentalist confidence-man, Mark Winsome, resembles a portrait of Emerson. Yet Melville's character from *The Confidence-Man* points out how easily the Emersonian rhetoric of power and self-reliance, a rhetoric that empties itself of practical meanings and references, could be taken up by the industrialists to justify their materialism.[1] Or we may want to see Ahab, glorying in his "inexorable self," as another parodic echo of Emersonian idealism as he exclaims, "What things real are there but imponderable thoughts."[2] My point is not that there is some recoverable line of influence between these two writers but that conditions in Jacksonian America established a rhetoric where their interests converged. Jacksonian America provided a common medium of political, social, and economic turmoil that strained each writer's literary strategies. Emerson's gradual metamorphosis from icono-

[1] On the possible connections between Emerson and Winsome, see Merton M. Sealts, Jr., "Melville and Emerson's Rainbow," *ESQ: A Journal of the American Renaissance* 76 (1980): 53–78, and Tom Quirk, *Melville's Confidence Man: From Knave to Knight* (Columbia, Mo.: Univ. of Missouri Press, 1982), pp. 126–28.

[2] Herman Melville, *Moby-Dick; or, The Whale*, ed. Harrison Hayford and Hershel Parker (New York: W. W. Norton, 1967), pp. 423–33. (Hereafter cited in text as MD.)

clast to sage reflects an accommodation to society's demands. Melville moved defiantly in the opposite direction. Deriding early successes like *Typee* and *Redburn* as "nursery tale[s]," Melville complained to Hawthorne that "what I feel most moved to write, that is banned,—it will not pay."[3] When he came to write the books he wanted, the public found not their own ideas in some alienated majesty but their neurotic compulsions and fears. His "strange vagaries," as one reviewer called his later works, became increasingly more aggressive in their willful mystification.[4]

What remains constant in their writings is American democracy, especially the increasing political chaos of the 1840s and 1850s. Rather than insist on Melville's works as simple political allegories, I want to describe how they recreate the complex relationships between authority, autonomy, and representation by engaging the highly charged rhetoric of the day.[5] Ahab is not Andrew Jackson, but the *Pequod* is a ship of state in which captain and crew act out a variety of political relationships. Moreover, Melville himself engages us as readers in narrative relationships that reenact the bonds of authority and obedience of the novels. Beginning with *Moby-Dick,* Melville creates an essential link between his narrative strategy and the world represented in the narrative. The kinds of communication that occur in his novels, the commands between captain and crew and the subtle equivocations of the confidence game, reenact the relationship between Melville's narrator and the reader. Ishmael and Ahab, the narrator of *The Confidence-Man* and his hero, share the same desire to establish their authority over a compliant and credulous audience. Confidence and belief become the prizes for which they struggle; language, both the battleground and the weapon. The "real clash," to borrow from Nabokov, "is not between the characters but between the author and the world."[6] Beginning with Ishmael's assertive playfulness, the nar-

[3] *The Letters of Herman Melville,* ed. Merrell B. Davis and William H. Gilman (New Haven: Yale Univ. Press, 1960), pp. 93, 128.

[4] Watson G. Branch, ed., *Melville: The Critical Heritage* (London: Routledge and Kegan Paul, 1974), p. 378.

[5] The best research on Melville's relationship to the political and social issues of his time is Michael Paul Rogin's *Subversive Genealogy* (Berkeley: Univ. of California Press, 1983).

[6] Vladimir Nabokov, *Speak, Memory* (New York: G. P. Putnam's Sons, 1960), p. 290.

rative voice in Melville's works becomes progressively more equivocal and sinister. Finally, in *The Confidence-Man*, Melville abandons the confidential tone of *Redburn* and the powerful rhetoric of *Moby-Dick* for the confidence-man's insinuating ventriloquism.

Melville tests the possible variations in the conflict between authority and obedience (the institutional and psychological terms of social control) and between the "inexorable self" of autonomy and the conditioned self of heteronomy (the individual's experience of simultaneous freedom and control). Between Ahab's demand for "instantaneous obedience" (MD, 129) and the confidence-man's game of possession lies the faint hope of democratic friendship which unites people in political ties of sympathy and common interests. Although these issues are present in almost every work of Melville, they are most clearly presented in *Moby-Dick* and *The Confidence-Man*. In the following chapter, the two aspects of fictional authority—the vision of authority found in his novels and the relationship of authority in which we as readers participate—reinforce each other. Like Charles Brockden Brown before him, Melville employs his narrative authority as a means to implicate his readers in subtly political relations.

Ishmael and Narrative Authority in *Moby-Dick*

Emerson's prose has the air of resonant absence about it, but we experience it as assertive and imperative. We find it unsettling because we feel commanded to some unkown mission. Unable to locate the voice of authority outside of us, we should seek it within our self-reliance. *Moby-Dick* too begins with an imperative, but its first line, "Call me Ishmael," unsettles us because its familiarity carries with it the force of command.[7] Uncertain of our true relation to the speaker, we hesitate momentarily in order to determine whether we are addressed as peers or subordinates. Contained in this command are questions of authority and compliance which

[7] The first chapter has prompted a number of excellent discussions. Of particular interest are Howard P. Vincent, *The Trying-Out of Moby-Dick* (New York: Houghton Mifflin, 1949; Kent, Ohio: Kent State Univ. Press, 1980), p. 55; Paul Brodtkorb, Jr., *Ishmael's White World* (New Haven, Conn.: Yale Univ. Press, 1965), p. 51; Warner Berthoff, *The Example of Melville* (Princeton: Princeton Univ. Press, 1962), pp. 119–21; Warwick Wadlington, *The Confidence Game in American Literature* (Princeton: Princeton Univ. Press, 1975), pp. 87–92.

proceed from the absence of the speaker. To whom are we granting authority? What are Ishmael's qualities that we can judge and warrant? What are the consequences of our acquiesence?

Confronted with a speaker of ambiguous intentions, we are doubly mystified by his assumption of an obviously fictive name. With this self-assured gesture, Ishmael almost capriciously teases those readers who, like Melville's upstanding publisher John Murray, wish to believe his "books are not fictions."[8] Ishmael's control exhibited in the first sentence includes our access to the facts in the second: "Some years ago—never mind how long precisely—having little or no money in my purse, and nothing particular to interest me on shore, I thought I would sail about a little and see the watery part of the world." Ishmael's elusiveness, combined with his insistence that he set the limits of our knowledge, makes us dependent on his disembodied voice.

Ishmael's appropriation of this fictive name by which he authors himself, contradicts the claims of verisimilitude that Melville had made in his earlier first-person narratives, *Typee, Omoo*, and *White-Jacket*. This first-person narration introduces us to a different world from those novels as it orients us to Ishmael in a special way. Besides warranting Ishmael's recounting of his past life, the autobiographical narration permits him to speak without hesitation to us, drawing us into the story through the rush of his words, or, perhaps more accurately, weaving us into the design of his narrative. Unlike Melville's earlier narrators who had insisted on the truth of their stories, Ishmael purposely blurs the borders of fact and fiction, always testing the boundaries of our credibility without irrevocably crossing them. Whereas a third-person narrator is in a sense the product of the narrative itself, a first-person narrator like Benjamin Franklin in his autobiography has an independent existence.[9] Third-person narration blends past and present tenses into an imagined here and now; first-person retains the pluperfect and perfect layers of memory so that a narrator like Ishmael can look back on his younger days with experiential irony.[10]

[8] Murray's letter to Melville is found in Merrell B. Davis, *Melville's Mardi: A Chartless Voyage* (New Haven, Conn.: Yale Univ. Press, 1952), p. 61.

[9] See Käte Hamburger's study of narrative in *The Logic of Literature*, trans. Marilynn J. Rose (Bloomington, Ind.: Indiana Univ. Press, 1973), esp. pp. 58–59.

[10] Ibid., pp. 66–69, 100.

For my purpose, first-person narration is most significant in its ability to create, in Dorrit Cohn's words, an "existential relationship" with the reader.[11] In contrast to third-person narratives, which create a world neither past nor present, a first-person narration focuses on the present moment of utterance. There is a "real" voice here that assumes (in both senses of the word) a listener. Käte Hamburger has made the distinction between third-person (her term is epic) fiction, which is a mimesis or semblance of reality, and first-person narrative, which is a "feigned reality statement." In a feigned reality statement, she claims, "the first person narrator can speak about other persons only as objects. He can never free them from his own experience field."[12] Ishmael's apparent disregard for this rule does not disprove it, but instead clearly shows the nature of his narrative as both an autobiographical recovery of his experience and its fictive interpretation.

The obvious, oft-made point about Ishmael's play with the rules of fiction is that it calls attention to the nature of fiction itself.[13] However, since this narrative is grounded in the present tense, Ishmael's first sentence arrests us not only because the narrator assumes a fictional identity, but, more importantly, because he *commands* us to give him that identity.[14] We are immediately implicated in Ishmael's story almost against our will. His pressing directive subordinates the question of his fictiveness while establishing a bond of intimacy between himself and the reader. It matters less that Ishmael is a persona than that he has the power to command our cooperation. In short, the issue that confronts us first in *Moby-Dick*, even before Ahab steps out onto the quarter-deck, is not the interpretation of fiction but its authority.

As a speech act, Ishmael's first command sets the terms by which we evaluate his speech. An illocutionary act such as a warning, greeting, promise, or command, carries with it its own communicative purpose satisfied by the verbal gesture itself. Moreover, the

[11] Dorrit Cohn, *Transparent Minds* (Princeton: Princeton Univ. Press, 1978), p. 144.

[12] Hamburger, *Logic*, p. 313.

[13] On Melville's attitude toward fiction see Edgar Dryden, *Melville's Thematics of Form* (Baltimore: Johns Hopkins Univ. Press, 1968), pp. 151–95, and Nina Baym, "Melville's Quarrel with Fiction," *PMLA* 94 (1979): 909–23.

[14] See Cohn, *Transparent Minds*, p. 198, for her discussion of the "evocative present," the momentary illusion of the present tense in first-person narration.

act telescopes intention and performance: If I wish to promise something, my utterance "I promise X" offers both my intention to promise and the actual promise itself. Underlying each illocutionary act are the rules and conventions governing the act's meaning for speaker and listener. Saying "I do" in a marriage ceremony has meaning only because the various cultural conventions, laws, and the couple's beliefs infuse them with meaning. Likewise, my promise is legitimate only if the person to whom I promise accepts the reciprocating conditions of the promise. This act warrants these conditions and reiterates the relationship between the participants. In a command, there must be a commander who utters the speech act and a subordinate who literally "under-stands" the rules legitimizing the act. Obedience warrants the positions and reinforces the conventional identities of the actors as well as the power of the rules themselves.

Returning to Ishmael's first sentence, we see its position calls attention to the nature of our relationship with the speaker. Ishmael's request (for it may be only that) relies on our trust in the conventions of fiction (the introduction of the narrator), cultural traditions (that of the Biblical Ishmael), and language (the efficacy of a speech act). But our dependence reveals the arbitrariness of the rules which construct his authority. Like Ishmael and Queequeg tied by the monkey-rope, we are joined to the narrator as in a "joint stock company of two" (MD, 271). And like them our security is balanced by our loss of autonomy. Ishmael's insistent control over the narrative continually emphasizes the contingencies of the relationship: Bound to him, we are always reminded of our precarious position.

Establishing narrative authority, then, raises the immediate question of the reader's autonomy and self-sufficiency. In addition, the locutionary act elides the problem of the narrator's veracity, replacing it instead with the issue of his success at creating and sustaining this bond of authority. Without being completely aware of it, we have entered a novel in which the principal issues involve authority, obedience, belief, and the question of failure or success. In a novel that becomes increasingly concerned with Ahab's authority over his crew, Ishmael's first words precipitate the action and set the rules. He becomes, in other words, the linguistic and imaginative counterpart of Ahab himself.

Even with the wealth of possible consequences contained in this first sentence, we read Ishmael's command without stopping to consider its effect on us and the future events of the novel. But the circularity of the narrative (one of the novel's many circles) inevitably brings us back to the beginning and Ishmael's intention for telling the story. To use Edward Said's term, Ishmael's beginning is "transitive" as it "foresees a continuity that flows from it. This kind of beginning is suited for work, for polemic, for discovery."[15] We return to the beginning of *Moby-Dick* after the destruction of the *Pequod* and the salvation of Ishmael aware of the import of these preliminary actions. Like Clara Wieland's narrative, Ishmael's goal is to recover events in order to understand the causal links between intention and consequences. In part he seeks to understand Ahab and Ahab's vision of the whale "as the monomaniac incarnation of all those malicious agencies which some deep men feel eating in them" (MD, 160). Thus, for him and the reader, the actual battle with Moby Dick, suspended (with the emphasis on the suspense) through long descriptions of whaling, is a return to a beginning and the recreation of intention, because we see and experience for the first time the impetus for the voyage in Ahab's antagonist. Yet despite its obvious importance as the agency for Ishmael's confrontation with natural and personal extremities, Ahab's story is contained within Ishmael's search for his own motivation: "Chief among these motives was the overwhelming idea of the great whale himself" (MD, 16). The distinction between Ahab's goal and Ishmael's is crucial. Ahab seeks revenge on Moby Dick; Ishmael is driven by the "idea" of the whale and his desire to represent it. Their stories are woven together, but each must be understood to unfold independently, both temporally and generically, of the other. The goal of Ishmael's narrative is not revenge but representation and revelation.

The relationship between authority and intention (Ishmael's term is "purpose") helps distinguish the two forms of authority at stake here by their differing goals. The complete title, *Moby-Dick; or, the Whale,* neatly describes the either/or paradigm that informs the two narratives. Ahab's quest for Moby Dick finds its parallel in

[15] Edward Said, *Beginnings: Intention and Methods* (New York: Basic Books, 1975), p. 76.

Ishmael's search and research for the "Whale." Even as Ahab's presence rules over the narrative of the *Pequod*'s voyage, the cetology chapters function as the field of action for Ishmael's labor. The capture and trying-out of the whole form a frequently comic analogue to Ahab's mad hunt for Moby Dick. The cetology chapters act as the warp of the novel's fabric, while Ahab's story is the inflexible, goal-directed, and linear woof. Provisionally, then, for the distinction between the two forms of authority—Ahab's institutional and charismatic authority and Ishmael's epistemic and narrative authority—Ishmael's position as the first-person narrator provides the parodic distance from which to view Ahab's control on board the ship.

Even as the first sentence of "Loomings" raises the question of authority and represents it as a fait accompli, the remainder of the first chapter sets the course we will follow. Ishmael's assertive presence is particularly remarkable because his voice fades in and out of the narrative, losing its distinct identity and sense of personal continuity in chapters like "The Quarter-Deck," then reaffirming its existence apart from the *Pequod* as (and because) it tells the *Town-Ho*'s story. His power as a storyteller comes from the high degree of sympathy he shares with his subjects, a quality that we see in his power of mimicry. Although he will later assume the parts of pedant and tragedian, in "Loomings" Ishmael's voice and concerns are authoritative. His first command is repeated in a number of imperatives: "Look," "Go," "Circumambulate," "Take," and so on. Most striking is his use of the imperative "Look," the same directive that Ahab continually speaks to his men as a means to attract and focus their attention. Ishmael's role as the reader's cicerone, revealed through his imperative, guiding language, is necessitated by our dependence on him. As he commands us to see the crowds "fixed in ocean reveries," we participate in the central perceptual act of the novel.

Characteristically, Ishmael subverts his authority, never letting us rest secure in his vision. By alternating command and question, Ishmael continues to set the rules of his narrative but also keeps the conventions before us as if a reminder of our necessary part in his work. The rhetorical quality of some questions momentarily disengages us from his voice. Other questions—for example, "Who ain't a slave?"—reveal the linguistic resemblance between speech act and question.[16] A speech act contains a number of unspoken questions about its appropriateness to which the listener must respond in order to complete the act successfully. In *Moby-Dick*, questions function aggressively at decisive moments to capture attention and win assent, as when, for example, Ahab's litany of questions to his men on the quarter-deck subtly unites captain and crew in an awareness of their common purpose. Ishmael's questions, on the other hand, demand a less authoritarian, more conditional, assent on our part.

Finally, the first chapter introduces Ishmael's role as a common seaman and participant within the distinct hierarchies of authority aboard the ship. Our subordination to Ishmael's narrative becomes the analogue to his own acknowledgment of the inevitable loss of autonomy within the institutions and relationships of society:

> What of it, if some old hunks of a sea-captain orders me to get a broom and sweep down the decks? What does that indignity amount to, weighed, I mean, in the scales of the New Testament? . . . Well, then, however the old sea-captains may order me about—however they may thump and punch me about, I have the satisfaction of knowing that it is all right; that everybody else is one way or the other served in much the same way—either in a physical or metaphysical point of view. (MD, 15)

Perceiving the world as a vast chain of command, Ishmael belligerently makes us question our allegiances and ties, even as we submit to his authority. Recognizing the inevitable but fluid ties between authority and autonomy, Ishmael introduces us to the law of the sea: We are loose-fish and fast-fish too.

"Loomings" fulfills part of its implied function by anticipating the various voices and forms of authority and autonomy in the novel. It fulfills the other function by weaving our compliance into the fabric of the novel itself. Ishmael's narrative authority, by which I mean the reader's initial understanding and acceptance of the narrative's particular conventions and ground rules, becomes

[16] For the relationship between illocutionary acts and questions see Paul Ricoeur, *Interpretation Theory* (Fort Worth, Tex.: Texas Christian Univ. Press, 1976), p. 14, and Mary Louise Pratt, *Toward a Speech Act Theory of Literary Discourse* (Bloomington, Ind.: Indiana Univ. Press, 1977), p. 13.

only one of a number of relationships involving authority in the novel. Institutions, families, most relationships, create the hierarchies of command and subordination; Ishmael seeks to uncover the source and powers of those relationships tying individuals together in the *Pequod*'s doomed enterprise. To understand the extent to which these issues of authority and autonomy underlie Melville's other works and their particular relevance to *Moby-Dick*, I mean to trace the gradual evolution of Captain Ahab as his supreme commander.

Authority and Obedience from *Typee* to *Moby-Dick*

Part of the power of Melville's earlier works (*Typee, Omoo*, and *Mardi*) lies in the rather peculiar confrontation between the descriptive realism of the novels and the escapist adventure of romance. Confrontation seems the appropriate word because resistance to the confining, ordered life of shipboard life becomes the impetus for escape into the romance of South Sea society. For Tommo, Omoo, and Taji, the three protagonists of these early novels, life aboard ship is routinized, oppressive, and institutional. In an odd way, this is the world of the novel of manners, a theatrical world in which identity is acted out according to prescribed roles with the captain as the tyrannical director. Seeking open-ended freedom and adventure, rather than the strictures of society, these heroes rebel against their father-captains because of their superiors' demands and rules. In *Typee*, for example, Tommo defends his desertion from the *Dolly* by calling the captain's actions "unmitigated tyranny."[17] Under similar circumstances, Omoo and Taji escape the structured world of shipboard authority. Having seen the most artificial and extreme forms of authority aboard whalers and U.S. navy ships, Melville remained fascinated by the consequences of rebellion.

Seeking freedom, each of these protagonists cannot avoid the ties of authority but merely moves from one form of subordination to another. Restricted by the taboos of the Typee, crippled by physical pain, Tommo regresses to childlike dependence on his

[17] Herman Melville, *Typee*, ed. Harrison Hayford et al. (Evanston, Ill.: Northwestern Univ. Press and Newberry Library, 1968), p. 21.

captors. Only after the threat to his own identity by the tattooing of the natives does Tommo escape. Taji, a rover like Tommo and Omoo, deserts his ship only to be drawn into an endless search for Yillah, a feminine embodiment of metaphysical truth who represents absolute freedom. What unites these characters is the fact that rebellion quickly assumes another form of authority. The seeming impossibility of achieving freedom and autonomy spurs them on searches that contradict their intentions. Like Ishmael's pointed question, "Who ain't a slave?" these novels propose a similar problem: In what ways does the search for freedom serve to enslave us?

The following two stories, *Redburn* and *White-Jacket*, also use the ordered shipboard society to explore the extremes of a codified, legalistic authority as it impinges on an individual's sense of freedom and identity.[18] However, these works clearly anticipate the full expression of these questions in *Moby-Dick* (published two years later) as they combine the theme of rebellion from authority with a subtle dramatization of the hidden springs of compliance and command. What interests Melville, it seems, is not simply obedience or rebellion but the psychological forces of repressed fear and anger against paternal rule that twists obedience to rules into a subservience to overpowering personalities. Moreover, as he asks why the crew should be in awe of a malicious personality like Jackson in *Redburn*, Melville also depicts the degeneration of legitimate authority into the despotic tyranny maintaining the structured order aboard the *United States* in *White-Jacket*: That ship "is no limited monarchy, where the sturdy commons have a right to petition, and to snarl if they please; but almost a despotism, like the Grand Turk's." The source of this hierarchical order is the captain: "The captain's word is law; he never speaks but in the imperative mood."[19] Here, and more explicitly in *Moby-Dick*, the captain's authority hinges on his ability to make language an agent of his office, or, to put it more extremely, to make language itself the authority as it presents and maintains the captain as the representative of institutionalized laws, themselves constructed out

[18] Michael Rogin has detailed the intricate interconnections of paternal and institutional authority in *Subversive Genealogy*, chapters 2 and 3.

[19] Herman Melville, *White-Jacket*, ed. Harrison Hayford et al. (Evanston, Ill.: Northwestern Univ. Press and Newberry Library, 1970), p. 23.

of language. Like Eve Effingham, Melville asks what happens when the codes of authority maintained by that language support tyranny.

In these novels, however, the eloquence of law—Weber's rational-legal authority—is challenged by the unarticulated and charismatic authority of personality. Sustained by psychological factors and expressed in the subtle, volatile bonds between actors, charisma involves the linking of desires, perhaps the transfer of filial affections of a son onto the image of another, who uses those feelings to maintain his own desire for mastery. In *Redburn* and *White-Jacket*, Melville presents these two competing forms of authority as the struggle between the aristocratic and democratic. On the one hand, the captain stands aloof as the delegated, but absolute, dictator; Captain Claret of *White-Jacket* and Captain Riga of *Redburn* are despotic representatives of naval law who manipulate the forms of their office to maintain order, as well as to achieve personal ends. In contrast to them stand the democratic leaders of the crew: Jack Chase of *White-Jacket* and Jackson in *Redburn*. Between them they exhibit the possibilities of democratic leadership to be enlightened and benevolent (in the case of Chase) or to achieve its power through demagoguery, coercion, and fear (as does Jackson).

Aboard the *Highlander* both Captain Riga and Jackson attract young Wellingborough Redburn. For the fatherless Redburn, Captain Riga initially presents an image of possible paternal affection: "I had made no doubt that he would in some special manner take me under his protection, and prove a kind friend and benefactor to me; as I had heard that some sea-captains are fathers to their crew."[20] Like Melville himself, Redburn is the son of a ruined merchant, the scion of an aristocratic American family, and he expects the deference to family ties that society once held. And like Fenimore Cooper, Redburn discovers the power of patrimony no longer exists in this country. In a series of disappointments, Redburn's images of paternal authority and his ties to the past—his father's guidebook, the statue of Admiral Nelson, England itself—

[20] Herman Melville, *Redburn: His First Voyage*, ed. Harrison Hayford et al. (Evanston, Ill: Northwestern Univ. Press and Newberry Library, 1969), p. 67. (Hereafter cited in text as RB.)

are shown not only to be worthless to Redburn but also corrupt and oppressive.

In Jackson, Melville provides Redburn with an alternative to the paternal image of the aristocratic Riga. Like Welbeck and Arthur Mervyn, Jackson frees Redburn from his family while subjecting the young hero to a power lying outside the legal forms of his rank or the traditional duties of family. Whereas Tommo's flight from authority leads to childlike dependence, Redburn discovers the uncanny and contradictory rule of Jackson: "He had," Redburn says, "such an over-awing way with him; such a deal of brass and impudence, such an unflinching face . . . he was by nature a marvelously clever, cunning man, though without education; and understood human nature to a kink" (RB, 57). Unlike the benign vision of Jack Chase, Jackson "seemed to be full of hatred and gall against every thing and every body in the world; as if all the world was one person, and had done him some dreadful harm, that was rankling and festering in his heart" (RB, 61). We see here the prototype of Ahab's monomania, his projection of inner anger onto the world, and the resulting fascination over the sailors who find some link with him. Both Jackson and Ahab combine keen penetration into human drives with their own overwhelming and compelling sense of the world's ultimate malevolence.

Jackson's power over the men arises from his very bitterness and anger. "His wickedness," Redburn comes to understand, "seemed to spring from his woe" (RB, 105). Jackson's horror and power, like Ahab's, is the "woe that is madness" (MD, 355), which holds a demonic fascination for Ishmael. Jackson uses his rage to control his subordinates, but there seems to be no particular origin for his anger. We glimpse the general source of Jackson's woe by looking at the world Redburn encounters. Poverty, social injustice, and oppression flourish in England just as Redburn himself experiences the humiliation of poverty in America. Deformed by his hate, Jackson nevertheless comes to mirror the bitterness and impotent defiance felt by all. The sailors obey him first of all because he has the institutional authority of office, but they remain in awe of him because he represents their own frustrated lives. In Michael Bell's words, he "is a democratic leader, exerting power not through the channels of institutionalized authority, as does Captain Riga, but through his almost magnetic authority over the minds of the men."[21]

It is in Redburn himself that we see Jackson's ability to capture and represent the desires of another. Like Arthur Mervyn before him, Redburn's poverty and diffidence drive him from the impotent paternal authority and corrupt institutions into Jackson's power. Jackson terrifies the young man, in part, because he becomes Redburn's alter ego. As he begins the voyage, Redburn admits, "I began to feel a hatred grown up in me against the whole crew—so much so, that I prayed against it, that it might not master my heart completely, and so make a fiend of me, something like Jackson" (RB, 62). The danger of Redburn's transformation into another Jackson reiterates the fear of democratic leadership held by many men of letters. The identification of representative and constituent here restates Emersonian representation as the constituent's will to power. The curious bond between Welbeck and Arthur Mervyn, Cooper's demagogues, and Emerson's description of Napoleonic power expresses the writers' constant skepticism in democracy's ability to create legitimate ties of authority. Subverting the already degenerating ties of family and the oppressive authority of institutions, democracy relies on extrainstitutional means of exacting obedience. Psychological coercion, flattery, social pressure replace the rule-bound directives of a traditional or rational-legal society.

Disillusioned with Captain Riga, fearful that his resentment will overpower him like Jackson's, Redburn searches for a way to escape dependency. Comparing his position with that of a young Chartist, he contemplates revolution: "I thought he must be some despairing elder son, supporting by hard toil his mother and sisters; for of such men political desperadoes are made" (RB, 206). But Redburn turns out to be neither a revolutionary nor a self-destructive tyrant like Jackson. What has been missing from this discussion up to this point is a third term, the mediating point between absolute authority and complete dependence. Like Ishmael, Redburn is an isolatoe, although one trying desperately to associate himself with the past and rise in society. We must remember

[21] Michael D. Bell, "Melville's Redburn: Initiation and Authority," *New England Quarterly* 46 (1973): 568.

that subordination is not the only political relationship; the body politic can also be based on the equality of its members. That is, friendship, as Ronald Beiner has pointed out, is "the political relationship par excellence."[22] Working from Aristotle's conception of *philia*, Beiner states, "What friends hold in common is a common view of what is just, and it is to this extent that friendship is a form of community. . . . When the citizens have the same judgment about their common interest, when they choose the same things, and when they execute what they have decided in common," they achieve political friendship.[23] I wish to suggest that friendship, including mutual sympathy and a community of interests, can serve as an alternative to authority.

In *Redburn*, like the other heroes of the novels, Redburn flees the ship to seek companionship. Harry Bolton proves to be a false friend to Redburn because he clearly seeks the privileges of aristocratic society, wasting his money on the experiences of that class. While Harry replaces Redburn as the weakest member of the crew, Redburn joins the community of sailors, finding in them the alternative to both Jackson and Riga. They mitigate Redburn's desire for a father replacement and provide a community of shared interests, in this case, a community of the disillusioned and cast out. Melville's novels rarely end with their heroes' absolute freedom or complete absorption into their communities; rather, the characters enlist themselves to the duty of searching for freedom, like Taji, or free themselves from inner turmoil by surrendering to society, like Redburn. Thus Ishmael's command in the opening lines of *Moby-Dick* includes the potential for isolation or community.

For Melville, like Emerson, the issues of authority and obedience result in questions of identity. The institutional rules upholding the captain's office and shipboard hierarchy impinge upon each sailor's definition of self; sailors like Tommo, Taji, Omoo, and even Ishmael who seek a freedom outside of those social codes, who seek self-reliance, are faced with the more disturbing task of either projecting a new identity from within or having one imposed on them externally. As Richard Sennett says, "the authority controls reality" by setting the categories by which we understand

[22] Ronald Beiner, *Political Judgment* (Chicago: Univ. of Chicago Press, 1983), p. 79.

[23] Ibid., p. 80.

the world. Ahab is Melville's most famous authority figure for the reason that he imposes his vision of the world so completely on his crew. To understand the means by which he achieves this ultimate authority we must return to the quarter-deck of the *Pequod.*

* * *

In *Moby-Dick,* the delineation and dramatization of Ahab's power and ascendancy occur chiefly within a short span, from "The Specksynder" (chapter 33) through "Midnight, Forecastle" (chapter 40). The effect of these chapters is to usurp Ishmael's voice of authority and substitute Ahab's, whose presence has previously been felt as an ominous background to the comic encounters of Ishmael, Queequeg, and the *Pequod*'s owners. Ahab's usurpation of his crew's purpose has the same effect on the narrative itself as it swerves from the absurdly comic play of "Cetology" to the darker, demonic fears of "The Whiteness of the Whale." In these chapters we move from a rather abstract dissertation on the traditional forms of authority aboard a whaling ship to the confrontation between Ahab and his crew on the quarter-deck in which his purpose of hunting the white whale is melded with theirs. Briefly, the action involves the transformation of Ahab's authority from legitimate and institutional to charismatic, that is, from Captain Riga's to Jackson's. By blurring the distinction between the two, Ahab is able to alloy the routinized conformity of the men with the powerful internal drives that originally compelled them to hunt the sperm whale.

"The Specksynder" begins as a general discussion of the traditional hierarchy aboard whalers. Compelled by Ishmael's characteristic love of facts, the chapter simply explains that the European custom of dividing the ship's authority between the chief whaling master, the specksynder, and the ship's commander was generally ignored on American whalers. Ahab ostensibly encompasses all three roles aboard the *Pequod.*[24] Setting out to emphasize the Americanness of this particular ship, the chapter evolves into a description of the ceremonies associated with the captain's authority. Like other captains, Ahab uses the traditional, legitimating artifices of his rational-legal office to distinguish his superiority: "Though the only homage he ever exacted, was implicit, instantaneous obe-

[24] See Vincent, *Trying-Out,* p. 144.

dience yet even Captain Ahab was by no means unobservant of the paramount forms and usages of the sea" (MD, 129). Disdainful of most conventions, especially those that would tie him to the responsibilities and civilities of genial society, Ahab nevertheless uses them to assert his power. These forms are the mask through which he would strike to clutch the inscrutable whale, but he finds them necessary as means to his end. In their very theatricality, these rituals are the only means by which Ahab can express and play out his authority, which is by its very nature conventional. Asserting this point himself, Ishmael tells us, "be a man's intellectual superiority what it will, it can never assume the practical, available supremacy over other men, without the aid of some sort of external arts and entrenchments, always, in themselves more or less paltry or base" (MD, 129). Using social forms to hunt the whale, Ahab, if successful, promises the destruction of these rituals and the human significance which they enable and express.

The following two chapters, "The Cabin-table" and "The Mast-head," serve to elaborate the captain's ornate social ceremonies and then oppose them with the malevolent vortex they conceal. In part, Ahab's complete control over his officers results from the ritual, "the witchery of social czarship which there is no withstanding" (MD, 131), of his meals. Yet his authority resides less in the ceremony itself than in his mates' willingness and desire to participate in the rite and to grant it meaning. "They were like little children before Ahab," and, like children, their obedience is rewarded by the security of the ceremony's repetition. In its ability to define, distinguish, and separate, Ahab's authority continually reestablishes the identity of the mates within the ceremonies. The danger which threatens the security of ritualized identity is revealed in the following chapter, "The Mast-head," replacing the order of the ritualized meals with Ishmael's warning of the "deep, blue, bottomless soul, pervading mankind and nature" (MD, 140) that lies beneath the mariners' feet. Lulled by these "Descartian vortices," antithetical to the routine of the sailors' daily lives, individual identity is erased by the absence of distinction and individuation, only to return in the hideous fall from the mast-head. Ishmael's warning appropriately introduces the next chapter, "The Quarter-deck," in which Ahab makes his Mephistophelian pact with the crew to hunt for Moby Dick.

Ahab's strategy on the quarter-deck is a masterful fusion of democratic demagoguery and religious ritual. Like Captain Claret, Ahab "never speaks but in the imperative mood." The initial questions to his crew galvanize the men with a commanding directness evoking their sense of purpose in order to weld it to his own. Echoing Father Mapple's ability to "condense" his scattered audience, Ahab easily transfixes his crew with a similar religious sentiment and dramatizes their unvoiced desires. The ritual of question and response, heightened by his own animation, introduces the elaborate ceremony and invocation of nailing the doubloon on the masthead: "Whosover of ye raises me a white-headed whale with a wrinkled bow and a crooked jaw; whosoever of ye raises me that white-headed whale, with three holes punctured in his starboard fluke—look ye, whosoever of ye raises me that same white whale, he shall have this gold ounce, my boys!" (MD, 142). His imperative, "look ye," like Ishmael's (and Father Mapple's) similar commands to the reader, focuses the crew's attention on the symbol of his obsession and unites their individual motives with his own design. Randomness, chance, and autonomy are replaced by Ahab's order and goal. The gold doubloon becomes the mirror for each man's reason to catch the whale.

By setting the value of the whale through the doubloon, Ahab warrants the creation of public meaning out of private desires. The coin mediates desire and possession because, as Sharon Cameron has commented, "those who project meaning or value onto the coin in the form of their own image of the world then want to possess the coin, (re)appropriate it, but now with its private value acknowledged and made public, reified by others *as* monetary value or 'currency' rather than as arbitrary image."[25] Emerson had said, "There are all degrees of proficiency of knowledge in the world." The sailors are those who "live to the utility of the symbol; esteeming health and wealth a final good" (CW, 2: 132). Ahab's use of the doubloon, like Jackson's use of the bank to symbolize the enemy of the people, does not define the whale's value according to the economic marketplace but substitutes private value for public exchange.[26]

[25] Sharon Cameron, *The Corporeal Self* (Baltimore: Johns Hopkins Univ. Press, 1981), p. 22.

[26] See Pitkin, *Concept*, p. 100: "Symbolic representation seems to rest on emo-

These theatrics also align the captain and crew: "At times his hate seemed almost theirs; the White Whale as much their insufferable foe as his" (MD, 162). An unconscious desire for revenge against a world intent on their destruction forces the men to accept Ahab's challenge, and his hate summons and focuses these men's resentment against "the universal cannibalism of the sea; all whose creatures prey upon each other, carrying on eternal war since the world began" (MD, 235–36). This primeval warfare against uncaring nature, unsparing even of "creatures which itself hath spawned" (MD, 235), drive the men onto the whaler and into battle with the whale.[27] It is the "instinct of the knowledge of the demonism in the world" (MD, 169) that motivates them; each man has his secret terror or hate which Ahab extracts and infuses with his own. In Ahab's words, his "one cogged circle fits into all their various wheels, and they revolve" (MD, 147).

With this pronouncement, Ahab aligns himself with the captains of American industry, those men who turn their workers into the machines of the Lowell Mills. Opposed to Emerson's hero of metaphor, Ahab's power is metonymic as it exists in the contiguity of his purpose with the crew's. Ahab, like Emerson's Napoleon, succeeds in transforming the men into appendages. As Michael Rogin says of the captain, "Ahab carries to its extreme the egotistic, bourgeois desire for power, to be alone in the world and possess it."[28] To possess the world in this sense is not to consume it as Emerson's Plato, taking it up within himself and transforming into symbol, but to attach nature (the "Not Me") to the body as another object. Because of his belief in the autonomy of the will, Ahab particularizes nature and through this tropic displacement hopes to overcome it. We should remember, however, Emerson's warning against the mystic's mechanical fastening of nature to single theological ideas, rather than to the dynamic process of emblematic, spiritual creation. For Emerson, it is a short step from Swedenborg's creation of nature as a static representation of moral laws to

---

tional, affective, irrational psychological responses rather than on rationally certifiable criteria."

[27] See Merlin Bowen, *The Long Encounter* (Chicago: Univ. of Chicago Press, 1960), pp. 75–76. See also Robert Zoellner, *The Salt-Sea Mastadon: A Reading of Moby-Dick* (Berkeley: Univ. of California Press, 1973), pp. 136–45, for a discussion of Ishmael's "hypos," which include his fear of both nature *and* human nature.

[28] Rogin, *Subversive Genealogy*, p. 120.

Napoleon's commodification of nature. Ahab succeeds in making the white whale stand for all nature and, at the same time, in making his sailors accessories of his quest and of himself. Near the end of the novel, Starbuck meditates on his plan to murder Ahab but his own will continues to belong to Ahab, even as he implicates the reader in this weakness: "And say'st the men have vow'd thy vow; say'st all of us are Ahabs" (MD, 422).

Ahab's power over the crew may involve the capitalist's ability to link individuals within a mechanically purposive system, but he also tries literally to mesmerize his men. In the odd ritualistic scene with the mates' crossed lances, where he "would fain have shocked into them the same fiery emotion accumulated within the Leyden jar of his own magnetic life" (MD, 146), Ahab's invocation of animal magnetic power extends his institutional authority into the realm of the charlatan. What appears a satanic ritual on the quarter-deck is also actually a parody of mesmeric therapy, in which patients were attached to a magnetized jar (like a Leyden jar) and "recharged" with electromagnetic power.

This allusion to magnetism makes Ahab a mock transcendentalist mediator between the individual and universal principles. Believers in this power found it working in public occasions, such as Ahab's oration on the quarter-deck in which he attempts to draw sympathy from his crew. Sympathy, according to one theory, is created when "nervo-vital fluid [is] thrown from a full, energetic brain, upon another of kindred feeling. That brain's being roused affects another, and still another, till the whole assembly are brought into magnetic sympathy with the speaker, and by him are moved as the soul of one man."[29] Ahab's challenge of revenge on Moby Dick, like his later challenges during the lightning storm, has the same effect. However, like Ahab's image of the men as "cogs" in his machine, this power works metonymically as it passes contiguously from individual to individual.

Melville's purpose in using mesmerism is to show that Ahab's power is, in part, fraudulent quackery. Testing his magnetic power on Starbuck, Stubb, and Flask on the quarter-deck, Ahab discovers

[29] John Bovee Dods, *Six Lectures on the Philosophy of Mesmerism* (New York: Fowler and Wells, 1850), p. 27. See also J.P.F. Deleuze, *Practical Instruction in Animal Magnetism*, trans. Thomas C. Hartshorn., rev. ed. (1843; reprint, New York: Fowler and Wells, 1886).

it is a failure: " 'In vain!' cried Ahab; 'but, maybe, 'tis well. For did ye three but once take the full-forced shock, then mine own electric thing, *that* had perhaps expired from out me' " (MD, 146). Ahab's power reaches its natural limit, but the effect of the ceremony on the crew is to increase their awe. In "The Candles" and "The Needle," he uses similar electric and magnetic phenomena to reassert his demonic control over the crew. Making ambiguous and self-dramatizing passes over the binnacle in an attempt to remagnetize the crew, Ahab is interrupted by Ishmael's interjection: "Whether indispensable to the magnetizing of the steel, or merely intended to augment the awe of the crew, is uncertain." As he has many times before, Ahab directs his men to "Look ye," and his triumph is assured: "One after another they peered in, for nothing but their own eyes could persuade such ignorance as theirs; and one after another they slunk away" (MD, 425).

Whether through mesmerism or constituted powers, Ahab's authority is allied with vision. His ability to focus his crew's desires and thereby unite their wills rephrases Ishmael's initial directives to the reader in demagogic, almost demonic terms. Like Ishmael, Ahab can transform the practical (the binnacle) and the arbitrary (the doubloon) into mystifying objects of contemplation. Ceremony enacts the credibility of action and infuses common objects with religious significance. When the men stare into the binnacle or contemplate the doubloon, the question becomes not what they see but *how* they see.

The epistemological connection between vision and authority is enacted in "The Doubloon" as each character steps up to the coin and (re)states its meaning. Unlike the scene on the quarter-deck, in which the doubloon gains a mystical symbolic status, here the men "read" what the coin visually represents. It is a critical commonplace to explain that their widely variant readings suggest the solipsism involved in the crew's and reader's inability to locate absolute, objective truth. Pip's reading, "I look, you look, he looks; we look, ye look, they look" (MD, 362), thus serves as a marker of isolated, autonomous perception. But this is not entirely true, for Pip's conjugation of the verb enacts the systematic differentiations of language. The subject changes but the system's meaning remains constant. In fact, conjugation implies language's order, pattern, and (through its etymology) the relationship between sexuality and connection. It is true, as Stubb comically says, that Pip has been studying *Murray's Grammar*, but the effect of Pip's pronouncement is to explore the ways in which individual perception is regulated within language's conventional patterns.

Combining his verbal and dramatic forms with the individual motives of the men, Ahab binds them to his cause: "All the individualities of the crew, this man's valor, that man's fear; guilt and guiltlessness, all varieties were welded into oneness, and were directed to that fatal goal which Ahab their one lord and keel did point to" (MD, 445). Melville insightfully depicts the place of epistemological uncertainty and pluralism in this process of demagoguery. Narcissus-like, each man is mirrored in the quest for the whale: "That same, we ourselves see in all rivers and oceans. It is the image of the ungraspable phantom of life; and this is the key to it all" (MD, 14). We see here the ruthless solution of a sacrificial crisis as the men project their violence synecdochically onto the whale. But Melville also anticipates the problem of ritual: If social order is the end of ritual, then it is achieved at the cost of individual identity. By melting thirty individuals into a single identity, Ahab creates the analogue, the mirror actually, of the whale's whiteness out of all colors, making the *Pequod* as terrifying a vision as Moby Dick.

To judge Ahab's authority we must finally distinguish between its means and its ends. Part charismatic leader, part confidence-man, Ahab uses the power of language to ritualize knowledge into belief. The ease with which he molds the crew to his purpose results from their own terror and desire for revenge; from this instinctive fear he constructs belief. Institutional authority works by separating and defining the relations between individuals. The charismatic leader, however, depends not on the conventions of authority but its representation through various symbols. It is symbolic authority, based not on knowledge but belief that seeks to unify and to destroy difference. Ahab's goal is the circumvention, indeed the obliteration, of communally based and generated conventions, to go beyond the idea of authority itself. His failure to achieve this goal, especially seen in light of his success in persuading his men to fulfill his means, calls that authority into question. In other words, authority seeks the union of intention and goal—it seeks its continuation and fulfillment in itself. But Ahab desires it only as a means, never as an end, because he knows he must break its bonds. With his utter, and anticlimactic, failure we must question this confusion of ends for means. We are brought around to the beginning of the novel and Ishmael's own authority as he enlists our help for his own search for the whale.

Ishmael and Epistemic Authority

Ahab's failure to capture Moby Dick and the *Pequod*'s apocalyptic destruction warrant Ishmael's authority as the Job-like witness, as narrator. Returning to the novel's beginning, having ourselves witnessed the consequences of Ahab's authority and the embodiment of his purpose in the whale, we find Ishmael asserting his own authority as raconteur, tour guide, and American scholar. Clearly his authority is of a different sort from Ahab's; Ishmael has a story to tell and information to impart, but he lacks the institutional authority granted by a ship commander's office. His authority is *epistemic*, that is, he is an authority *in* something, in this case in the information and facts concerning whales and whaling. Like the Sub-Sub Librarian who collected extracts and quotations about whales, Ishmael presents himself as an expert in whale lore and facts, one who has dived deeply into the literature. Unlike the librarian, however, Ishmael sets himself the task of going beyond mere collecting; rather, he seeks to instruct us out of his own experience, "comprehending," to use Emerson's term, a whole spectrum of knowledge from the common to the grotesquely comic within his imagination.

Ishmael's epistemic authority, like Ahab's power over his crew, is dependent on the coincidence of our belief with his. And like the captain's control we can measure the forms of authority by testing the degree to which he can successfully fulfill his purpose of "realizing" the sperm whale. Mocking the failures of others to create a realistic representation of a whale, either by their lack of first-hand knowledge or the clumsiness of the representation, Ishmael must provide us with a vision of the whale's bulk and power. In effect, the book *becomes* the whale, thereby marking itself as a counterpart to the *Pequod*'s mirroring of Moby Dick. Although working under different conventions from Ahab's office, Ishmael too depends on the persuasive possibilities of language, the fact that authority is embedded in language's ability to create or call up the intersubjective relations of command and obedience. The issue of Ishmael's authority, therefore, raises the corollary problem of autonomy within this relationship. As both epistemic commander within his own work and subordinate sailor within Ahab's narrative, Ishmael demonstrates the links between the two. Able to command the reader's compliance in his first sentence, Ishmael proceeds to test the limits of his authority and our obedience. The effect of his cetology chapters, as Richard Brodhead notices, "is gradually to break down our sense of incredulity and to move us closer and closer to entertaining these beliefs ourselves."[30] Unlike Ahab, Ishmael comes to break the demonic spell holding the reader in order to preserve a saving skepticism.

The purposive nature of authority, the fact that it is employed to express and link the intentions of the participants, finds two versions in Ahab and Ishmael. Whereas Ahab replaces his crew's intentions with his own on the quarter-deck, Ishmael begins his narrative with the reasons for his interest in the whale. Compelling him to write the story is his understanding of what drove him onto the *Pequod* in the first place: "Now that I recall all the circumstances, I think I can see a little into the springs and motives which being cunningly presented to me under various disguises, induced me to set about performing the part I did" (MD, 16). From his vantage point as the experienced narrator, he realizes that "chief among these motives was the overwhelming idea of the great whale himself." Rather than insisting on the literal and particular, as Ahab incarnates his hate in Moby Dick, he proves himself to be a bit of a scholar as he ships aboard to entertain the abstract, but "overwhelming," idea of the whale.[31] Variously functioning as low comedy, sermon, and textbook, the cetology chapters finally serve as autobiography, for Ishmael too must confront the "dead blind

[30] Richard Brodhead, *Hawthorne, Melville, and the Novel* (Chicago: Univ. of Chicago Press, 1976), p. 139.

[31] It appears this opposition between the two quests reflects the composition of the novel itself. It is likely the adventure tale of Ahab's hunt came first, to be balanced later by Ishmael's complexities in the cetology chapters. See Leon Howard, *Herman Melville* (Berkeley: Univ. of California Press, 1951), p. 162; James M. Barbour, "The Composition of *Moby-Dick*," *American Literature* 47 (1975): 343–60; and Robert Milder, "The Composition of *Moby-Dick*: A Review and a Prospect," *ESQ: A Journal of the American Renaissance* 23 (1977): 203–16.

wall" of the whale in order to understand better his own "springs and motives."

In his attempt to enlist an authority counter to Ahab's, Ishmael creates what Edward Said calls the authority of a beginning: "The necessary creation for a beginning is also reflected in the act of achieving discontinuity and transfer; while in this act a clear break with the past is discernible, it must also connect the new direction not so much with a wholly unique venture, but with the established authority of a parallel adventure."[32] For both men the whale looms as the ultimate goal, a goal requiring the warranting of their authority by subordinates. In seeking revenge, however, Ahab's goal actually includes its own origin. Ishmael, true to his namesake, seeks to escape his origin by confronting the idea of the whale. In the first chapters of *Moby-Dick,* Ishmael maintains the ironic distance on his younger self, the young man who followed Ahab's mad orders, as a means of breaking with the past and therefore charting a new course.

Moby-Dick thus offers us a series of parallels between Ahab and Ishmael.[33] Each of the two epic whaling quests requires the hero to test the boundaries of conventional knowledge. Leading these separate, but related, quests are the different authorities of Ahab and Ishmael. As we have already seen, Ahab's authority begins, at any rate, as institutional and coercive; it commands the men's actions.[34] But his search also travels beyond the ability of language to represent any object or idea. Ishmael's authority too is contained and created by language. His epistemic authority, however, exists in our confidence in his ability to share knowledge, that is, to create a relationship based on our gradual accumulation of information within his created categories. He contains the dual functions of the cicerone: He guides us, entertains us with his loquacity, and, like Cicero, attempts to "move" us.

The two strands of the novel are clearly marked in the narrative.

[32] Said, *Beginnings,* p. 33.

[33] On the connections between Ahab and Ishmael, see Sharon Cameron, *Corporeal Self,* p. 44, and Bainard Cowan, *Exiled Waters: Melville and the Crisis of Allegory* (Baton Rouge: Louisiana State Univ. Press, 1983), pp. 136–37.

[34] Ahab is also likely modeled on contemporary political figures like Daniel Webster, John Calhoun, and Andrew Jackson. See Alan Heimert, "*Moby-Dick* and American Political Symbolism," *American Quarterly* 16 (1963): 498–534, and Bercovitch, *American Jeremiad,* pp. 192–3.

Ahab's story is told as a fictional account, using the conventional past-tense and third-person epic fiction as a marker. The cetology chapters generally exist in the present tense and maintain a consistent first-person stance. Formally the two stories are woven into the novel. "The straight warp of necessity" is Ahab's story, "not to be swerved from its ultimate course" (MD, 185). Ishmael's chapters are "free to play [their] shuttle between given threads." Resisting Ahab's relentless, grim pursuit, these chapters present a mind's free play over a universe of objects and ideas. Parody, symbolism, and double-entendres proliferate among the great chunks of facts lifted intact from other books on whaling. In turn, these "facts" accumulate, generate insights into the whale and coalesce to form the shape of a whale. Following the etymology of *instruct*, "to build on," Ishmael literally uses facts to construct a representation of the whale much different from Ahab's doubloon. These chapters serve to create a spatial form existing apart from the time-bound vision of Ahab.[35] These facts in turn provide support for Ishmael's claim for authority.

The facts of Ishmael's cetology chapters, like all facts, are human constructs, and by their human origins can be used as emblems, or symbols, or representations. Criticism on *Moby-Dick* has modified Charles Feidelson's work on Melville's symbolism by contrasting Ahab's allegorizing of the whale with Ishmael's approach to emblems. For Michael Rogin, Ahab is able to unify the crew and the narrative by presenting Moby Dick as the allegorical emblem: "He projects a single, allegorical meaning on the white whale. The allegorist inhabiting a secure universe knows that his allegory is only a representation and not the thing itself."[36] By privileging the transcendental signified over its symbol, Ahab demeans the emblem's status as an object with representational power. We cannot *know* what the whale symbolizes except through a kind of Emersonian intuition.

Ishmael's symbols, however, are said to proliferate meanings endlessly, thereby raising "the spectre of solipsistic subjectivism."[37]

[35] Brodhead, *Hawthorne*, p. 158, appropriately cites Frank Kermode's distinction between *chronos* and *kairos*. Ishmael sees time as *chronos*, the perpetual present of unfolding time; Ahab sees it as *kairos*, in which "meaning is derived from its relation to the end."

[36] Rogin, *Subversive Genealogy*, p. 116. See also Cowan, *Exiled Waters*, p. 152.

[37] Rogin, *Subversive Genealogy*, p. 116.

But do his symbols actually do this? Rather than being interested in what a symbol may symbolize, and therefore entering into the question of subjectivity, he simply asks, What does a symbol represent? and thereby places the question in social, rather than psychological or metaphysical, terms. The difference is crucial. Ishmael constructs his image of the whale out of what it looks like but also provides the conditions by which we come to know the whale as a process. For Ahab, Moby Dick is really an arbitrary means to his end, but for Ishmael the "idea" of the whale is an end in itself. We can ask answerable epistemological questions about the whale's suitability as a symbol, but not about the "imponderable thoughts" that it symbolizes. Ishmael here diverges from Emerson's American Scholar, for he is interested in the processional forms of thought, not Thinking as a universal act. Like the Scholar, though, he wants to "comprehend" (that is, know and contain) the criteria for true knowledge and how such knowledge can be communicated.

Motivating Ahab's and Ishmael's quests is the shared desire to possess truth. As Ishmael claims, "Unless you own the whale, you are but a provincial and sentimentalist in Truth" (MD, 285). Perhaps as much a problem as defining truth is the issue of possession, that is, of defining oneself in relation to objects or people (and we must remember that slavery is central to *Moby-Dick*) that lie outside of the recognizable boundaries of the self. The men aboard the *Pequod* are demonically possessed by Ahab as they become appendages, unified not by their proximity to his body, or by loyalty to an ideal, but by their obedience to his will. Because Ahab orients himself to the physical world as particular and natural means to some supernatural end, even Moby Dick exists merely as the particular emblem of some metaphysical truth. In this way Ahab represents nineteenth-century capitalism's use of nature for quasi-religious ends. For Ishmael, however, to possess the whale's truth is to speak for it, representing the thing in an act of language: "The real owner of anything is its commander" (MD, 393). Within the novel, the problem of ownership is repeated in a number of ways. Ostensibly, the principal owners of the ship, Bildad and Peleg, apportion a certain degree of ownership to the crew in "lays." It is Ahab who is the true commander of the men and ship and therefore its owner.

Like Franklin, Ishmael conceives of ownership and truth as a kind of linguistic possession. By equating ownership with command, Ishmael describes it as a speech act, which is both conditional and active. He counters, in other words, Ahab's claim that truth lies outside of language and the conventions of human interaction by locating it in the rule-bound rituals of language and authority. I hesitate to make him sound like a pragmatic man of the world who refuses to speculate on metaphysical matters, but his place in the novel is preserved by an aggressive skepticism, or, as he says, he remains "neither believer nor infidel" but one who regards "doubts of all things earthly, and intuitions of some things heavenly . . . with an equal eye" (MD, 314). For Ishmael, possession is enabled by our ability to command, to tell stories, to communicate knowledge about the whale's significance within the realm of his epistemic authority. To possess this significance, however, he must be able to locate and express it. Like Ahab, he faces the specter of failure: His own authority over the reader and his search for truth will fail if he does not successfully rarefy the whale's bulk into some form of certitude.

In his "inexorable self," Ahab stands apart from the crew, isolated yet "owning" them as their commander. As absolute authority aboard his ship, he also believes himself absolutely autonomous. Peering at the doubloon, he sees "all are Ahab" (MD, 359), meaning that his crew are mere extensions of himself as they have united their fortunes and motives with his. His monomania arose, in part, from the fusion—the integration—of body and soul: "His torn body and gashed soul bled into one another; and so interfusing, made him mad" (MD, 160). Just as he collapses body and soul, Ahab attempts to subordinate the external world to his will: "What I've dared, I've willed; and what I've willed, I'll do" (MD, 147). The power of Ahab's autonomy is to make his private revenge public and to integrate his crew into his mad purpose. Ahab's power of extension is not the narcissistic projection of the self *onto* the world, but the reification of the self and all relations into the metonymic contiguities of causality. Unlike Emerson who proposes an intuitive Reason to achieve transcendental self-reliance, Ahab believes he can use natural laws, including the laws of causality, as a means to his transcendental end.

It has often been noted that Ishmael exemplifies the potential loss of identity. On the mast-head, he warns us to beware the confusion of our thoughts with their attachment to the world:

> Lulled into such an opium-like listlessness of vacant, unconscious reverie is this absent-minded youth by blending cadence of waves with thoughts, that at last he loses his identity; takes the mystic ocean at his feet for the visible image of that deep, blue, bottomless soul, pervading mankind and nature; and every strange half-seen, gliding, beautiful thing that eludes him, every dimly discovered, uprising fin of some undiscoverable form, seems to him the embodiment of those elusive thoughts that only people the soul by continually flitting through it. (MD, 140)

What does this youth's identity, almost lost to the ocean, consist of and how does the mistaken connection between thoughts and nature occur? At first we assume that the "elusive thoughts" comprise the identity, the sense of self lost in the projection of those thoughts onto the ocean. But separating these thoughts from the ocean, and reminding the youth of their absolute distinction, is the corporal body as it moves and then falls through the air. What causes the confusion in the first place is the youth's mistaking of the figural connection of metaphor—here the identification of the "mystic ocean" and the "bottomless soul"—for some literal correspondence.

In "A Squeeze of the Hand," we see Ishmael gladly losing the sense of an autonomous self for the "affectionate, friendly, loving feeling" of squeezing sperm until he asks, "Why should we longer cherish any social acerbities, or know the slightest ill-humor or envy! Come; let us squeeze hands all round; nay, let us all squeeze ourselves into each other; let us squeeze ourselves universally into the very milk and sperm of kindness" (MD, 349). The differences between the two kinds of self-loss are clear. Isolated, the youth is threatened with metaphysical destruction by the loss of his sense of a corporal self. Ishmael loses his self *through* the physicality and ritual of his activity with his mates. The integrity of self is abandoned for the ecstatic pleasure of friendship, of inhabiting momentarily a corporate self. Coming as it does after Pip's abandonment and his terrifying vision of God's repetitive, purposeless power, this scene provides a human balance to such absolute isolation.

Isolation and incorporation. These are the poles in the struggle between authority and autonomy, but they do not exhaust the permutations of the relations. Following the evocation of his experience squeezing sperm, Ishmael pulls back and evaluates:

> Would that I could keep squeezing that sperm for ever! For now, since by many prolonged repeated experiences, I have perceived that in all cases man must eventually lower, or at least shift, his conceit of attainable felicity; not placing it anywhere in the intellect or fancy; but in the wife, the heart, the bed, the table, the saddle, the fire-side, the country; now that I have perceived all this, I am ready to squeeze case eternally. (MD, 349)

Removing himself from the memory of that ecstatic experience, separating the metaphysical goal of absolute, corporate fusion from the daily experience of domestic happiness, Ishmael once again orients himself toward the reader and linguistically asserts his presence in "I." The interblending of selves he has just described presents the loss of personal autonomy resulting from Ahab's absolute authority. Like Emerson's experience on the bare common in *Nature*, Ishmael can find only proximate representations of that moment. However, he locates this "attainable felicity" not in the mind's autonomous play but in the closure of perception upon familiar objects. Unlike Ahab's appropriation and mastery of external objects, Ishmael's relations to the world do not make the objects extensions of the self. Rather, he finds pleasure in losing the self slightly as he engages these objects perceptually, never confusing them for the pleasure they evoke. Isolation is a terror for Ishmael, as it becomes for Pip, but it arises not only from abandonment at sea (Ishmael himself experiences this) but also from the (mistaken) belief of Ahab's claim for an autonomous, self-created, and self-willing identity. Cameron fails to remember Ishmael's own disclaimer that the squeezing of the sperm is not a solution. As he turns from the corporate self created in the squeezing of the sperm, a protective self to be sure but one created not in reaction to Ahab's autonomy but *by* the captain's absolute authority, Ishmael settles for the contingent and conditional social ties of heteronomy.

Identity for Ishmael is unstable, for it exists only in relational terms. His initial claim to an identity can be completed only by the reader, thus linking his authority to our mutual loss of autonomy and the creation of identity. The instability of this identity, as Cameron points out, is inevitable: "The very idea of identity, however, is contingent upon a dependable outside from which the self differentiates itself, as the very idea of interpretation consists upon a plurality of perspectives, a relativism against which a clearly delineated self or a particular interpretation takes a stand."[38] The idea of personal and individual autonomy is not only a fiction, but as Ahab reveals, it is a dangerous one in that it destroys the relational ties of society, culture, and even language that enable identity to be formed and enacted. Within the novel we find images of salvation in Ishmael's "wedding" with Queequeg, the union of Christian and cannibal, their mutual dependence through the monkey-rope, the union of life and death that continues to make Ishmael's identity and survival contingent on his ties to others.[39]

Ishmael's claim for the contingencies of authority and social ties over the unity of autonomy reminds us as readers of the very odd relationship engendered by the act of reading. When he turns to us, asking, "And what are you reader, but a Loose-Fish and a Fast-Fish, too?" he once again announces the special conditions by which we have united ourselves to his narrative, conditions, he makes clear from the beginning, we have only voting rights to create. The conditions include the tradition of Biblical exegesis, of paternal authority, of institutional rules which precede and impinge upon us, but which also help establish the continuity of our created and assumed identities. We are Fast-Fish, for he possesses us; we are Loose-Fish, for we warrant the relationship, grant him the identity of Ishmael as well as the epistemic authority of the scholar. Resulting from this assent is the incorporation, the "joint-

[38] Cameron, *Corporeal Self*, pp. 56–57.

[39] Carolyn Karcher, *Shadow over the Promised Land: Slavery, Race and Violence in Melville's America* (Baton Rouge: Louisiana State Univ. Press, 1980), p. 77, writes, "The ultimate difference between Ishmael and Ahab is that Ishmael's marriage with Queequeg has made it possible for him to retain his human values and allegiance to his fellow man in the face of the overwhelming evil and woe he sees in the world."

stock company of two," of ourselves within the body of the novel as we join Ishmael. If this novel has the bulk and appearance of the whale, then we are Jonahs working out the peculiar acts of authority and disobedience and social interactions of that story.

Both failed searches are extensions of their different uses of authority. Ahab's authority enacts its own self-destruction as it seeks to go beyond its limits; Ishmael's, from the willful and whimsical subversions of his own authority. His cetology chapters are hermeneutic inquiries into the question of the whale's identity, an identity, which like Ishmael's own, turns out to be contingent on the inquirer's. Unlike Ahab, whose purpose to catch the whale never varies or swerves, Ishmael circles his subject, first classifying and then presenting the background before cutting in. Ishmael's intention is to capture the "grand hooded phantom" that drove him, Ahab-like, onto the *Pequod*. Roughly described, his method is to move from external views—the description of the whale's whiteness and its capture—through the various stages of cutting-in and trying-out, finally ending with a discussion of the whale's skeleton, fossils, and immortality. However, it is futile trying to connect the whale's external features with an internal, incorporal "self," corresponding to Ishmael's own sense of identity created in the interweaving of internal and external. Each attempt to own the whale by interpretation is frustrated by the whale's indeterminacy. As a result, the cetological systemization of whales remains unfinished, the significance of the whale's whiteness is that it has no meaning because it incorporates all meaning; Moby Dick is unlocatable because he is ubiquitous in both time and space. The whale is the undecipherable hieroglyphic: "How may unlettered Ishmael hope to read the awful Chaldee of the Sperm whale's brow?" (MD, 293). Ishmael finally admits: "Dissect him how I may, then, I but go skin deep. I know him not, and never will" (MD, 318).

It is clear that Ishmael's quest to own the whale, like Ahab's, does not succeed. As Richard Brodhead states, "Ishmael's scientific procedures are almost without exception extravagant failures."[40] What we should notice, however, is not the failure but its extravagance; Ishmael purposely mars his cetology chapters by adulterating the serious claims to authority with self-parodic exaggeration. With-

[40] Brodhead, *Hawthorne*, p. 152.

standing the temptation that destroys Ahab, Ishmael admits and demarcates the limits of his knowledge and the danger present in successfully completing his search for identity. If Ahab claims that "all my means are sane, my motive and object mad," then Ishmael shares the means of authority, but provides an alternate ending.

We can see the intentional subversion of Ishmael's authority by his mimicry of Ahab's imperative voice at the beginning of the narrative and his continual parody of the captain's imperious tone. He employs the same stylistic constructions as Ahab in order to call attention to the common linguistic basis of their authority. For example, Ahab's incantation as he nails the doubloon to the mast finds its counterpart in the periodic rhythms and force of Ishmael's ciceronian sentences. His epic invocation in "Knights and Squires" is typical of this particular style:

> If, then, to meanest mariners, and renegades and castaways, I shall hereafter ascribe high qualities, though dark; weave round them tragic graces; if even the most mournful, perchance the most abased, among them all, shall at times lift himself to the exalted mounts; if I shall touch that workman's arm with some ethereal light; if I shall spread a rainbow over his disastrous set of sun; then against all mortal critics bear me out in it, thou just Spirit of Equality, which hast spread one royal mantle of humanity over all my kind. (MD, 105)

Bearing echoes of Father Mapple and Ahab (and further of various orators of the day), Ishmael's homiletic style has the extravagance of parody. However, the building of the conditional, if-then, ciceronian period reflects the entire contingent nature of belief and action of the novel. Variations of this construction, like Ahab's hortatory pronouncements, or Fedallah's "if-then" prophecy, are used to incite action by instilling belief in their absolute, rather than conditional, truth. As in many tragedies, Ahab's destruction comes from an ironic misapprehension of language. He confidently attacks Moby Dick, in part, out of a mistaken trust in Fedallah's mysterious prophecy, but is tricked by his own hubristic faith in language. Having used language to mystify his crew, Ahab cannot interpret the warning veiled in the conditional sentence and thereby becomes the victim as well as the victimizer of language. Ishmael's parody of this style foregrounds its artificiality, rendering harmless its potential danger.

By such actions Ishmael undermines his epistemic authority and comments on Ahab's misuse of institutional authority by calling into question its linguistic source. Using a variety of voices, Ishmael reminds us that language's ability to name and describe a whale remains removed from any actual ties to its power and reality. His description of the whale's spine reflects his method of analysis: Beginning with the overwhelming size of universal matters, Ishmael inevitably "tapers off at last into simple child's play" (MD, 378) because verbal play once again points out the conventionality of language and all knowledge. Issued in commands, or even in the declarative sentences of his cetology chapters, language affects and engages the listener or reader, but we must not mistake the signifiers for the thing signified. It is Ahab's belief that he can break through this cardboard-mask reality into whatever lies beyond. For him, and in contrast to Ishmael, "the world beyond artifices of the visible—the supposed reality—is not unknowable but only unknown."[41] Encountering that reality, Ahab and his crew sink into its silent vortex. Saved by Queequeg's coffin, on which are carved "a complete theory of the heavens and the earth, and a mystical treatise on the art of attaining truth" (MD, 399), Ishmael floats above the mute waters: "The unharming sharks, they glided by as if with padlocks on their mouths; the savage sea-hawks sailed with sheathed beaks" (MD, 470). Despite its inability to express absolutes, language protects Ishmael from the abyss over which he hovered and attaches him to the world of conditionally shared beliefs and values in which we first encounter him.

Ishmael's first command demands our trust in him as the autobiographical narrator of the story. His subsequent narration involves an intricate strategy calculated to undermine our confidence in all forms of authority. At stake is the understanding that human desires can be evoked, reified, and associated with demonic designs by language. We must fill up the world with conditional expressions of human truth—the genial, even tragic, stories we share. This genial skepticism of Ishmael that we first encounter in his

[41] James Guetti, *The Limits of Metaphor: A Study of Melville, Conrad, and Faulkner* (Ithaca: Cornell Univ. Press, 1967), p. 35.

voice is empowered by Ahab's demonism which we follow throughout the course of the narrative, but it resists his conclusions. Perhaps skepticism is the wrong term, for Ishmael provides us with incremental stages of intellectual growth, corresponding to the unfolding stages of the novel: "Through infancy's unconscious spell, boyhood's thoughtless faith, adolescence's doubt (the common doom), then scepticism, then disbelief, resting at last in manhood's pondering repose of If" (MD, 406).[42] Significantly, Ishmael's final stage of understanding is his own ubiquitous and powerfully evocative grammatical construction of the conditional. "If" presents us finally with an awareness that has moved disbelief into an acceptance of what we can know through the conditional linkage of language, identity, and culture. If "Silence is the only Voice of our God," Ishmael understands how language is our best defense and hope.[43] Turning from *Moby-Dick* to *The Confidence-Man* we will see how the creation of authority aboard the *Pequod* is finally transformed into the game of confidence on the *Fidele*.

The Authority of Confidence

Ishmael's description of maturity in a frightening, oppressive world as "manhood's pondering repose of If" provides us with a substantial link between *Moby-Dick* and the later, darker fictions, particularly *Pierre* and *The Confidence-Man*. In *Pierre*, Plotinus Plinlimmon's pamphlet on "Horologicals and Chronometricals" is part of a lecture series entitled "EI," a word of characteristically ambiguous meanings, chief of which is "if." In *The Confidence-Man*, working his game on a miser, who doubtingly stutters, "If, if now, I should put, put—" the Confidence-Man answers, "No ifs. Downright confidence, or none. So help me heaven, I will have no half-confidences."[44] The fascination this word seems to have held for Melville lies in its power simultaneously to assert and retract possible meanings, mediating in an "if-then" construction between a

[42] The editors of *Moby-Dick* have suggested that this speech might belong to Ahab (see p. 494). However, it is clearly connected with Ishmael's final understanding and his own linguistic interests.

[43] Herman Melville, *Pierre*, ed. Harrison Hayford et al. (Evanston, Ill.: Northwestern Univ. Press and Newberry Library, 1970), p. 204.

[44] Melville, *Confidence-Man*, p. 75. (Hereafter cited in text as CM.)

hypothetical primary cause and its logical, but equally fictional, consequence.[45] As it projects a series of potential meanings, which extend from what we know to what we might conceive to be true, this word enacts our ability to create a fictional world of "as if" which the narrator of *The Confidence-Man* tells us, "should present another world, and yet one to which we feel the tie" (CM, 183).[46] From this use we can also see how "if" acts as a mediating form between experiential knowledge and what might be called absolute knowledge, that is, between human, horological time and God's chronometrical knowledge.

In his study of language and politics, David V. J. Bell has made a similar claim for the relationship between linguistic paradigms and the structures of authority, influence, and power.[47] Authority, according to Bell, is a simple imperative command to "do *X*," which is followed either by its successful completion in obedience or in its failure. Power and influence, however, involve conditional "if-then" paradigms in which the person addressed assesses the consequences of his actions contained within those paradigms. Power, for example, is a first-person conditional statement, "If you do *X*, I will do *Y*." The speaker's intentions, conditioned by the addressed listener's actions, may be either punishment or reward, but his power in the relationship comes from the listener's ability to be coerced by the potential force held in reserve by the speaker. Influence, on the other hand, involves a third-person conditional paradigm: "If you do *X*, then he will do *Y*," or, "If you do *X*, then *Y* will happen to you." Here the speaker seeks not to coerce the listener through implied force, but to move the listener by presenting evidence of events or consequences resulting from the listener's actions. The best example of this paradigm is the jeremiad in which the prophet figure warns his backsliding listeners of their impending punishment by God for their sins. As we will see, variations of these three paradigms are also the source of the confidence game in Melville's novel.

[45] On Melville's use of hypothetical constructs, see Gary Lindbergh, *The Confidence Man in American Literature* (New York: Oxford Univ. Press, 1982), pp. 15–38.

[46] See Hamburger, *Logic*, pp. 58–59, for another description of literature's "as-if" proposition.

[47] David V. J. Bell, *Power, Influence, and Authority: An Essay in Political Linguistics* (London: Oxford Univ. Press, 1975).

Recent criticism of Melville has shown how the dark, repressed forces of a character like Pierre rebel against paternal and institutional authorities in symbolic incest and murder, deconstructing the repressive institutions of family and society, and canceling the terms of human interaction. True enough, but Melville was also fascinated by the way language and its fictional constructions work equally well to channel and represent desire. Authority's inherent conventionality works to express and link desires, bridging isolatoes within a particular society and culture. In the fiction after *Moby-Dick* Melville's critique of social repression and irrational motivation involves the ways in which language constructs the matrices of human identity and interaction. And his critique of conventions, from the institutions aboard ship in *Typee* to Captain Vere's adherence to "forms, measured forms," includes the way people misuse language to create rigid categories of meaning.

Benito Cereno reflects the gradual shift in Melville's works from images of institutional authority to the processes of individual compliance. Authority becomes less an appointed office than a momentary status, a theatrical role created in the drama of persuasion and skepticism. Unstable because unlegitimated by a fixed social control, authority constantly seeks to perpetuate itself against the ever-present danger of rebellion, reminding us of Ishmael's declaration: "I myself am a savage, owing no allegiance but to the King of the cannibals; and ready at any moment to rebel against him" (MD, 232). The association of authority with theatricality effectively defines politics as the "space of appearances in which men show themselves and their deeds in public."[48] In *Benito Cereno*, the defiant rebel Babo is able to deceive the benign Captain Delano by stripping away Benito Cereno's institutional authority while appropriating its theatrical power. Meanwhile, Babo's self-conscious display of authority over Benito Cereno destroys the Spaniard's class presumptions. For Babo, as Warwick Wadlington succinctly puts it, "iconoclasm and image making are the same."[49]

Like Ahab, Babo rules the *San Dominick* through a combination of terror and ceremony. The elaborate ritualistic inversions of power, like the shaving of Cereno, parodically recreate the bond

[48] Beiner, *Political Judgment*, p. 12. He is actually paraphrasing Hannah Arendt's discussion in *The Human Condition* (Chicago: Univ. of Chicago Press, 1958), p. 199.

[49] Wadlington, *Confidence Game*, p. 134.

between master and slave while presenting them as a spectacle to Amasa Delano, a show in which he remains the observer. This spectacle reveals not so much Delano's distance from the events but rather his failure to understand his own participation and implication in their significance. In *White-Jacket,* and throughout *Moby-Dick,* Melville uses the elements of the *theatrum mundi*—stage directions, dramatic dialogue, costuming, asides—to emphasize the theatrical basis of human action. Even as Delano gazes into the crowd of sailors "as from a stage-box into the pit," he never fully realizes his own role in the drama.[50] Anticipating the Confidence-Man, Babo is both actor and director of action and so prepares us for radical confidence by leading us into doubt. For as we learn later, "Distrust is a stage to confidence."

* * *

Within the period from *Moby-Dick* to *The Confidence-Man,* from Ahab to Pierre to Babo to the Confidence-Man himself, we can trace the gradual replacement of the "corporal self" by a sense of identity constructed by the speaking voice and its accompanying theatrical gestures. This theatricalization of self renders identity unstable and disperses it into the linguistic and interpersonal relations by which we express and construct our knowledge of beings.[51] As the last stage of this process, the Confidence-Man is the most difficult to fathom for the very reason he has no depth; his character is as evanescent and transient as the costumes he wears. As he metamorphoses from the lamb-like man who first steps aboard the *Fidele,* through the crippled Negro, the man from the Black Rapids Coal Company, herb-doctor, PIO officer, and the cosmopolitan, his identity and the meaning of his word *confidence* acquire a multiplicity of references. Oddly enough, his rhetoric achieves the same emptiness as Emerson's: Language for both serves less as a common carrier of information than as a smooth and pointed tool for insinuation and penetration. *Moby-Dick* is a novel about uncovering intention and origins, just as *Benito Cereno* is about missing and repressed intentions. The Confidence-Man seems a thinly realized character because the game of confidence

[50] Herman Melville, *Benito Cereno,* in *"Billy-Budd, Sailor" and Other Tales,* ed. Harold Beaver (New York: Penguin, 1967), p. 257.

[51] In contrast, Rogin, *Subversive Genealogy,* p. 221, claims that theatricality turns the self into a prison.

has no clear intention. As the one-legged man warns, "Money, you think, is the sole motive to pains and hazard, deception and deviltry, in this world. How much money did the devil make by gulling Eve?" (CM, 32). To evaluate the Confidence-Man's purpose, we must begin with his game and its ability to create the momentary bond of confidence necessary for authority to flourish.

The Confidence-Man reduces the insights of *Moby-Dick* into their most radical formulas. Gone are the repeated actions of an identifiable character expressed through the continuities of plot, replaced by the enactments of the confidence game itself. And replacing the wolf-like Ahab, powerful in his inexorable self, is the Confidence-Man and his portmanteau self, confident that "where the wolves are killed off, the foxes increase" (CM, 4). Like Ahab and Babo, the Confidence-Man cleverly employs ceremonial structures to attach himself to his victims. Although his elaborate rituals are not always successful, like the herb-doctor's elaborate diagnostic ritual and the Philosophical Intelligence Officer's obsequiousness, they establish the conditions and rules—the momentary stage setting—of each encounter. The omnipresent metaphors of impersonation, playacting, and disguise serve to elaborate the conventionality inherent in the concept of play.[52] The metaphor aptly describes the characters' self-conscious awareness that they are performing before one another. "To do, is to act," says the wooden-legged man, "so all doers are actors" (CM, 38). This insight distinguishes this novel from *Moby-Dick*, in which Ahab is the stage director to his subordinates who remain only dimly aware of their manipulation. When the characters aboard the *Fidele* cannot discern the boundary between performance and sincerity, or trust one another's intentions, they have lost the basis of community.

This confusion reflects Melville's increasing interest in the relationship between theatricality and control. Ahab's stage combines legitimate authority, which restricts his power as much as it enables it, with coercive chicanery. The Confidence-Man is an unrestrained actor, but he inhabits a world in which all beings are actors whose roles seem unsubstantial at best. Victim and victimizer share a fundamental distrust of the world's substantiality; only those

[52] For a discussion of the theatrical metaphor, see Barish, *Antitheatrical*, pp. 311–14.

characters who distrust all performance remain protected from his advances. A good example of this game of confidence occurs in the anecdote of Mocmohoc's warfare with the Wrights and the Weavers. Having waged war on the Indian Mocmohoc for years, the white settlers eventually and gradually grow to trust him, even to the point of visiting his camp where they are treated well. Their residual distrust, however, prevents them from entering Mocmohoc's tent in a group and some wait outside to guard against treachery. When one day they all confidently enter Mocmohoc's tent, they are treacherously murdered. Mocmohoc defends his actions, for " 'twas they who broke their covenant first, in coming all together; they that broke it first, in trusting Mocmohoc" (CM, 148). If the moral of this anecdote supports the misanthropy of "NO Trust," it also suggests that the victim is never passive but participates in, even furthers, his own gulling. Unable to perceive Mocmohoc's unwavering purpose through the duplicity of his acts, the Wrights and Weavers forget the conventions that tied them to the Indian in the first place.

In his own games, the Confidence-Man performs verbally rather than visually. Replacing the ritualized ceremony built up over time that united Mocmohoc and his victims are the social codes of interaction elicited by language's illocutionary force. Disturbing the various linguistic interactions manipulated by the Confidence-Man are doubts about the intention lying behind these speech acts as well as doubts about the meanings of the words themselves. Much of the victims' (and reader's) confusion arises from ambiguities of syntax. As Cecilia Tichi has noted, "by depersonalizing dialogue, divorcing speeches from speakers, and restraining visual evocation, Melville forces his readers to focus largely upon the entity of language, itself horrendously corrupted and abased."[53] The fault of this corruption, the fact that language provokes only mistrust, lies not with the Confidence-Man but with the Jacksons and Websters. Daniel Webster's ringing defense of the Fugitive Slave Law, Justice Shaw's judgment to return Simms to slavery, among many examples, emptied traditional rhetoric of its ability to convey moral ideas which unite listeners within a community.[54] This is not

[53] Cecilia Tichi, "Melville's Craft and the Theme of Language Debased in *The Confidence-Man*," *ELH* 39 (1972): 643.

[54] See Rogin, *Subversive Genealogy*, pp. 140–51, for the rhetorical consequences of the Fugitive Slave Law.

to equate the Confidence-Man with any particular political figure; rather, he shares with the orators the goal of confidence, but he must work against the doubt they have already created. His success, like Ishmael's, can be seen by the degree to which his rhetoric attracts and implicates his victims in a momentary victory of confidence.

As he progresses through his identities, moving from silence to verbosity, the Confidence-Man's rhetorical strategies likewise become more cunning and complex. The least successful of his masquerades is the deaf-mute in cream colors who initiates the deceptions. Competing with the wanted poster ("as if it had been a theatre bill") for the crowd's attention, the mute offers direct but ineffective homilies such as "Charity never faileth" for the crowd's benefit. With "no badge of authority about him" (CM, 4), the man's wisdom draws only the listeners' animosity. Franklin's Father Abraham had similarly tried and failed to move his audience with the traditional wisdom of proverbs. The Confidence-Man's succeeding incarnations discard the deaf-mute's simple declarations for more effective and ambiguous rhetorical effects.

Upon the transformation of the man in cream colors into his contrary, the Guinea Negro, the rhetorical seduction of confidence begins in earnest. The crowd answers the Guinea Negro's pleas for confidence by following neither the one-legged man's skepticism nor the Methodist's trust. Instead, they promise him conditional trust: If his friends vouch for his character, then they will give him their confidence. Their doubt and need for empirical proof establishes the pattern of behavior and the linguistic paradigm that become the method of the confidence game itself. Contingency and the conditional construction, which neither imply absolute confidence nor deny it, become the Confidence-Man's means for gaining his victims' trust. In other words, he turns their lack of confidence against them, creating in its absence the possibility, the "fiction," of its future presence. It is soon afterwards that the third incarnation, John Ringman, approaches the merchant with a plea couched in this same phrasing: "Would you not loan a brother a shilling *if* he needed it?" (CM, 21; my emphasis). Like Bartleby's famous "I would prefer not to," this question obscures intention and insinuates much without becoming an overt command. With its added personal appeal, the question claims more of the listener than the situation warrants, but, of course, his victim ignores its conditional nature and responds to its emotional appeal by emptying his wallet.

The following strategies of the Confidence-Man involve variations and elaborations of this simple construction. As success follows success, he gains, as the herb-doctor says, "some little modest confidence in himself" (CM, 107). His own success depends on the tension raised by his proposals between his victims' professed beliefs and their actions. In other words, the conditional nature of his proposals draws his listener out on stage, forcing that person to act consistently within the role he or she has already played. For example, he traps the merchant in a moral contradiction. After the merchant has given money to the Guinea Negro, he is confronted by the Confidence-Man once again: "Since you are of this truly charitable nature, you will not turn away an appeal in behalf of the Seminole Widow and Orphan Asylum?" (CM, 33). In order to save face, the merchant complies. Somewhat later, meeting a woman who claims to have confidence, he demands that she "prove it. Let me have twenty dollars" (CM, 44). Both victims hesitate, caught between their instinctive distrust and the need to preserve their identities through consistent action. They both overcome doubt because any failure to prove their confidence would dislocate their sense of a consistent, continuous self. They must also construct a link from his demands to his good intentions, make *him* consistent in other words, in order to satisfy their self-doubts about their contradictory impulse. He legitimates their identities as philanthropic individuals as long as he remains consistent. "If you were other than I have confidence you are," says the merchant to the Confidence-Man, "hardly would you challenge distrust that way" (CM, 56). The Confidence-Man's metamorphic power explodes the myth of stable identity and his ability to move them destroys the idea of an autonomous, self-regulating identity.

Prompted by his success, the Confidence-Man gains revenge on the world that denied him complete confidence as the cream-colored man. Posing as the Black Rapids Coal man, he tempts the miser, who is unable to decide to trust him: "If, if now, I should put, put—" (CM, 75). To this the Confidence-Man shoots back, "No ifs. Downright confidence, or none. So help me heaven, I will have no half-confidences." Much like Ahab's desire for "flat obedience to . . . flat commands" (MD, 422), he now trusts his own powers.

Whereas earlier he had used the conditional constructions to draw out his victims, he can abandon it at times for more direct means. In every case, however, his aim is the same: to test the limits of his victim's belief, to insinuate his doubt at that point where belief and action meet, and to create a bond of confidence as the victim seeks to complete his or her sense of identity. Often, as with the miser who hands over his money, he catches the person in a contradiction between a professed skepticism and the secret desire for confidence and certainty. Other times, as with the merchant and woman, he betrays the existence of feelings that contradict their own philanthropic actions. However, as Warwick Wadlington states, "The paramount issue is not what is believed but the personal temper than informs belief."[55] Unwilling to rest with the "pondering repose of If," each victim, like Pierre before them, seeks to rescue a consistent identity through strict adherence to prescribed roles in the face of their often inconsistent emotions. The people protect their belief in a unified self against the existence of desires that would contradict that belief.

Like Ishmael, the Confidence-Man is a mimic, but in this third-person narrative he remains contained within the bounds of the narrative itself, unable to insinuate himself in our confidence with a sophistic tale. Ishmael's epistemic authority derives from his intention to guide and impart information; the Confidence-Man has no intention, only the goal of confidence. When his first attempt to influence the audience with inscribed language fails, he turns to his power to fictionalize and appropriate stories. He never achieves the authority of command, for social institutions (we see this most clearly in "Bartleby") are incapable of sustaining human relations; they isolate and entomb their victims. His game is conditional and momentary; he achieves authority not through his personality (he has none in the traditional sense), but in his victims' granting of his identity (much like the reader's first interaction with Ishmael) from their projected belief in his power or intention.

As the Confidence-Man establishes the rules of provisional belief by which the victims measure the consistency of their identities, the narrator engages the reader in his own narrative version. Such an attempt to implicate and interweave the reader is typical of Mel-

55 Wadlington, *Confidence Game*, p. 147.

ville: As the characters seek to preserve a consistent identity, the narrator asks us to believe in them for the very reason that they must fail in the attempt. After the merchant's benevolence is shaken by his momentary confession of doubt, the narrator meditates: "While to all fiction is allowed some play of invention, yet, fiction based on fact should never be contradictory to it; and is it not a fact, that, in real life, a consistent character is a *rara avis*?" (CM, 69). As Leo Bersani has discussed, the internal consistency of characters in realistic fiction represents the society's belief, or wish to believe, in its order and integrity. The internal is regulated by the external by containing an individual's antisocial desire within those socially produced objects by which desire seeks to satisfy itself.[56] For Melville, internal inconsistency is a result of society's incoherence, a chaotic state that survives by repression and the valuing of strict moral consistency.

To preserve the Union at all costs, even at the cost of condoning slavery, became the goal of politicians like Daniel Webster, but it resulted in the tortured logic and rhetoric which actually separated belief in justice and equality from legislative acts created to maintain the Union. The victims of the Confidence-Man's game likewise seek to preserve the unity of their identity through consistency, but he is able to reveal the discrepancy between their actions and beliefs and uses it to extort their confidence in him. The confidential structure of his game, the if-then situation, traps the victim in his or her claim of belief and simultaneously calls that belief into question.

The Confidence-Man's most radical attack is on the cherished American belief in individualism and autonomy. To the popular notion of the Franklinesque self-made man and the politicians' praise for self-reliance, Melville, like Emerson, would ask: What is the identity of the self and how can it be defined apart from other selves and society which always seem to impinge on its self-reflections? In *The Confidence-Man,* identity is such an unstable, contingent element that the characters' identities tend to overlap and commingle. Authority aboard the *Pequod* and confidence aboard the *Fidele* create identity out of the conventions of social interaction, the theatricality of self-presentation, and individual desire.

[56] Leo Bersani, *A Future for Astyanax* (Boston: Little, Brown, 1976), pp. 51–88.

The ideal of "A Squeeze of the Hand," however, is missing from *The Confidence-Man*. Seeking to contain and preserve themselves and dominate others, the victims give themselves over for the brief moments of confidence—and the *Fidele* steams toward disaster.

To an even greater extent than Ahab, the Confidence-Man's power rests in his ability to use language as a tool to influence and bond. Eliciting his victim's belief, the Confidence-Man proceeds to test the categorical nature of that belief, soon allying belief uncomfortably with disbelief. For example, the self-assured Confidence-Man approaches Pitch from the woodsman's supposedly impregnable misanthropy. Pitch has resisted the reliance on confidence, as he says, because "St. Augustine on Original Sin is my text book" (CM, 125). Safe in his belief in man's fundamental corruption (and relying like Redburn on traditional authority), Pitch relents when the Confidence-Man points out that St. Augustine's seemingly inconsistent religious conversion might prove an analogue to his boys. When Pitch later considers the interchange, he moves from uncertainty back to skepticism:

> He revolves, but cannot comprehend, the operation, still less the operator. Was the man a trickster, it must be more for the love than the lucre. Two or three dirty dollars the motive to so many nice wiles? . . . Fain, in his disfavor, would he make out a logical case. The doctrine of analogies recurs. Fallacious enough doctrine when wielded against one's prejudices, but in corroboration of cherished suspicions not without likelihood. Analogically, he couples the slanting cut of the equivocator's coat-tails with the sinister cast in his eye; he weighs slyboots sleek speech in the light imparted by the oblique import of the smooth slope of his worn boot-heels; the insinuator's undulating flunkyisms dovetail into those of the flunky beast that windeth his way on his belly. (CM, 130)

Revolving on a cycle of commitment and disengagement from the confidence game, his thoughts return to the certainty of his belief in original sin. It was, he comes to believe, the Confidence-Man's doubtful doctrine of analogies that successfully undermined his skepticism by drawing on the "cherished suspicions" that his boys might be reformed and converted. Belief lies at the heart of this Missourian's mistrust; he has cultivated doubt, in the form of doctrine, in order to prevent sentimental charity from ruling his judgment. Were he to stop there, we could conclude that he has regained his proper skeptical attitude and saved himself from the confidence game. However, with the last twisting reflection of the Confidence-Man as serpent, we see that his analogical thinking is as fallacious as his enemy's. The analogy between the Confidence-Man and Satan restates his belief in original sin, but with the added irony that he recognizes the logical seduction of analogies, making the doctrine of original sin now as suspect as the doctrine of trust. He is caught in the paradox of his skepticism: If he doubts all, then he must doubt even his disbelief. From the suggestion that good and evil might arise in the same person or event, he retreats into a world where doctrinal consistency overcomes experiential discontinuity.

The Confidence-Man's encounter with Pitch reiterates the participatory nature of the game. A Confidence-Man's momentary authority is acquired by his victim's participation in his own gulling. The confidence game is a "trans-action," a process conjuring the victim's belief, mistaken or not, in the game as a conditional representation of the world. The Confidence-Man should not, therefore, be equated with the corrupt politicians and the businessmen whose language he employs. His victims choose the means of their gulling by responding to the corruption of the language, seeking to gain themselves in the game. Although he has been linked to Satan's corruption of Adam and Eve, the devilish part of the Confidence-Man's game is that there is no Fall, only the revolutions of the dilemma, that point where one is trapped like Pitch in self-contradiction. In a logical dilemma, a person must make a choice between contradictory alternatives arising from the terms of a proof unfolding in an if-then construction. Johann Huizinga in his study of play has noticed how the nature of a logical dilemma involves the interactions of the game: "The question calculated to catch your opponent is properly called the dilemma, the answer to which, by forcing him to admit something else not covered by the original proposition invariably falls out to his disadvantage."[57] The horns we discover at the end of the novel are not a satanic altar

[57] Johann Huizinga, *Homo Ludens*, trans. R.F.C. Hull (Boston: Beacon Press, 1955), p. 112.

but merely the "horns" of the dilemma all of the victims face in their desire to find certainty and consistency in the presence of ambiguity and disjunction.[58]

The power of the Confidence-Man over his victims lies not in his personality but in his ability, and their willingness, to merge their beliefs and identities in the game itself. Thus we see the interdependence of characters and the doubling of their identities. The mistrustful miser clings to the herb-doctor much as "the less strong of the Siamese twins habitually leans against the other" (CM, 108). Similarly, Pitch and his antagonist (again the herb-doctor) reveal their identical habits of analogical thinking. To Charlie Noble, Frank Goodman (the Confidence-Man) says, "Our sentiments agree so, that were they written in a book, whose was whose, few but the nicest critics might determine" (CM, 158). The act of confidence requires a doubling of identities through which the Confidence-Man and victim briefly incorporate. Although this may appear similar to Ahab's usurpation of his crew's identity, the confidence game, at least practiced by *this* Confidence-Man, has no goal like the white whale, and therefore no intention. The identity is conditional rather than authoritarian, and mutual, like Ishmael's and Queequeg's "joint stock company," or our attachment to Ishmael by the thread of his story.

What unsettles us most about the Confidence-Man is not his ability to create these momentary bonds of confidence but their apparent calculations. This disturbing quality, as Warwick Wadlington says, suggests that "the strictly objective, descriptive truth of his hortatory statements is a matter of ultimate indifference to him."[59] If he can probe the contradictory motivations of the passengers aboard the *Fidele*, his own remain undefined. We finally reach a point in puzzling out the Confidence-Man's reasons for the game where we must locate them not in his devilish or angelic intentions but in the very creation of shared beliefs which is the game. In other words, he shared with Ishmael a longing for union

58 The *OED* (1971 ed.) describes a dilemma in this way: "a form of argument involving an adversary in the choice of two alternatives, either of which is (or appears) equally unfavorable to him. (The alternatives are commonly spoken of as the 'horns' of the dilemma.)" The term "horns of a dilemma" arose from mistakenly attributing the etymology of *dilemma* to the Greek word for *horn*.

59 Wadlington, *Confidence Game*, p. 158.

as well as Ishmael's disregard of absolute truth; both create pleasurable hypothetical situations which serve most importantly to link individuals by their potential credibility. In doing so (again like Ishmael), he makes the particular belief so agonizingly conditional that it is impossible for his victims (and I am including the reader among them) to hold that truth as anything more than a relative construct. Manipulating language in order to compel his victims to commit themselves, the Confidence-Man then tests the limits of the commitment. His conditional, quasi-syllogistic arguments call for his victim to affirm or deny the logical consistency of his or her own belief, most often catching the victim in the dilemma.

For example, Charlie Noble's statement, "If Truth don't speak through the people, it never speaks at all" (CM, 163), expresses the same contradictory, either-or, conditions that compel Pitch to choose his authority. As the Confidence-Man's double, Charlie Noble employs the same strategy as his antagonist. The irony of this particular conditional statement, however, cuts several ways. If we accept it, as the cosmopolitan appears to do, we are implicated in the mindless coerciveness of mass society intolerable to Emerson and Cooper. If we deny it, as the novel's constant irony and undercutting of belief seem to demand, then we are left without any truth at all, or with truth's compass, "whose needle indifferently respects all points on the horizon alike."[60] Denial means the terrifying possibility that "Silence is the only Voice of our God."[61] What remains after the confusing paradoxes of these logical conclusions is the pleasure and compelling power of the arguments themselves, those analogies and fictions which replace logic in the confidence game. He gains authority, like Ishmael, by moving the listener toward confidence and belief. "It is with fiction as with religion," the narrator says, making this essential link for us, "it should present another world, and yet one to which we feel a tie" (CM, 183). The "tie" is the conditional confidence of the game.

Much of the attraction of the Confidence-Man's fictions lies in their ability to create these ties. The Confidence-Man directly captures the merchant's sympathies with his story of Goneril, and indirectly drives home his point about confidence to his ungenerous

[60] Melville, *Pierre,* p. 165.
[61] Ibid., p. 204.

friend, Charlie Noble. Through the analogies created in each story, the victims (including the reader) are meant to interpret, judge, and draw conclusions about the characters and the Confidence-Man himself. From the Goneril story we presume to understand the man with the weed, in Colonel Moredock's history we see an analogy to the Missourian, and in Charlemont's tale the Confidence-Man aims at the connection to Charlie Noble. Yet in their orderly narratives, and moralizing conclusions, these tales are subtly seductive for the simple reason that they lend themselves to interpretation, in fact, demand to be interpreted. As in *Moby-Dick*, these interpolated tales are more consistent and intelligible than the novel in which they are told, but in their orderly Aristotelian quality they are also more clearly false when seen in the light of the novel's implicit theory of fiction. Inconsistent characters, discontinuous narrative, and opaque mystery are more true to experiential reality than Colonel Moredock's monomaniacal consistency, or the transparent parable of China Aster's tragedy. I find this an affirmation of fiction's seductive powers and its ability to preserve our awareness of the conditional ties which hold us to that hypothetical world.

Finally, it seems inappropriate to call the Confidence-Man a hero, for we understand neither his motivation nor his intention. His amorality and victimization of the merchant and Pitch seem repellent, although we find satisfaction in his unmasking of comparable confidence-men like Charles Noble. However, compared to the chilly Mark Winsome and his practical disciple Egbert, the Confidence-Man appears almost sympathetic. Our understanding of his actions involves discovering a purpose behind the inconsistent metamorphosis from the helplessly benign man in cream colors into the cosmopolitan. Changing from the deaf-mute into the talkative, attentive Frank Goodman, his color changes from the terrifying whiteness of Moby Dick to the rainbow colors of the butterfly. Like the butterfly's metamorphosis, however, the continuity of his transformation is arguable. To the PIO officer, the butterfly is substantially different from, and justifies, the miserable caterpillar. The cynical Pitch declares them the same creature: "The butterfly is the caterpiller in a gaudy cloak; stripped of which, there lies the imposter's long spindle of a body, pretty much worm-shaped as before" (CM, 124).

Our interpretation of the Confidence-Man's actions hinges upon the same terms of judgment. In either case, whether through Platonic, metamorphic transcendence or Aristotelian, metonymic evolution, we look for a connection between origin and end. However, if the Confidence-Man retains elements of his earlier form, it must include the deaf-mute's Christian message. We must, in this case, return to Pitch's meditation on the Confidence-Man's intention: "Was the man a trickster, it must be more for the love than the lucre" (CM, 130). Love of confidence is precisely his goal, but it is never entirely successful. From his earliest form as the lamb-like innocent, the Confidence-Man gains increasing confidence in himself, even as he fails to find it in others. With each confidence game he tests his fellow passengers and finds them lacking in true confidence. In his final guise as the cosmopolitan, he is remarkably unsuccessful against the more dangerous confidence-men—Charlie Noble, Mark Winsome, Egbert, and the child. He is not, as some have claimed, "basically evil," but rather neither good nor evil. As Pitch exclaims, he is "Diogenes masquerading as a cosmopolitan" (CM, 138), looking for one honest person, honest at any rate to himself.

The Confidence-Man asks us, "How can that be trustworthy that teaches us distrust?" (CM, 243). Lacking Ishmael's presence, the narrative seems intent on revealing the dangers of fiction, and thus undercutting its own justifiction and authority. The self-qualifying, opaque prose has the opposite effect of Ishmael's first chapter, which establishes a voice on whom we depend. The confusing use of pronouns and deictics obscures identities and tends to melt Confidence-Man and victim into disembodied voices; they become "phantoms which flit along a page, like shadows along a wall" (CM, 69). Seeking relief from indeterminacy, we are thrown into the interpolated stories and find there the elements of fiction—consistent plot, character, and moral—that we have vainly sought in the novel. The narrative authority that Ishmael claimed, and which we conditionally granted, seems so capriciously manipulated by the third-person narrator that we feel ourselves related to the victims of the Confidence-Man's strategies. Like the gulls, we are confronted with the ambiguity of the novel, the unbearable doubts that drove Pierre mad, and then are asked to have confidence in a novel, which, despite its assertion of realism, is self-consciously fictional.

It is here that we connect the questions of the Confidence-Man's intentions to that of the narrative. Narrative authority, like any kind of authority, implies a constructed intention. The Confidence-Man's victims construct intention from his game itself. We are left three possibilities mentioned by Frank and Charlie in their discussion of Shakespeare's intention. He meant, they claim, either to (1) open people's eyes; or (2) corrupt people's morals; or (3) he had "no express intention at all, but in effect opens their eyes and corrupts their morals in one operation" (CM, 171). Presented with these alternatives we become potential victims like Pitch: To choose between instruction and corruption means that we must construct an image of the world based on absolute categories. It is perhaps a bit of knavery that we are given such contradictory choices, but like all victims of the confidence game we participate in the knavery and reveal the desire to live in one fictive world or the other. The final option, however, is the one practiced by the Confidence-Man and his narrative counterpart. We never learn of his good or evil intentions; rather, we see in the consequence of his game the particular failures of confidence for each of his victims. In truth, he opens our eyes and corrupts our morals in the same "operation." By morals, I mean those professed beliefs in consistent ethical standards which are never practiced in this world. By pointing out the disjunction between belief and experienced practice, by describing the true inconsistencies of our characters (and his "characters"), Melville does not condemn the particular pieties or skepticisms, but, rather, the shocking neglect or abuse of them. As the third option suggests, the narrator is also an operator, but we must remember how Frank Goodman defines the operator: "He operators, he purges, he drains off the repletions" (CM, 196). The narrator's purpose, if we can hypothesize, is subversive and threatening to our rigid beliefs and prejudices, but in his desire to free us from the tyranny and absolute authority of ideas and the men who misuse them, his purpose is sanative.

CONCLUSION

Coming at the brink of the Civil War, *The Confidence-Man* proved to be Melville's most desperate attempt to lay bare the radical lack of trust propelling America into the abyss. This work's obscurity provides a measure of his determination to ignore the demands of critics and audience in order to attack the self-destructive impulses of American society. Like Cooper, he faced the complete loss of his dwindling audience as reward for his persistence. Melville's career recapitulates the dilemma of American writers: Attempting to gain a readership and establish authority, they inevitably ran counter to the demands of society. Some writers, like Franklin and Brackenridge, adapted their ambitions to the nation's expectations; others, like Cooper and Emerson, attempted to rewrite the nation in terms of their ideals. Those writers who proved to be confidence-men, able to inspire popular confidence in their authority, survived. They remained, however, always uncertain of their position. By becoming representatives, they remained at the mercy of the people.

A year before Melville dissected the inconsistencies of the nation's rhetoric and its actions, an obscure poet published a volume of poems that wholeheartedly embraced inconsistency. Walt Whitman created a position of power within American democratic society through both accommodation and manipulation. His success originated in the easy intimacy he established with his reader. The 1855 edition of *Leaves of Grass* was startlingly, at times vulgarly, self-revelatory, but its uncanny style caught the rhythm and intonation of the American voice. Just as Charles Brockden Brown had earlier called for a writer to "converse with his reader not as an author, but as a man," in "Song of Myself" Whitman creates a tone of familiarity in the first stanza: "I celebrate myself, and sing myself, / And what I assume you shall assume, / For every atom belonging to me as good belongs to you." These lines are brilliantly calculated to attract and implicate the reader, much like Ishmael's first sentence. Moving from the ritualistic invocations of the first line, the voice confidently addresses us as equals in the second, and slips into a conversational insouciance in the final, drawn-out declaration. The slight ambiguity of the directive "shall" in the second line, surprisingly similar to Ishmael's initial command, momentarily disturbs the egalitarian sentiments and reminds us of our dependence on this unidentified voice, who has set the terms of our relationship.

Whitman continues his assault on the reader's confidence in the 1855 Preface as he establishes the essential role for the poet in America. Like the men of letters before him, Whitman dignified the poet's calling at the expense of the politicians: "Of all nations the United States with veins full of poetical stuff most need poets and will doubtless have the greatest and use them the greatest. Their Presidents shall not be their common referees so much as their poets shall."[1] His pose culminates the various attempts by earlier writers to adapt their talents to the contradictions of American democracy. Encompassing the diversity of America within his democratic voice, the poet fulfills Brackenridge's previous attempt to unify America's babel of tongues. Like Cooper, he provides the generational continuity of tradition by uniting past and future, tradition and prophecy. Most important, Whitman seeks the office of Emerson's representative, witnessing the power of America, growing strong with its vitality and lending his genius in celebration: "The proof of a poet is that his country absorbs him as affection-

[1] Walt Whitman, *Leaves of Grass*, ed. Harold W. Blodgett and Sculley Bradley (New York: W. W. Norton, 1965), p. 712.

ately as he has absorbed it."[2] As Emerson had written of Shakespeare, however, the poetic representative had to share the fate of his country; the eventual succession of the Southern states were soon to mock Whitman's claims to office.

The coming of Civil War, Reconstruction, and America's economic boom revealed how insignificant the poet's role was in America, even as those events compelled Whitman to reiterate the centrality of his position. In "Democratic Vistas," the urgency of Whitman's claim is commensurate with his acknowledgment that America's "justification and success" lay "almost entirely on the future."[3] Looking around, Whitman saw only unfulfilled ideas: "Even to-day, amid these whirls, incredible flippancy, and blind fury of parties, infidelity, entire lack of first-class captains and leaders, added to the plentiful meanness and vulgarity of the ostensible masses—that problem, the labor question, beginning to open like a yawning gulf, rapidly widening every year—what prospect have we?" (513). The answer to these problems was simple: "View'd to-day . . . the problem of humanity all over the civilized world is social and religious, and is to be finally met and treated by literature" (463). Even as Whitman continued to diagnose the spiritual malaise of American democracy, the country moved even further away from his transcendentalist presuppositions.

By the end of the century writers were painfully aware of their positions. Their alter egos were no longer politicians but businessmen. Writing in 1894, William Dean Howells looked back over the century and accurately charted the evolution of authority and representation in America:

> Before the war, and during all the time from the revolution onward, it was undoubtedly the great politician, the publicist, the statesman [who was representative]. As we grew older, and began to have an intellectual life of our own, I think the literary fellows had a pretty good share of the honors that were going; that is, such a man as Longfellow was popularly considered a type of greatness. When the war came, it brought the soldier to the front, and there was a period of ten or fifteen

[2] Ibid., p. 729.

[3] Walt Whitman, *Leaves of Grass and Selected Prose*, ed. John Kouwenhoven (New York: Modern Library, 1950), p. 460.

> years when he dominated the national imagination. That period passed, and the great era of material prosperity set in. The big fortune began to tower up, and heroes of a different sort began to appeal to our admiration. I don't think there is any doubt but the millionare is now the American ideal.[4]

The transference of leadership from statesman to businessman left intellectuals like Henry Adams with their historical necks broken, but it also suggests how future literary strategies of representation would build on economic paradigms. And yet even here Benjamin Franklin's "The Way to Wealth" seems to have anticipated, or maybe inspired, the new course of empire. The economic terms with which Franklin had equated the authority of authorship were finally realized.

[4] William Dean Howells, *Traveler From Altruria* (New York: Hill and Wang, 1957), p. 138.

INDEX